Politics and Rhetoric of Italian State Steel Privatisation

The globally spreading privatisation wave that occurred in the 1990s deeply changed the structure of economic institutions worldwide. This turmoil overturned not only economic institutions, but shared cultural and societal institutions as well.

This book is the result of an investigation into the history of the privatisation of the steel industry in Italy, completed between 1994 and 1995. It explores the history of the Italian steel industry by looking at the interplay of local intertwined interests, political relations, and ideological formations that characterised an idiosyncratic hegemonic historical bloc. Rather than stigmatising this pattern as the legacy of a dysfunctional provincialism, the authors mobilise Gramsci's theory of hegemony to explain how the Italian privatisation process unfolded to accommodate economic pressures, political interests, and ideological constraints of a hegemonic social group, or aggregation of social groups. Thus, in reconstructing the privatisation of Italian steel, this book proposes a hegemony theory of privatisation and, more generally, describes a model that explains how political and cultural dynamics give rise to idiosyncratic local variations in globally spreading policies.

It will be of interest to researchers, academics, and students in the fields of business history, economics, sociology, and political science.

Edoardo Mollona is a full professor of business ethics and corporate strategy in the Department of Computer Science and Engineering at the University of Bologna, Italy.

Luca Pareschi is an assistant professor of organisation studies at "Tor Vergata", University of Rome, Italy.

Routledge International Studies in Business History
Series editors: Heidi Tworek and Ai Hisano

For more information about this series, please visit: www.routledge.com/Routledge-International-Studies-in-Business-History/book-series/SE0471

Politics and Rhetoric of Italian State Steel Privatisation

A Gramscian Analysis

Edoardo Mollona and
Luca Pareschi

Routledge
Taylor & Francis Group

NEW YORK AND LONDON

First published 2022
by Routledge
605 Third Avenue, New York, NY 10158

and by Routledge
4 Park Square, Milton Park, Abingdon, Oxon, OX14 4RN

Routledge is an imprint of the Taylor & Francis Group, an informa business

Library of Congress Cataloguing-in-Publication Data
A catalog record for this title has been requested

ISBN: 978-1-138-34443-3 (hbk)
ISBN: 978-1-032-24399-3 (pbk)
ISBN: 978-0-429-43851-6 (ebk)

DOI: 10.4324/9780429438516

Typeset in Sabon
by MPS Limited, Dehradun

Contents

Figures

Tables

About the Authors

Edoardo Mollona graduated cum laude in strategic management at Bocconi University in Milan (Italy) and received a PhD degree in strategic management/decision sciences at the London Business School. He is currently a full professor of business ethics and corporate strategy in the Department of Computer Science and Engineering at the University of Bologna. He conducts research on the relation between corporates and politics, with a specific focus on privatisation, and on the formal modelling of corporate behaviour. In this area of investigation, he has published books and journal articles and he has coordinated EU-funded research projects.

Luca Pareschi is currently an assistant professor at "Tor Vergata", University of Rome. Previously, he worked as a researcher at the University of Venezia "Ca' Foscari", and at the University of Bologna, where he received his PhD in management. While at the University of Bologna, during 2016–2019 he was in the team that coordinated the Horizon 2020 funded project PERCEIVE. Luca analyses words and texts and performs analysis with qualitative and semi-automated techniques. He is interested in how meanings emerge from texts, and in the performative power of such meanings. He deployed his competencies in neo-institutional theory, in the analysis of cultural industries and socio-political institutional processes, in the diffusion of European identity, and the evolution of academic fields of knowledge.

Acknowledgements

The authors wish to thank a number of people who, with their insightful comments and valuable information, facilitated our journey in writing this book. Enrico Gibellieri, deputy president of the European Steel Technology Platform (ESTEP) and, formerly, and last president of the Consultative Committee of the ECSC (European Coal and Steel Community), acted as our informant and made available his rich repertoire of archival data at the Historical Archives of the European Union at the European University Institute. Romano Prodi, president of the European Commission between 1999 and 2004, and chairman of IRI in the periods 1982–1989 and 1993–1994, as well allowed us to consult his dossiers in the same archive. Andrea Becherucci is the archivist who opened to us the doors of the Historical Archives; without his skills, care, and helpfulness, our work would have been more difficult and much less pleasant. Professor Maria Balconi, at the University of Pavia, was so kind to send to us her book that was, and still is, the fundamental guide to understanding the evolution of the Italian steel industry after the Second War World until the 1990s. Talking with Professor Ruggero Ranieri was extremely useful to complete our picture of the European steel privatisation process. Without the help of Angela Signorelli and Anna Ciarpella, it would have been very difficult for us to explore and use the rich database of documents at the Research Department of Assolombarda. In addition, thanks to the help of Pierluigi Molajoni, we had access to precious data held by the CIEE (Center for Information Service and Economic Studies) of Techint in Buenos Aires on the history of steel privatisation in Argentina. Anthony de Carvalho, Laurent Daniel, and Akihiko Shiga at OECD, as well, made available information and data on the history of the steel industry in Europe, and Federico Barbiellini Amidei, at the Bank of Italy, let us have access to financial data of state-owned Italian holdings. Vittorio Bardi, at the CGIL, enriched our analysis with the perspective of unions. Besides the data that was made available for our analysis, Andrea Goldstein, at OECD, contributed to our work with the valuable conversations we had along this long way. We would like to thank as well the colleagues who, in the context of the MEDEA project, which was funded by the European Commission in the seventh framework, provided insightful comments both in workshops and private conversations: Arianna Del Forno, Victoria Goddard, Andrea Fumagalli, Massimiliano Mollona, and Susana Narotzky. Renate Meyer and Markus Hollerer, at the Research Institute for Urban Management and Governance at the WU of Vienna, provided very instructive comments on our methodological approach. Finally, two colleagues generously donated their time to us either providing comments on earlier drafts of our work or by engaging in long conversations. Stewart Clegg, emeritus professor at the University of Technology Sydney and professor at the University of Sydney, gave us his immensely valuable support in our theorising on power. Alberto Burgio, at the University of Bologna, supported our interpretation of Gramscian theory with his insightful and knowledgeable comments.

1   Introduction

1.1 Our motivation in writing this book

Immersing for years into a research endeavour requires strong motivation. This research endeavour, as it is common for researchers, is connected to a pressing research question.

In our case, the research question was the following: *Why steel privatisation in Italy walked through a pattern, and produced an outcome, partially idiosyncratic in respect to comparable European countries?* While digging into this principal research question, however, we realised that our research illuminated another, more general, theoretical quandary: *How to explain local idiosyncratic variations in globally emerging patterns of policy-making?*

We started our study by investigating the privatisation of the Italian steel industry. We were intrigued by the peculiarity of the privatisation of the Italian state steel occurring in the 1990s when compared to the privatisation of the steel industries in other comparable European countries in the same period. However, soon we became conscious that our study was addressing the tension between the hegemony of a developing global order and the attempt of a local power system to defend specific interests.

Like Italy, in other European countries, such as France, Spain, and United Kingdom, where the state played a pivotal role in the post-WWII development and reorganisation of the steel industry, privatisations brought about the opportunity to take part in a global process of restructuring and concentration in the steel industry. In these countries, the pressure to increase the scale of production created the incentive for large integrated state-owned companies to sell their assets to foreign global producers. This process facilitated the concentration of the industry and opened the way to the creation of large private global groups able to both exploit economies of scale and enjoy an increased bargaining power, for example in respect to the concentrated upstream industry of iron extraction.

On the other hand, in the Italian privatisation process, which was completed between 1994 and 1995, Italian producers took the lion's

DOI: 10.4324/9780429438516-1

share. This was especially true for the production of flat products through integrated processes using large furnaces in which particularly strategic is the issue of exploiting economies of scale.

To explain this idiosyncrasy, we scrutinised the role of the complex tangle of local power relations. Our research theorises on how deep-seated meaning structures and political relations interact with economic pressures to produce local power formations able to explain observed local variations in globally unfolding waves of policy-making.

In stark opposition to the apparently self-evident statement that power relations and culture matter in explaining the evolution of economic institutions and policies is the general attitude to tackling the design and planning of economic policies as a politically neutral exercise in which the so-called technical solutions are there for all to see.

In general, such technical discourses, apparently deprived of political content, which stigmatise alternative worldviews as "ideological", produce two dysfunctional outcomes, we suggest. First, they make cognitively unacceptable any political discourse that deviates from a specific pedagogic practice (Oakes et al., 1998) that mobilises a specific technical language (Bourdieu, 1991). Second, and consequently, the reduction of the repertoire of considered alternatives forces a homogenisation of economic policies that, once applied to specific political and cultural contexts, may lead to counterintuitive and often undesired consequences.

In our case, we show how the widely accepted economic discipline inspired by the so-called Washington Consensus legitimised the European Commission to produce a discourse on the alleged virtues of markets with respect to state ownership that, in the late 1980s and 1990s, was enforced as unquestionable natural evidence. On the other hand, however, we document the attempts of a specific power system in Italy to respond to the global pressures to privatisations giving rise to idiosyncratic economic institutions.

While reconstructing the privatisation of the steel industry in Italy, in this book, we propose a hegemony theory of privatisation. By the means of the empirical evidence that we report and interpret, we explain how privatisation processes unfold to accommodate economic pressures, political interests, and ideological constraints of a hegemonic social group, or aggregation of social groups.

Therefore, we explain privatisations through the interpretive lens of Gramsci's theory of hegemony. Antonio Gramsci was a Marxist political thinker who focused on the "...relations of human thoughts, feelings, and will to 'objective' social process" (Kołakowski, 2008: 969). With the concept of hegemony, Gramsci described the process through which different ideologies struggle for supremacy until one, or a unique combination of ideologies, emerges as the winning one (Gramsci, 1975: 457, 1584). Hegemony ensues when an alignment is reached among ideology, political/organisational structures, and economic incentives (Gramsci, 1975: 1583–1585). The central interpretive device in our analysis is the concept of the *historical bloc*. A historical bloc is made of the complex and contradictory cluster (Gramsci, 1975: 1051) of (i) cultural "superstructures", which are shared understandings and meanings, (ii) material forces, or relations of production, and (iii) organisational structures, which wield power through bureaucratic and coercive power.

The idiosyncratic unfolding of the Italian steel privatisation, with respect to other European countries facing a similar crisis of overcapacity, reveals how idiosyncratic cultural, political, and economic forces explain the nature of a specific institutional change.

In France, Spain, and the United Kingdom, a globally legitimated industrial logic moulded privatisation processes, and national privatisations seem to participate in a globally planned restructuring process, with foreign producers playing a key role, whereas privatisations in Italy seem to respond to specific local pressures with domestic producers being the centre of the stage in the process.

The history of the Italian steel industry suggests that economic pressures to create large global champions could not find their way into the Italian steel industry due to the existence of a bundle of local intertwined interests, political relations, and ideological formations that characterised a specific hegemonic historical bloc.

Our work, we suggest, in re-proposing the conceptual device of historical bloc within Gramscian hegemony theory, provides a way to integrate discursive-cultural, economic, and political elements to explain the context-specific destiny of privatisation processes.

Ideology, which operates through discursive structures and hegemonic vocabularies, defines what policy or set of policies are legitimate. The narratives that defend the widely accepted rhetoric that private entrepreneurship creates value whereas state intervention in the economy is always deleterious and unproductive, Mazzucato explains (2013), has veiled the role of the state in producing valuable innovations in many fields and has legitimated the often hurried privatisation of many industries. Along these lines, in our book, we put particular emphasis on the analysis of the ideological-discursive structures that underpinned the steel privatisation process. In this light, the advantage of a Gramscian approach is one of integrating ideology, politics, and economic forces in explaining the socio-economic change.

In the conclusion of the book, we elaborate a model that presents privatisations as a process in which interest groups put in place discursive practices to legitimise new institutions or overrule existing ones. In our explanation, we do not disregard the economic interests of involved actors. However, we investigate such interests as complex objects. They are not just assigned in the abstract; rather they are, at least partially, socially and culturally constructed and are dependent on specific historical trajectories. This perspective contributes to explain why similar countries, belonging to the same supranational political and economic structures (European Union, World Bank, or International Monetary Fund), produced different privatisation patterns. In writing this book, we intended to take the wraps off the deep causal mechanisms and motives that underpin dramatic institutional change. Too often, the pedagogical rhetoric behind the application of economic rationality suppresses the analysis of hidden political conflicts that mould institutional changes. These conflicts trigger not only political manoeuvring but discursive struggles as well that work to assign specific meaning to issues. Along these lines, we investigated how local interest groups actively moulded the pattern of the privatisation of Italian steel. In this exploration, we were guided by the curiosity to understand how local cultural and political opportunity structures interacted with exogenously given and globally spreading pressures to generate a local mutation in privatisation policy.

Under a theoretical and methodological perspective, as is now clear to readers, this book adopts the theoretical lenses of Gramscian hegemony theory. Yet, in the course of our research, we embarked on a dialogue between Gramscian analysis and contemporary sociological research. We found particularly fruitful the interaction with research on social movement and neo-institutionalism. The bridge that we built facilitates, we believe, a reciprocal enrichment since the body of empirical research on framing and institutional entrepreneurship makes available a repertoire of concepts that allows an empirical grounding of Gramscian analysis of hegemony. Specifically, to empirically investigating the discursive strategies that actors applied in the fight for hegemony, we borrow from the literature on social movements the concept of *collective action frame* that are "action-oriented sets of beliefs and meanings that inspire and legitimate" action (Benford & Snow, 2000: 624). On the other hand, our analysis does not occur in an institutional vacuum. Therefore, we explore hegemonic practices considering the constraints in which these practices operate. We mobilise the concept of *institution*, and the connected concept of *institutional entrepreneurship*, as developed in neo-institutionalism (DiMaggio & Powell, 1983; Scott, 2014), to account for the coercive, normative, and cultural-cognitive constraints in which hegemonic practices occur and that aim to change. As well we borrowed from neo-institutional theory in sociology the concept of *field* (Fligstein & McAdam, 2012) that we find much more useful than the economic concept of *industry* to capture the population of actors and the repertoire of forces that shaped privatisations.

Finally, a caveat. In our work, we especially focused our empirical research on discourse. To this aim, we often mobilised post-Gramscian theorisation, such as Laclau and Mouffe analysis of discursively built political identities (1985), in which the discourse is constitutive of interests. Yet, in our interpretation, economic pressures maintain a key explanatory role. To be clear, we reject the "autonomization of the political" from the economic base as in Laclau and Mouffe (1985: 25). However, the analysis of our case suggests that the specific political and cultural structures of a field may differently mobilise the same economic pressures. Developing further the Gramscian idea that "economic and discursive dimensions are mutually reinforcing" (Levy & Scully, 2007: 977), we propose that the political organisation of a historical bloc crystallises the compromise between economic and cultural pressures that appear "inextricably linked" (Fligstein & McAdam, 2012: 43).

Along these lines, theoretically, our book mobilises the Gramscian concept of the historical bloc to score three objectives. First, the concept of the historical bloc explains the idiosyncratic configuration of local variation of globally spreading policies. Second, the concept of the historical bloc supports the explanation of why and how do countries privatise their industries. Third, the analysis of the dynamics alignment or misalignment of a historical bloc supports the explanation of institutional change and field fragmentation and settlement. Specifically, the process of misalignment is an endogenous explanation of why processes of institutional change start off, while alignment, or, better, realignments, explain why and how fields settle after an institutional change. In this respect, our bridging of Gramscian hegemony theory and institutional theory contributes to better articulate the dynamics of institutional changes.

1.2 Post-factum

The completion of the first draft of this book was concomitant with the sudden development of the vicissitudes of ILVA, the largest Italian steel-integrated producer that was privatised in 1995 and acquired by the private Italian group Riva.

In 2018, following the judicial problems of the owner, the Riva family, the company was again available on the market and was acquired by ArcelorMittal. At that time, we interpreted the event as the conclusion of a long process initiated 30 years before. More interestingly, the sale of ILVA to ArcelorMittal seemed to finally consummate the fate of European steel-integrated production. Indeed, in 2006, the same group had acquired state-owned steel makers in France, Luxembourg, and Spain. In the United Kingdom as well, in 2007, the Indian group Tata acquired privatised state-owned steel production.

The event, as well, sounded like the conclusion of the story we started to tell; it looked to us as the precipitating of a system towards its end-state equilibrium. After almost 30 years from the beginning of the privatisation process, and the decisive intervening of criminal offences of the Italian laws for environmental protection, the Italian steel industry was converging towards the same destiny of other European countries.

To us, this ending testified that the strength of material forces, precisely the pressure towards the concentration of the industry, found their way to domesticate local cultural and political structures. After all, we could be satisfied with how our theory was able to explain the 30-year delay.

However, to the surprise of most, the end of the drama of ILVA was not written yet.

On the 5th of December 2019, ArcelorMittal announced that it would renounce implementing the content of the sale contract and would abandon ILVA to its destiny.

A number of voices tried to explain what exactly happened and, more importantly, what is going to happen.

Briefly, on 2nd November 2019, the Italian parliament did not ratify a law that assured ArcelorMittal immunity from criminal offences related to environmental law. Without the immunity, the executives of the company explain, ArcelorMittal cannot take the risk to start operations.

Two facts help explain why one of ArcelorMittal demands was not at all unacceptable. First, the immunity was included in the original agreement. Second, since the plant of ILVA became unlawful, starting the operations entailed the risk of being immediately prosecuted even if the company had started, contemporaneously, to address the investment to make the plant compliant with legal standards. Of course, the immunity only regarded events that occurred before 2015. Indeed, the immunity law was not tailored for ArcelorMittal, rather it had been previously conceived of to preserve the activity of the commissioners that the government indicated to manage the company in the period between the conviction against the Riva family and the sale to a private investor. On any manager eventually taking the responsibility to manage ILVA, a risk was pending in the form of a notice of criminal offence. It was to move away from this deadlock that the government issued the immunity law for ILVA administrators. The agreement with ArcelorMittal only included the upholding of the immunity.

The pursuit of ambiguous political tactics underpins the coalescence of a majority able to abolish the immunity in the Italian parliament. We do not want to dig deeper into the motivations of those who pressured to modify the legal context that was in the background of the agreement with ArcelorMittal. It suffices to say that a number of politicians who had previously voted in favour of the immunity changed their minds and voted against it.

Some commentators suggest that the abolition of the immunity was a pleasant gift for ArcelorMittal that, after testing the constraints in reducing workforce and willing to leave the Italian investment, used the abolition of the immunity as the *casus belli* for breaking the agreement.

At present, ILVA is back in the perimeter of the Italian state; this unexpected occurrence advises that we were too hurried to certify the end of the history of Italian privatisation of steel.

As far as our research is concerned, independently of the tortuous route that the future of the Italian company may take, the recent development of the ArcelorMittal investment proves that our theorising on the explanatory strength of power relations in moulding local economic policies and institutions holds tight. Without the knowledge of the web of local power relations, it becomes hard to explain the evolving features of the Italian steel industry. The schizophrenic adventures of ArcelorMittal further convinced us that our research question has a much wider application, and a contemporaneous breath, than the explanation of steel privatisation. This is particularly interesting in times when global pressures seem to be the sole force in place to influence the creation of institutions.

We moved from the assumption that Italian steel privatisation was an idiosyncratic case in Europe with local economic and political forces playing a pivotal role. While we are writing these lines, Invitalia, a state-owned company, holds 50% of the equity of Acciaierie d'Italia Holding S.p.A, which incorporated ILVA, and is going to acquire 49% of the equity of JWS Steel, the Indian company that had acquired the production site located in Piombino. In addition, Arvedi, an Italian producer, acquired AST, a company owned by the German ThyssenGroup after being privatised. The control over the production of steel came back into Italian hands, public or private, after a journey that lasted 25 years.

1.3 *Caveat*: against indisputable *technical* solutions

Our account, we hope, is a call to consider power structures when analysing possible evolutions and consequences of economic policies. In our story of Italian steel, we reported a sequence of failures; the management by the state-owned IRI led to bankruptcy but the private management, retrospectively, did not perform much better in the long term.

The large steel production site located in Piombino, the coastal area of Tuscany, a region in the centre of Italy, was acquired by the Italian group Lucchini. After a dramatic financial crisis, and subsequent reorganisation, the company was first bought by the Russian group Severstal and then transferred into the private hands of the Algerian group Cevital, in 2015. Yet, the agreement with the Algerian group was rescinded due to the violation of a number of commitments by the acquirer. In 2018, the Indian group JSW Steel acquired the production site; in 2020, however, it was not entirely clear yet the destination and industrial plan to relaunch production and, as mentioned before, the state-owned Invitalia is buying back almost half of the equity. As for AST – Acciai Speciali Terni – acquired by the German ThyssenGroup, the company produced oscillating economic performances and, in 2012, was sold to the Finnish company Outokumpu. With the acquisition, however, the Finnish company reached a market share that produced a domain market position, according to the anti-trust European authorities. Therefore, in 2014, ThyssenKrupp bought back AST. In July 2021, ThyssenKrupp put AST on the market again and Arvedi, an Italian producer, acquired the company in September 2021.

Probably the most successful case is the privatisation of Dalmine, a company that performs and is still in the hands of the Rocca family, the original acquirer.

As for the adventures of ILVA, we may say that the recent developments cast puzzling light on the benefits of privatisation. The Riva Group, which acquired the company after privatisation, went through a debated judicial ordeal. In 2012, the top management of ILVA was investigated for environmental crimes and poisoning. As a consequence of the investigation, the company was put under external administration and, in 2015, went into bankruptcy and the production site was rented out to ArcelorMittal with a connected option to buy the company at the end of the rental period. In addition, the prosecutor's office in Milan started to investigate for alleged responsibilities of the top management in the bankruptcy of the company. In 2019, the tribunal acquitted the members of the Riva family for the accusations regarding responsibilities in the bankruptcy. However, in 2021, the tribunal located in the city of Taranto, where the ILVA plant is located, condemned Fabio and Nicola Riva for the accusation of environmental crimes.

While painting this portrait, one may suggest that the attempt to sell ILVA to ArcelorMittal is a welcome strategy to finally entrusting an efficient global producer with the task of unleashing the productive potential of the largest European furnace. Yet, the previously described unfolding of the agreement with ArcelorMittal suggests that this was not exactly the case.

More importantly, what the case of ILVA, and the historical account in our book, implies is that privatisation is not always the panacea, or the magic bullet, to revive industries or companies. These latter are complex systems of interlaced institutions, political and economic interests, and discursive formations.

1.4 Global versus local interests: the dubious behaviour of ArcelorMittal

Adopting the perspective that we offer in our book, the attempt to preserve a local power system, or a *historical bloc*, explains why Italian steel privatisation differs from other European countries especially in the limited role played by large global groups such as Tata Steel or ArcelorMittal.

For sure, this pattern might be stigmatised as a dysfunctional provincialism that protected an entrenched Italian corporatist agreement against the supposedly salvific pressures of market competition. Yet, on the other hand, with hindsight, the penetration of global players might have been a remedy not much better in the long term than the survival of an apparently asphyxial local power system.

A closer analysis of the recent vicissitudes regarding the ILVA-ArcelorMittal agreement brings about some shades in regards to the potential benefits that might have accrued from selling ILVA to a global producer.

Going back to the analysis of the facts occurring in 2019 and 2020, the principal motivation that ArcelorMittal put forward to justify the annulment of the contract for the acquisition of ILVA was the repeal of the law on immunity, on 2nd November 2019, by the Italian parliament. This was, as we illustrated, for sure, a very good reason for breaching the contract.

Yet, many have put forward the idea that the repeal of the immunity was only a pretext to abandon the Italian site forward. A number of elements underpin the interpretation.

On the 14th of November 2019, Sole 24 ORE, the more legitimate Italian economic newspaper, reported that in an alleged colloquium between the Mittal family and the then–Italian Prime Minister, Giuseppe Conte, the key issue to be resolved was the number of layoffs. Apparently, the diriment element was the request by ArcelorMittal to fire 5,000 employees, much more than what the original agreement planned.

As the president of the company, Laksmi Mittal, explains, in the third quarter of 2019, the company faced a crisis in the steel industry, with decreasing selling prices and increasing costs of raw materials and, in the second quarter, ArcelorMittal closed the income statement with a loss of € 572 million and an EBITDA falling by 61%. In the European industry, performances were worse than in the global market and, during 2019, ArcelorMittal announced to reduce production by 10%. The Italian branch of the company largely contributed to the negative performance so that the announcement of the abandonment of ILVA produced a 6% increase in the company's shares at the Amsterdam stock exchange after a 13% decrease since the beginning of the year.[1]

In a report by Morgan Stanley, mentioned by Sole 24 ORE,[2] it is calculated that if ArcelorMittal had to withdraw from the contract to acquire ILVA, the company would obtain an additional $1.2 billion cash derived from eliminating the future losses, which were calculated at $600 million, and the agreed investments. In addition, abandoning the ILVA plant would eliminate the downwards pressure in the LTIF index, the Lost Time Injury Frequency, which is the number of injuries occurring every million worked hours. The group LTIF is 1.36, which was growing compared to the 1.26 reported in the second quarter of 2019. One explanation of such growth was the impact of the Italian plant, which counts a much higher LTIF.

What is difficult to understand is how ArcelorMittal could not foresee the situation in advance, before agreeing to such a demanding contract. Both the structural problems of the plant, the needed investments, and the alleged redundancy of the workforce, were largely documented at the time of the public tender, in January 2016.

Moreover, while ArcelorMittal was rescinding its contract with ILVA, and the Italian government, the company was bargaining with the government of South Africa for the closure of a production site located in Saldanha, close to Capetown, with 1,000 workers at risk of being laid off. According to Kobus Verster, CEO of ArcelorMittal South Africa, despite the reduced tariffs of water and electricity, the cost advantage of the plant eroded. Previously, in 2003, ArcelorMittal bought a privatised steel maker, ISPAT, in Hunedoara, in Romania, stopping a large part of the operations and drastically reducing the workforce.

It is difficult not to speculate on the spurious use of a company's global operations by shifting production along the globe, exploiting, often temporary, cost advantages or, as in the case of Italy, closing a potential competitor.

In addition, interesting elements emerge from both the lawsuit put forward by the administrators of ILVA and the independent investigation conducted by the general attorney. First, from the bookkeeping of the company, it is not clear what happened to a $500 million worth inventory that ILVA was endowed with when ArcelorMittal took over.[3] Second, allegedly, in intercompany exchanges, ILVA acquired raw materials from a Dutch branch of ArcelorMittal at an unjustifiably high transfer price. It is suspected that these transactions were aimed at concentrating profits in the favourable Dutch fiscal regulation thereby avoiding fiscal pressures in Italy. In addition, the prosecutors investigate the possibility that a number of sales have been made through foreign branches of ArcelorMittal rather than directly to clients with the aim, again, to move profits away from Italy. Furthermore, the investigation of the general attorney revealed that the company was suffering from a dramatic financial crisis for months before the decision to rescind the contract. In an interrogatory, the chief financial officer of ArcelorMittal Italy, Steve Wampach, confirmed the financial crisis admitting difficulties in paying suppliers. At the same time, the presidents of the association of employers of Taranto (Confindustria Taranto), where the supply-chain of ILVA is located, and of Piedmont, in the North of Italy, where a large number of suppliers are located, both lamented that suppliers were experiencing difficulties in receiving their payments in due course from ArcelorMittal Italy.

The consequences on the Italian industrial system of the closure of ILVA would be striking and, paradoxically, the closure of ILVA would open the way of the Italian market to ArcelorMittal, as the president of Assofermet Acciai (the association of steelwork distributors), Tommaso Sandrini, advocated.[4]

In 2019, Italy was the second steel consumer in Europe. The core of the Italian industrial system consists of manufacturing in automotive, shipbuilding, and appliances, which need flat steel products and coils. In 2018, the Italian production of coils was around 8.5 million tonnes, of which 5 million tonnes are produced by ILVA, while Arvedi produces the remaining. The dependence on foreign, often extra-EU, producers, brings about a relevant element of instability. As Antonio Gozzi, CEO of the steel producer Duferco and past president of Federacciai (the association of Italian steel producers), suggests, while ILVA delivers in Italy within 1–1.5 months from the order, foreign producers deliver after 3–4 months in the best conditions. This implies that Italian manufacturers need to afford increasing costs connected to the maintenance of larger inventories. Thus, the loss of ILVA production, given the limited capacity of the other Italian producers of coils to cover the entire Italian demand for coils, forces Italian manufacturers to depend on foreign producers, increasing the instability of the industrial system.

Foreseeing the decrease in the production of ILVA, in 2019, Italian producers increased their order from foreign producers. Precisely, the market anticipated the loss of the amount produced by ILVA and ordered nearly 5 million tonnes. Half of this amount is ordered from countries outside the European Union. Only in the month of September 2019, coils imported from Russia doubled from 159,000 to 278,000 tonnes. Besides Turkish, Korean, and Russian producers, Indian producers such as Tata and ArcelorMittal are the candidates for filling the gap left by the closure of the installed capacity of ILVA.

1.5 How to read this book

To guide the readers through the book, we may say that our work is articulated in three main parts that are not necessarily developed in a strict sequence; yet, the three threads of works are embedded in an iterated dialogue.

1.5.1 The three directions for our investigation

The first area of work concerns the theoretical elaborations of the concepts that we used to interpret and guide the empirical analysis. The main role played by social scientists, we advocate, regards the maintenance of concepts. By maintenance, we mean the continuous adaptation of symbols to empirical objects. In this work, we bridged the neo-institutional analysis developed in economic sociology with Gramscian hegemony theory to explain the change in the institutional arrangement in the Italian steel industry in the late 1980s and 1990s. We thought that the neo-institutional theory of institutional change was able to provide a general perspective to interpret the phenomenon that we were interested in. Yet, we thought, the available panoply of concepts and assumptions of the theory was deficient in adequate conceptualisations of power dynamics. More specifically, we suggest that the theory was unable to explain why a specific institutional change reaches a state of settlement; also, we argue, the theory fails to provide a satisfactory account of how economic, cultural-symbolic, and political structures, together, explain the evolution of power systems.

The second area of investigation is the empirical analysis of the privatisation of the steel industry in Italy. Precisely, we were intrigued by the peculiarities of Italian privatisations and we felt the need to build a theoretical framework for explaining observed facts. Here, we collected and made sense of data of different kinds; we analysed the evolving economic dynamics of state-owned steel production, with a particular emphasis on the transfer of property rights, and the evolution of European and Italian economic institutions. Yet, the focus of our empirical analysis was on the discursive work that wrapped around the narration of privatisations.

Finally, the third part of our analysis is the attempt to contribute a theoretical process-model to explain the emergence of local institutional arrangements as the result of the materialisation of specific historical blocs. In the conclusive chapter of this book, the model explains the surfacing of institutional arrangements as the fragmentation and the settlement of historical blocs.

1.5.2 The structure of this book

In our attempt to adequately guiding the reader through the perils of this analysis, we articulated the book as follows:

Chapter 2 and chapter 3 include the theoretical analysis. More specifically, chapter 2 describes the concepts that we borrow from the neo-institutional theory in economic sociology. Here, for example, we describe the fundamental concepts of *institution, institutional entrepreneurship,* and *institutional field*. Chapter 3 reports Gramscian hegemony theory and explains why we find this theory useful for explaining our empirical context.

Chapter 4 and chapter 5 explain the methodology that we adopted. Chapter 4 reports the data collection and data analysis processes, whereas chapter 5 aims at guiding the reader into the interpretation of the results of our analysis of the discourse on privatisations.

Chapter 6, chapter 7, and chapter 8 include the gist of our empirical research. In chapter 6, we describe and interpret the period from 1985 to 1992, when steel privatisation emerged as an issue to threaten a consolidated power system. The conclusion of the steel privatisation process in the period 1993–1995 is the theme of chapter 7. In this chapter, we report the settlement of the power system connected to the steel industry as the consequence of the consolidation of a historical bloc. To provide a larger picture of the long stabilisation period that occurred in the discourse in the public sphere, in chapter 8, we analyse a sample of about 70,000 newspaper articles about privatisations in Italy, published during 1984–2014. By mobilising this body of information, we describe how the privatisation issue was accommodated in the public sphere, what different forms of resistance emerged and how the privatisation issue became *naturalised*.

To conclude, in chapter 9, we describe a process model of historical bloc fragmentation and settlement and we explain why, we suggest, the model may be of some help to explain how specific institutions evolve to reach idiosyncratic states of transitory and unstable settlement.

1.5.3 The logic of analysis: a conceptual map

In this book, we describe in turn fragmentation and settlement stages in the Italian steel field dynamics. Specifically, we argue that pressures to privatise and, later on, privatisations themselves produced fissures in the existing historical bloc and brought about pressures leading to the field fragmentation.

On the other hand, as the privatisation process unfolded, the field's actors weaved together alliances and compromises that stitched fissures and contributed to building a new historical bloc. It is the materialisation of a new historical bloc, we advocate, that determined the settlement of the field.

In this respect, through the lenses of the Gramscian theory of hegemony, we explain the fields' dynamics and contingent stabilisation of organisational fields (Levy & Scully, 2007). In our theory of fields' dynamics, thus, the fields' settlement occurs when a historical bloc ensues from "the alignment of material, organisational and discursive formation" and stabilises a field by "reproducing relations of production and meaning" (Levy & Egan, 2003: 806).

In what follows, we first describe the existing historical bloc, before the push towards privatisations occurred, and then we explain the fragmentation and the settlement of the field of steel production as, respectively, the misalignment and realignment of the structural elements of the field's historical bloc. These structural elements are material, political, and cultural-discursive in nature.

In the fragmentation stage, we as well highlight a number of economic exogenous jolts that contributed to producing the misalignment. Despite the crucial role of these stimuli, the focus of the section is on the interaction between the structural constraints and the agency that the field's actors enact to move the historical bloc towards a specific settlement.

When analysing the material structure of the Italian steel field, we developed the concept of *Composition of elites*. We mobilised the concept in order to describe how economic interests are distributed in the field, pool or divide actors, and, thereby, contribute to creating competitive or converging interests. In other words, the description of the *Composition of elites* illuminates the composition of the economic structure underpinning the steel field.

Walking through the conceptual bridge between the Gramscian framework and social movement theory, as built in the theoretical section, we use the general labels of *political* and *discursive opportunity structures* to describe, respectively, the political and the discursive-cultural elements that contribute to constrain or facilitate agency, or institutional entrepreneurship, in the Italian steel field. More specifically, structural elements, in our analysis, both constrain and constitute the field's actors (Clemens & Cook, 1999: 446). They are both recognised constraints and inducements to action, and forces that shape the identity and the cognition of individuals. In our explanation of fields' settlement, hegemonic practices both find their way within, and contribute to mould structural opportunities. Thus, we investigate the field dynamics by reconstructing hegemonic practices as overarching processes that aim at integrating structural material, discursive and political opportunities to stabilise a field through the consolidation of a power structure.

Notes

1 Sole24 ORE: 06/11/2019.
2 Sole24 ORE: 06/11/2019.
3 Sole24 ORE: 20/11/2019.
4 Sole24 ORE: 21/05/2018.

References

Benford, R., & Snow, D. (2000). Framing processes and social movements: An overview and assessment. In K. H. Cook, & J. Hagan (Eds.), *Annual review of sociology*, 26(2000): 611–639.

Bourdieu, P. (1991). *Language and symbolic power*. Cambridge, MA: Harvard University Press.

Clemens, E., & Cook, J. (1999). Politics and institutionalism: Explaining durability and change. *Annual Review of Sociology*, 25(1999): 441–466.

DiMaggio, P. J., & Powell, W. W. (1983). The iron cage revisited: Institutional isomorphism and collective rationality in organizational fields. *American Sociological Review*, 48(2): 147–160.

Fligstein, N., & McAdam, D. (2012). *A theory of fields*. Oxford: Oxford University Press.

Gramsci, A. (1975). *Quaderni dal Carcere*. Torino: Giulio Einaudi Editore.

Kołakowski, L. (2008). *Main currents of Marxism*. New York, NJ: W.W. Norton & Co.

Laclau, E., & Mouffe, C. (1985). *Hegemony and socialist strategy: Towards a radical democratic politics*. Second edition. London, UK: Verso.

Levy, D., & Scully, M. (2007). The institutional entrepreneur as modern prince: The strategic face of power in contested fields. *Organization Studies*, 28: 971–991.

Levy, D. L., & Egan, D. (2003). A neo-Gramscian approach to corporate political strategy: Conflict and accommodation in the climate change negotiations. *Journal of Management Studies*, 40: 803–829.

Mazzucato, M. (2013). *The entrepreneurial state: Debunking public vs private sector myths*. London: Anthem Press.

Oakes, L., Townley, B., & Cooper, D. (1998). Business planning as pedagogy: Language and control in a changing institutional field. *Administrative Science Quarterly*, 43(2): 257–292.

Scott, W. R. (2014). *Institution and organization*. Fourth edition. Thousand Oaks: Sage.

2 Institutional theory

2.1 Isomorphism in privatisation policies

2.1.1 Introduction

The first tenet from which this book departs is that from the mid-1980s a striking process of convergence towards similar neoliberal policies occurred that materialised into a global massive movement of privatisation of economic activity.

2.1.2 The concept of isomorphism

While the explanation of the heterogeneity of the organisation of economic activity has been a core endeavour in social science, a thread of work developed in the second half of the 1980s that worked to explain exactly the opposite: why organisations tend to converge towards the homogenisation of organisational forms and behaviours. The concept that best captures this process of homogenisation is *isomorphism* (DiMaggio & Powell, 1983), that is, a constraining process that forces units in a population to resemble each other (1983: 149). According to a first view, which DiMaggio and Powell label *competitive*, isomorphism stems from the competition for survival and the connected pressures that force organisations to converge towards the adoption of specific organisational forms that successfully adapt to environmental constraints (Hannan & Freeman, 1977).

The key intellectual contribution that DiMaggio and Powell made available is the concept of *institutional* isomorphism. To describe this perspective, the authors suggest that "organizations compete not just for resources and customers, but for political power and institutional legitimacy, for social as well as economic fitness" (1983: 150). By taking this conceptual angle, DiMaggio and Powell suggest that the pressures that force organisations towards isomorphism are not only economic but are socio-political and cultural as well. The core message is that

DOI: 10.4324/9780429438516-2

isomorphism is the consequence of the operation of institutions of a different nature that constrain behaviour.

2.1.3 Institutionalism and the concept of institution

The concept of institution, however, is ubiquitous in social sciences. In *new-institutional economics* (Commons, 1924, 1932, 1934; Williamson, 1975, 1981, 1982, 1985; North, 1986; Veblen, 1909), economists mainly address coercive institutions such as laws and regulations. In sociology, a *neo-institutional* approach (DiMaggio & Powell, 1983; Meyer & Rowan, 1977; Scott, 2014) provided an articulated description of institutions to explain the isomorphism among economic actors. From this perspective, institutions include, beyond laws and regulations, norms and cognitive institutions as well. Norms are the constraints that emanate from the shared values and moral principles of a specific community. For example, professional communities share specific deontological principles. On the other hand, cognitive institutions are schemata, mental models, and routines that individuals employ to address problems of a different nature. Therefore, in neo-institutionalism, the institutions that bind behaviour include social norms and decision-making routines. Consequently, in respect to neo-institutional economics, in neo-institutionalism, institutions influence behaviour by not only constraining individuals but also constituting them (Clemens & Cook, 1999). That is, individuals not only adapt to the rules that are recognised as constraints but they may as well adopt specific behaviours without perceiving constrictions. In the last case, institutions produce their effect by participating to mould individual's objectives and identity.

Here, however, a note is necessary to tease out the subtlety, and ambiguity, that underpins the interpretation of human behaviour in new institutionalism. In early new institutionalism (DiMaggio & Powell, 1983), a component of rational (Levy & Scully, 2007) choice is reformulated in a cognitive version (Ingram & Clay, 2000). That is, individuals abide by the limitations brought about by institutions to minimise cognitive costs. As Levy and Scully put it, "non-compliance could risk formal sanctions, social ostracism, or economic costs" (2007: 973). For example, by violating coercive institutions individuals may be obliged to pay sanctions, or to be deprived of personal freedom. On the other hand, the violation of social norms entails social costs such as stigma and ostracism. Finally, as for cognitive institutions, isomorphism of economic actors would, again, result from the attempt to minimise costs of a different nature. By adopting, for example, cognitive institutions such as the mental models that are shared by a given community, individuals enact a mimetic behaviour that minimises both economic costs, which may derive from adopting a deviant behaviour, and cognitive costs eventually arising from the process of reconstructing original mental models and of searching for novel decision-making routines. Regardless of the different underpinning mechanisms, however, institutions have the effect to produce models of behaviour that are taken for granted as the consequence of their repeated usage and of the legitimisation that they receive from some form of authority (Clemens & Cook 1999: 445).

Neo-institutional approach, therefore, despite the common interest for institutions, provided a more articulated image of institutions in respect to the *choice within constraints* framework of *new-institutional* economics, in which institutions are mainly laws and formal regulations. Namely, neo-institutionalism produced two key innovations. First, the concept of cognitive institution and, second, the concept of *embeddedness*. By portraying social actors as immersed in a tangle of institutions of various kinds, the concept of *embeddedness* highlights the complexity of the constraints driving human behaviour. The idea of embeddedness emphasises the constituting, rather than constraining, nature of institutions. That is, institutions contribute to shaping the very sense that social actors assign to phenomena. This perspective, within the neo-institutional body of research, paved the way to the concept of *institutional logic* (Friedland & Alford, 1991; Thornton et al., 2012). Institutional logics influence actors' behaviour by moulding the meaning that they assign to real-world facts. Through the concept of institutional logics, a clear cultural proximity emerges between the social constructionism of Berger and Luckman (1966) and the interests of neo-institutional research in the symbolic institutions and systems of meaning that support individuals in interpreting their social environment and in building their identity (Thornton et al., 2012: 79). In this framework, institutional logics are socially built structures of cultural symbols and material practices that incorporate values and beliefs and that are employed by individuals to give meaning to their material life, organise their time and space and reproduce their lives and experiences (Thornton et al., 2012: 2). With the introduction of the concept of institutional logic, the process has been completed of immersing social actors into institutions that not only constrain and regulate but contribute to constituting social identities as well.

This is a key turning point. In DiMaggio and Powell (1983), human behaviour is driven by a cost-avoidance rationale. Accordingly, individuals avoid non-compliance to institutional constraints to minimise material sanctions, social stigma, or cognitive costs without necessarily internalising the logic and prevalent social identity that underpin those institutions (Thornton et al., 2012: 87). On the other hand, the conformism that institutional logics produce derives from the internalisation of a specific social identity. This emphasis on the search for approval and symbolic remunerations, which ensues from the need to adhere to a social identity, is the key engine of the internalised conformism that institutional logics produces. In practice, the institutional logic approach does not deny that individuals comply with the pressures of coercive and normative constraints. Yet, social identity will guide individuals to select specific subsets of coercive and normative constraints to comply with.

2.1.4 Isomorphism in the global diffusion of policies: institutionalism and the world society theory

The mechanisms underpinning isomorphism typical to neo-institutional analysis – coercion, normative pressures, and mimicry – have been used to explain the global spread of privatisation in the 1990s.

The institutional approach to the study of the international spread of privatisations dates back to the work of Ikenberry (1990). The author suggested that, besides global economic and technological trends, which might also push international policies to converge, privatisation policies are internationally adopted through the three mechanisms of external inducement, emulation, and policy bandwagoning, in addition to social learning.

To explain the global diffusion of policies and practices, institutional scholars extended the analysis of policy isomorphism from organisations to nation-states in a "world society" approach (Jepperson & Meyer, 1991; Meyer et al., 1997). According to this theoretical perspective: "Many features of the contemporary nation-state derive from worldwide models constructed and propagated through global cultural and associational processes" (Meyer et al., 1997: 144–145).

This thread of research applied the neo-institutional theoretical repertoire to the worldwide spread of central bank independence (Polillo & Guillén, 2005) and stock exchanges (Weber et al., 2009).

The adoption of neoliberal and market-oriented reforms in infrastructure industries in a sample of countries, in particular, was explained by Henisz et al. (2005) using a similar neo-institutional approach. They explored the role of international forces that push countries to adopt specific policies. The authors considered the role of typical neo-institutional mechanisms of isomorphism such as coercive isomorphism, normative emulation, and competitive mimicry.

More specifically, in their empirical study, Henisz et al. analysed the adoption of neoliberal reforms in telecommunication and electricity industries. Their hypothesis is that the mechanisms of isomorphism are precursors for predicting the occurrence of four dependent variables that define neoliberal and market-oriented reforms: privatisation, formal separation of the regulatory authority from the executive branch, de facto elimination of executive political influence on the regulatory authority, and the opening of the retail market to multiple service providers.

In their study, empirical testing strongly supports the hypothesis that privatisations in the electricity industry are determined by mechanisms of coercive isomorphism. Namely, the authors found a strong statistical relationship between a country's exposure to international lenders (such as the IMF) and the probability of privatising the electricity industry.

Interestingly, the argument of coercive isomorphism also emerges in empirical economic literature. Brune et al. (2004) suggest that there is a consistent and strong relationship between IMF lending and privatisation, as privatisation was greater in countries with larger outstanding obligations to the IMF. The study is based on empirical analysis of privatisation over the 1985–1999 period. Their results show that privatisation revenues were higher in the countries of East Asia and the Pacific (13.3% of 1985 GDP) than in North America and Western Europe (8.9% of 1985 GDP). Most importantly, the variable measuring outstanding obligations to the IMF was positive, large, and statistically significant, whereas the estimated parameter for World Bank debt was negative and insignificant. The authors conclude that IMF lending had a positive impact on privatisation revenues, inferring that the imposition of IMF conditions in a country won the approval of global capital markets for its privatisation program.

2.1.5 The spread of neo-liberal policies and privatisations: the "privatization wave" isomorphism in steel privatisation

The global diffusion of neoliberal economic policies, as crystallised in the 1990 Washington Consensus, weakened the shared consciousness that considered state-ownership as a naturalised institution in many countries. The globally spreading "privatisation wave" (Bortolotti & Pinotti, 2008) forced political elites to consider privatisation as a legitimised policy especially in those countries where privatisation could counter increasing public debt.

In the European steel industry, the privatisation of British Steel occurring in 1988 paralleled the privatisation of French steel where the largest state producer, Usinor-Sacilor, was privatised in 1995 and pre-empted Spain's steel privatisation where Aceralia was privatised in 1997.

In Great Britain, British Steel, the stronghold of state steel, was privatised in 1988 and merged with Dutch Koninklijke Hoogovens to give birth to Corus in October 1999. Corus was then sold to Indian Tata Steel in March 2007.

In France, in 1982, the socialist government had nationalised the two largest steel producers, Usinor and Sacilor, that were in desperate economic and financial conditions as the consequence of the dramatic crisis that hit the steel industry in the late 1970s. In 1987, the incoming right-wing government merged the two companies and created Usinor-Sacilor which was privatised in 1995 to become Usinor in 1997.

In Spain, the beginning of the 1990s signalled the outset of a comprehensive process of public steel restructuring led by the PSOE government. In 1990, a debt-free company was created, the Corporación de la Siderurgia Integral (CSI) that acquired the assets of ENSIDESA, the largest state-owned steel producer, along with other private companies. In 1997, CSI was transformed into Aceralia to be privatised. The privatisation process included a strategic alliance with Arbed, a company from Luxembourg. Beginning in 2001, the French company Usinor merged with Arbed and, thereafter, Aceralia, Usinor, and Arbed merged into Arcelor. Finally, in 2006, the steel producer Mittal acquired Arcelor to create ArcelorMittal.

2.2 Privatisations as institutional change

2.2.1 Introduction

The privatisation of an industry is an institutional change in which private ownership replaces state ownership of means of production.

But what do we mean by institutional change? The concept of institutional change, which is a central conceptual anchor of neo-institutionalism, brings about at least two issues.

The first issue regards the paradox of embedded agency. That is, if the actors are embedded in institutional logics or, more generally, in social and symbolic structures, that constitute them, and unconsciously drive their behaviour, how can they change the logics along with the power relations that are crystallised in these logics? To address this conundrum, neo-institutionalists propose the concept of an institutional entrepreneur who is an actor able to, first, overcome the cognitive limitation of embeddedness and, second, to resist, and rise above, the pressures of extant coercive and normative institutions.

Yet, and this is the second issue we address, to empirically investigating what is the set of institutions that mould specific human behaviour, for example, the decision to privatise a state-owned enterprise, researchers need to set the boundaries of actors' embeddedness. For this purpose, neo-institutional research relied on the concept of *field*.

2.2.2 The locus of institutional change: the concept of field

As anticipated in the foregoing, the concept of field delimitates the area of social and symbolic interaction that embeds social actors and exerts pressures to conformity.

As suggested by Scott (2014: 17–18), neo-institutional research in sociology borrowed the concept of field from the French scholar

Bourdieu to "better situate" the locus in which institutions are shaped. According to Bourdieu, a field is a field of power (Bourdieu, 1977, 1985, 2005), a battleground that is comparable to a field of physical forces, a site of action and reaction (Bourdieu, 2005). From this angle, fields are spaces in which power relations are created.

In the seminal work of DiMaggio and Powell (1983: 148), the organisational field is a recognised area of institutional life. As the original focus of the model was the economic activity of organisations, DiMaggio and Powell included in the field suppliers, clients, and any other organisation that contribute to shape the playground, and the connected system of rules, in which firms operate. In a more general definition, Greenwood and Suddaby (2006: 28) explain that what the actors of a field have in common are the shared institutional logics that contribute to define organisational boundaries and identities and that constitute the key principles regulating reciprocal interaction. An organisation field, Scott explains, is "a community of organizations that partakes a common meaning system and whose participants interact more frequently and fatefully with one another than with actors outside the field" (1994: 207–208). In a broader interpretation, Lawrence and Phillips (2004) propose that two elements characterise a field. First, a field is constituted by a set of institutions that include, beyond formal rules and taken-for-granted practices, shared symbolic systems. Second, a field materialises in a web of interacting organisations. This portrait of fields suggests, in the analysis of Levy and Scully (2007), a dialectical mechanism of codetermination between institutions and organisations and implies that heterogeneous organisations, in reciprocal conflict, populate fields. Along this road, Hoffman (1999: 352) advocates that fields' constituents are often armed with opposing perspectives rather than with common rhetoric and the process of institutional change may more resemble institutional war than isomorphic dialogue. From the perspective that Hoffman conveys, a field cannot be defined by a common market or technology, for example by referring to an SIC code. Rather, what defines a field is the volume of interactions, and the amount of information exchanged, within a population of organisations along with the reciprocal awareness of common issues and discourse. As Hoffman puts it, a field is formed around the issues that become important to the interests and objectives of a specific collection of organisations (1999: 352). Extending this perspective, in their study of the introduction in Austria of the managerial mantra of shareholder value, Meyer and Höllerer (2010) focused on the concept of issue field. An issue field includes the set of competing and relevant actors who engage in the "politics of signification" (Benford & Snow, 2000), that is, the activity of assigning specific meanings to contested issues.

Therefore, increasingly, neo-institutional research addresses fields not only as areas of institutional life (DiMaggio & Powell, 1983: 148) but rather as "arenas of power relations" (Brint & Karabel, 1991: 355) in which institutional wars occur (White, 1992) and that "become centres of debates in which competing interests negotiate over issue interpretation" (Hoffman, 1999: 351). These power struggles mould fields' dynamics (Fligstein & Mara-Drita, 1996; Ingram & Rao, 2004), and actors who pursue specific interests push fields towards a state of settlement (Schneiberg & Soule, 2005; Davis & Thompson, 1994; Fligstein, 1996; 2001; Rao & Kenney, 2008).

2.2.3 The engine of institutional change: the concept of institutional entrepreneur

As Henisz and Zelner (2012) lament, the concept of embeddedness brings about a picture of human behaviour deprived of autonomy and determined by the effect of institutional logics. In this respect, neo-institutionalism indeed developed as a theory of isomorphism rather than of agency. This is especially compelling in the case of cognitive institutions that function as elements that are constitutive of identity. This portrayal of actors as embedded in social structures brings about a conundrum: how individuals, whose values, interests, and ideas of rationality are determined by institutions, are able to change these very institutions? The concept of institutional entrepreneur intervenes to make available an explanation for the occurrence of institutional change.

Institutional entrepreneurs, Maguire et al. explain, are actors who have interests in particular institutional arrangements and who leverage resources to create new institutions or to transform existing ones (2004: 657). Institutional entrepreneurs are capable of strategic manoeuvring (Levy & Scully, 2007: 974) and are capable of conceiving institutional strategies as patterns of organisational action concerned with the formation and the transformation of institutions, fields, and the rules and standards that control those structures (Lawrence, 1999: 167). The action of an institutional entrepreneur is, thus, political in that it is aimed at reshuffling power relations and at differently accommodating interests (Fligstein, 1996; Greenwood & Suddaby, 2006; Maguire et al., 2004). Given the political dimension of institutional entrepreneurship, a legitimate question is who is then able to play the role of the entrepreneur. To become an entrepreneur, a heroic cultural and cognitive effort is requested to break the chain of largely taken-for-granted identities and models of behaviour. Additionally, to turn extant institutional arrangements down, the entrepreneur should collect and organise a large number of resources. Who has the motivation and the stamina to accomplish this endeavour?

A well-established idea is that the actors who are more prone to challenge dominant institutions are those who occupy a marginal position in the field and are the less privileged. These actors are more frequently exposed to the clash between their interests and the pressure of hegemonic institutions. Consequently, they perceive what Seo and Creed (2002) define as misaligned interest contradiction, that is, a misalignment between privileged and marginal interests. Since their marginalisation makes them less embedded into socialisation processes, they are more likely to activate a process of praxis that entails the shift from unreflective participation in institutional reproduction to an imaginative critique of existing arrangements and practical action to change (Seo & Creed, 2002: 231). Thus, a recognised narrative advocates that it is reasonable to assume that actors who are peripheral in a field more easily escape isomorphic pressures and are more likely the engines of institutional changes being these latter, less represented, and embedded, in the institutions of the field.

In the neo-institutional literature, however, another thread moves from a different perspective. The line of reasoning that this viewpoint follows grounds on the issue of resources availability and legitimisation. It is true that marginal actors, this is the argument, are less embedded in the cognitive and cultural institutions of a field. On the other hand, the assumption of marginality implies ipso facto that these actors lack resources and legitimisation. Along these lines, Greenwood and Suddaby (2006) put forward that are the actors that maintain a central position in a field who are more likely to play the role of entrepreneurs. The idea behind this hypothesis is that elites more easily change the rule of the game. First, given economic and political power, central actors become immune to coercive and normative processes because their market activities expand beyond the jurisdiction of field-level regulations (2006: 27). This is the phenomenon that Greenwood and Suddaby refer to as boundary misalignment (2006: 27). For example, companies that operate on global markets expand the horizon of their organisational processes and structures, and the relationship with clients, well beyond local interests and constraints. The claim of Greenwood and Suddaby is that field-level governance systems operate at the local level and are weakened when they deal with actors that operate at the global level and are able to exploit the boundary misalignment between the global boundaries of their activity and the local boundaries of governance systems. As Greenwood and Suddaby explain, by the 1990s, the static regulatory structures of fields became inappropriate for the expanding scale and sophistication of larger players (2006: 38).

Not only central actors are less constrained by the coercive and normative institutions of their field. In addition, they can resist cultural and cognitive pressures as well. This is because they are able to develop a richer cultural repertoire. For example, multinational and global companies maintain multiple relationships with clients and institutions in different countries. The richness of their perspective endows them with alternative institutional logics and, therefore, puts them in the position to play the role of boundary bridging. That is, these actors bridge their original field with other fields, and are able to perceive how different logics, eventually located in different fields, better suit their interests.

2.2.4 The content of institutional entrepreneurship: the link with research in social movements

To study how the political manoeuvring of institutional entrepreneurs influences the state of fields, a thread of literature in institutional research mobilised the conceptual repertoire developed by the studies on Social Movements (SM) (Fligstein, 1997; Rao, 1998; Rao et al., 2000, 2003; Morrill et al., 2003; Hensmans, 2003; Ingram & Rao, 2004; Hargrave & Van De Ven, 2006; Schneiberg et al., 2008; Schneiberg & Lounsbury, 2008). Namely, the research on how groups are able to rally new political constituency around specific issues (McAdam et al., 1996: 7) offered useful theoretical lenses for investigating the content of power struggle underpinning fields' dynamics.

As Rao et al. (2003: 796) explain, the neo-institutional analysis that is inspired by the research on SM walks over two avenues. The first strand investigates the dynamics that occur in cultural domains focusing on the framing and discursive activities that influence cultural codes, narratives, and symbols. A second perspective explores how actors' manoeuvring challenges political structures, policies, and governance structures.

2.2.4.1 Framing and the power of discourse

To mobilise collective action and modify the state of fields, institutional entrepreneurs provide "common meanings and identities" (Fligstein, 1997) by manipulating cultural symbols "to produce new sets of interests for actors" (Fligstein & Mara-Drita, 1996).

Since actors can "sign on to an institutional project under a new cultural frame" (Fligstein & Mara-Drita, 1996) and "entrepreneurs are skilful political operatives employing frames as mobilisation devices" (Rao, 1998: 948), a bridge has been created between social movement theory and the literature on institutional change (Rao, 1998; Hensmans, 2003; Schneiberg et al., 2008).

More specifically, the literature on framing in social movements looks at the ways social actors produce and maintain "action oriented sets of beliefs and meanings that inspire and legitimate" action (Benford & Snow, 2000: 624).

Neo-institutional theorising extensively grounds on this conceptualisation to explain institutional entrepreneurship and field dynamics. Change is analysed as the result of the "mobilization of collective action, which is contingent on the mobilising potency of action frames" (Creed et al., 2002b: 478). In this perspective, agents of change are "signifying agents" who are engaged in "the politics of signification" (Snow & Benford, 1988).

Recent work on institutional entrepreneurship focuses on how discourse is constitutive of institutions (Phillips et al., 2004). In this light, a fundamental tenet of recent neo-institutional literature is that institutions are not just social constructions but social constructions constituted through discourse (Phillips et al., 2004: 638). Hence, power is itself constituted through discourse (Clegg, 1998: 31) and analysis of agency is increasingly focused on the ability to manipulate discourse and to enact "politics of signification" (Benford & Snow, 2000: 625).

Successful institutional entrepreneurs produce texts that draw on discourses from other fields to create new institutions or to delegitimise existing ones (Greenwood et al., 2002; Phillips et al., 2004: 648; Maguire & Hardy, 2009). Entrepreneurs' legitimacy to speak grants power (Maguire et al., 2004) and the literature points at several strategies to gain legitimacy (Suchman, 1995), such as storytelling (Lounsbury & Glynn, 2001), theorisation (Greenwood et al., 2002; Rao et al., 2003), the use of rhetoric and the exploitation of contradictions embedded in dominant institutional logics (Greenwood & Suddaby, 2006), the framing of contested issues (Meyer & Höllerer, 2010), of new standards (Garud et al., 2002) and problems (Tracey et al., 2011), the creation of legitimating accounts (Creed et al., 2002b), persuasion (Maguire et al., 2004: 676), the use of impression management (Elsbach & Sutton, 1992), and the formation of discourse alliances (Hensmans, 2003; Meyer & Höllerer, 2010).

Along these lines, a research thread investigates arenas of power dependencies and strategic interaction where "multiple field constituents compete over the definition of issues and the legitimation of different organizational forms" (Hensmans, 2003: 356) and analyses the competition for the definition of institutional arrangements as a struggle over the meaning to be assigned to contested issues (Meyer & Höllerer, 2010).

Following this discursive turn in neo-institutional analysis, increasingly scholars investigate this political activity as the struggle to assign meaning to contested issues in order to legitimise or delegitimise institutions.

Here, two mechanisms recur as fundamental in this political activity. The first mechanism is the mobilisation of existing cultural categories for gaining legitimacy (Creed et al., 2002a, b). Actors use existing discourses as part of their framing (Cornelissen & Werner, 2014: 209).

In Rao (1998), for example, emergence of consumer watchdog organisations as an organisational form follows from aligning framing activity with common societal discourses. The concept of discursive opportunity structures, as described by Koopmans and Statham, points at the need for actors to use frames that are aligned within dominant discourses (1999: 231) to be effective (McCammon et al., 2007: 745). In their framing activity, actors have a toolkit (Swidler, 1986) of discourses to select from.

The second mechanism that characterises political struggles is the clustering of actors around frames that represents a compromise upon which a field can settle. In this respect, actors build discursive alliances by coupling more or less aligned frames (Meyer & Höllerer, 2010; Hensmans, 2003) and by using "compromise frames" (Fligstein & McAdam, 2011, 2012), "frame bridging" (Snow et al., 1986), or "integrated frames" (Rao & Kenney, 2008).

2.2.4.2 *The political activity of the skilled institutional entrepreneur*

Despite the emphasis on discourse and framing, neo-institutional research acknowledges that the politics of signification is "embedded in more comprehensive political struggles" (Meyer & Höllerer, 2010: 1254) and power relations (Rao & Kenney, 2008). Skilled entrepreneurs, Phillips et al. suggest, need resources, formal authority, and centrality to maximise text diffusion or prevent other actors from being able to disseminate their texts (2004: 648). When adopting a new frame, social actors produce "judgements about the types of power within a field that might facilitate or impede adoption" (Gray et al., 2015: 131) since "change can be blocked through a concentrated power structure (elite domination)" (Greenwood & Hinings, 1996: 1046) or facilitated by fragmented political elites (Zelner et al., 2009). From this angle, the size of coalitions (Rao & Kenney, 2008) and the composition of elites (McAdam, 1996: 27) are crucial for the success of discursive practices.

As Hardy and Maguire advocate, for example, in addition to discursive practices, institutional entrepreneurship requires the creation of "relations among actors, such as collaborations, coalitions, and alliances" (2008: 209). Researchers advocating this political perspective suggest that much of the literature on institutional change "ignores the power relations that pervade institutional fields" (Hardy & Maguire, 2017: 213; Munir, 2005; Willmott, 2015). Accordingly, assessing the size of coalitions (Rao & Kenney, 2008) and the composition of elites (McAdam, 1996: 27) is crucial for the success of discursive practices. As Cornelissen and Werner warn, explaining meaning struggles and emerging settlements requires accounting for differences in "political interests between actors and groups" (2014: 211).

2.2.5 The structural constraints to institutional entrepreneurship

This tradition of studies that focuses on fields' politics and dynamics inherited from the research on social movements a structuralist penchant that innevates the analysis of agency as embedded in cultural and political constraints (Schneiberg & Lounsbury, 2008: 652).

More precisely, the strategic behaviour of institutional entrepreneurs is conceived of as constrained by both *discursive opportunity structures* and *political opportunity structures*.

2.2.5.1 The concept of discursive opportunity structures

Taking a discursive perspective, the subversion of a societal order, in neo-institutional research, becomes a "framing contest" (Ryan, 1991). Previous frames are seen no longer as appropriate (Fligstein, 2001; Maguire et al., 2004), and the suture of fields' fragmentation occurs in the form of "compromise frames" (Fligstein & McAdam, 2012), bridging frames (Snow & Benford, 1988), and integrating frames (Rao & Kenney, 2008). This contest, however, requires appropriate social skills to "take what the system gives" (Fligstein, 2001: 106), recombine "available discursive elements" (Hensmans, 2003: 362), and navigate the cultural texture of logics of a field, that is, its deeply ingrained societal beliefs and practices (Friedland & Alford, 1991). The "latent meaning structure" of a field (Meyer & Höllerer, 2010), the "multiplicity" of the field's logics (Hoffman, 1999: 2001) and the ideological incompatibility (Rao & Kenney, 2008) and "relative incoherence" of these latter influence how a field settles around new frames (Ansari et al., 2013; Granqvist & Laurila, 2011) and when sufficiently large discursive alliances coalesce (Meyer & Höllerer, 2010; Hensmans, 2003).

Therefore, when addressing institutional change, Cornelissen and Werner encourage scholars to study *discursive opportunity structures* (Koopmans & Statham, 1999: 231; McCammon et al., 2007: 745) as "the opportunity provided by salient discourses that are alive and have momentum at a particular point in time" (2007: 210).

2.2.5.2 The concept of political opportunity structures

Besides cultural, discursive, and symbolic constraints, institutional entrepreneurship faces political restraints. In this political perspective, neo-institutional scholars (Meyer & Höllerer, 2010: 1254; Gray et al., 2015: 118) recognise the role of *political opportunity structures* (Tarrow, 1994, 1996; McAdam, 1996; Diani, 1996; Hargrave & Van De Ven, 2006; Meyer & Höllerer, 2010; Gray et al., 2015).

More precisely, actors willing to modify the state of a field exploit the freedom of movement available in political opportunity structures (Tarrow, 1994, 1996; McAdam, 1996; Diani, 1996; Hargrave & Van de Ven, 2006; Gray et al., 2015). In general, a political opportunity structure is made of "not necessarily formal, permanent, or national signals to social or political actors which either encourage or discourage them to use their internal resources to form social movements" (Tarrow, 1996: 54). In describing typical dimensions of political opportunity structures, McAdam (1996: 27) mentions, for example, the relative openness/closure of the institutionalised political system and a state's capacity and propensity for repression. In the list, however, the key role is played by the composition of the elites and the availability of alliances. Namely, McAdam refers to the stability/instability of that broad set of elite alignments that typically undergird a polity and the presence or absence of elite allies. In this perspective, the analysis of institutional change and fields' settlement needs to engage with the assessment of the structure of political opportunities.

2.3 Explaining local variations in institutions and policies

2.3.1 The Italian case as a local variation to be explained

In the late 1980s, Italy started a privatisation process leading to the demise of the entire system of steel production.

Steel privatisation in Italy followed the privatisation of British Steel in 1988, paralleled the privatisation of French steel where the largest state producer, Usinor, was privatised in 1995, and preceded Spain steel privatisation where Aceralia was privatised in 1997.

Considering steel privatisation processes in France, Great Britain, and Spain, however, the privatisation of state steel in Italy presents idiosyncratic features. Privatisation in the former group of countries was embedded within a shared industrial logic oriented by the idea that privatisations were to be considered as a part of the restructuring of the global steel industry. In this logic, as we have anticipated, the steel industry was privatised by merging producers of different countries and by selling these conglomerates to global producers.

Steel privatisation in Italy deviated from this pattern. Retrospectively, in the privatisation of Italian steel, local interest groups more actively moulded the pattern of the process.

In 1995, occurred the last and probably the most emotionally poignant event in this process: the privatisation of ILVA's integrated plant of Taranto, one of the largest of Europe, and the reification of the very idea of the state-owned enterprise in Italy. The company, which was sold to a private Italian group, Riva, was the largest producer of flat steel products and was owned by IRI (Institute for Industrial Reconstruction), one of the most important Italian institutions, a state agency that was created in 1933 for giving shape to the Italian industrial structure. After the Second World War, IRI was maintained to orchestrate the re-construction of the Italian productive system.

The dismissal of ILVA, so important in the economic history of Italy, so entrenched in the culture of the country's industrial relations, and so imbued of political interests, was a dramatic institutional change. The endogenous pressures generated by state fiscal deficits, the exogenous pressures of the steel industry crisis, and the pressures from the EU to reduce installed capacity all conjured up to explain the privatisation.

The privatisation process in Italy began in the second half of the 1980s when the internationally spreading, and mounting, "privatization wave" (Bortolotti & Pinotti, 2008) forced leading political elites to consider privatisation as a policy to counter skyrocketing public debt. In particular, pressures to privatisation were particularly strong in the steel industry since state steel producers experienced dramatic financial tensions and the steel industry had suffered pathological problems of overcapacity in the previous ten years. The government was held by a coalition labelled "Pentapartito" since five parties were involved: Partito Socialista (PSI), along with Democrazia Cristiana (DC), Partito Socialdemocratico (PSDI), Partito Liberale (PLI), and Partito Repubblicano (PRI). As expected, the debate concerning privatisation was complex and heated: unions opposed privatisations, together with the Communist Party. Moreover, in the government coalition coexisted PLI and PRI, a typical expression of laic liberal thought, inclined to principles of the free market, but also PSI and DC, these latter two parties being representative of statist approach. Nevertheless, the privatisation of the steel industry started during the government of the prime minister Bettino Craxi, in the period 1983–1986, with the sale of Cornigliano, a large plant in the north of Italy owned by Finsider. The plant was conferred to COGEA, a new entity. One year later, 67% of the equity of the consortium was transferred to a group of private producers. To follow the main steps in the steel privatisation process, we can rely on Figure 2.1, which reports the share of private capital in the steel industry, together with the most important events that occurred.

A second step in Italian privatisation runs from 1991 to the beginning of 1994. In this period, Italy experienced a strong economic and political turmoil. Mounting public debt raised international concerns on the ro-bustness of the Italian economy and the Italian currency, which was especially dramatic in the face of impending pressures to accomplish the financial and economic parameters set by the Maastricht Agreement to be included in the European Union. Also, large parts of the political leading class were implicated in a vast anti-bribery investigation known as *mani pulite* (clean hands), from the name of the trials, or *Tangentopoli*

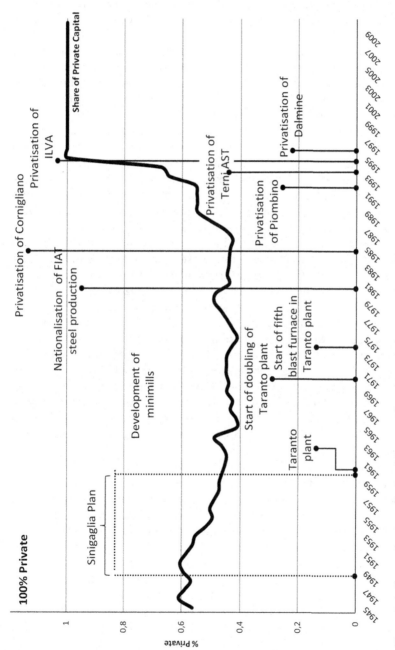

Figure 2.1 Share of private and public capital in the Italian state steel (1945–2009).
Source: elaboration by the authors.

(City of bribes), which is the name that journalists gave to this system based on bribery.

The European Union pushed Italian governments to privatise steel production since it did not consider the commitments of state-owned producers to cut their debt and the government to stop state transfers to indebted firms convincing and plausible. At the end of 1991, the decree DL 386/1991 was issued. The decree institutionalised privatisations by stating that state-owned enterprises could be restructured and sold. The decree opened the way to large-scale privatisation and was followed by decree DL 333/1992, which decided the transformation of major state-owned holdings into public companies to facilitate their privatisation.

This shock was managed by two governments that lasted one year each the government led by Giuliano Amato and that led by Azelio Ciampi. The first man was a socialist who had worked in the preceding governments as an economic expert and who had been Treasury Minister; the latter had been the governor of the Bank of Italy and was renowned as belonging to the elite of the Italian technocracy. To give a feeling of the mounting pressures in Italy at the beginning of the 1990s, in July 1992, Mr. Amato enacted a financial law worth nearly 100,000 billion of Italian lira, the largest in the second post-war world, to cover the public deficit. The same government pushed forward the privatisation process by transforming in law n° 359 8/8/1992 the decree n° 333 of 11/7/1992 that changed large state holding owned directly by the Minister of Treasury – IRI, ENEL, and ENI – into private companies whose equity was held by the same Ministry. This technical step was meant to be preparatory to the re-organisation of state-owned holdings to be conducted through mergers and, among other means, privatisation of the state holdings. In this window of opportunity for privatisation, in 1992, a large plant located on the western coastal area of Italy was spun off the Italsider group to create a new firm – Acciaierie e Ferriere di Piombino – participated by the state and the private company Gruppo Lucchini.

The last period, occurring from 1994 to 1996, was characterised by a change in the leading political coalition. A new coalition came to power led by Mr. Silvio Berlusconi and supported by parties newly created, such as Forza Italia (a party created by Mr. Berlusconi himself), Lega Nord (that supported a federal organisation of the government), and two small parties that inherited the tradition of the dissolved Christian Democrats (CCD and UDC). Mr. Berlusconi's government lasted for only one year and was substituted by a government led, again, by independent technocrats. Interestingly, in this last period, most of the important decisions were taken concerning the privatisation of the steel industry. Indeed, the privatisation of the steel industry was concluded between 1994 and 1995. For example, The decree 332/1994[1] was issued. The decree gave the final push to the privatisation process by removing constraints and accelerating privatisations. Namely, the decree made it easier to use, among accepted privatisation methods, the direct sale.

In 1994, AST, a state-owned company producing stainless steel, was sold to Kai Italia, owned by Thyssen Krupp and few Italian entrepreneurs. One year later, Thyssen Krupp reached 75% shares of Kai Italia. Between 1994 and 1995, as anticipated in the foregoing, ILVA Laminati Piani, the larger state-owned company that included a large part of the remaining state-owned capacity for flat products, was sold to a private producer, Riva. In 1995, Acciaierie e Ferriere di Piombino was completely privatised as the state sold its share of equity to Gruppo Lucchini. Finally, in 1996, Dalmine, a pipe producer, was privatised by direct sale of 84% of the equity to the Techint Investment Netherlands (owned by the Rocca family).

2.3.2 Explanations of local variations of privatisation policies in economics

A rich body of empirical literature in economics has examined how country-specific political contexts may induce or inhibit the adoption of privatisation policies. At least three lines of research are worth mentioning.

First, economists refer to partisan theory and public choice theory to suggest that, in general, the presence of right-wing governments is associated with a higher likelihood of privatisation while the presence of left-wing governments leads to the contrary (Biais & Perotti, 2002; Bortolotti et al., 2003; Bortolotti & Pinotti, 2008). Empirical studies exploring privatisation processes in OECD countries have found significant statistical evidence that the presence of right-wing governments is associated with a higher likelihood of privatisation (Bortolotti & Pinotti, 2008). However, when tested in developing countries, the hypothesis that left-wing governments are associated with a lower likelihood of privatisation does not find significant empirical support (Boubakri et al., 2005a, 2005b).

Second, Dinc and Gupta (2011) examined the role of region-specific political factors influencing the likelihood of privatisation. They found that privatisation is significantly delayed if a firm is located in a politically competitive constituency where the governing and opposition party alliances have won similar shares of the vote. In addition, no firm located in the state from which the minister with jurisdiction over that firm is elected is ever privatised. Furthermore, the government also delays the privatisation of firms that are located in districts where the opposition party has more voters' support. The authors argue that the government attempts to minimise the effects of a political reaction by delaying privatisation in districts where the governing party faces more competition from the opposition; therefore, the dispersed benefits and concentrated costs of privatisation appear to have a significant effect on the pattern of privatisation sales.

Third, the "war of attrition" argument (Alesina & Drazen, 1991; Spolaore, 2004) suggests that a lower political fragmentation favours executive stability and allows incumbent governments to privatise a sizeable fraction of their SOE sector sooner, as the constituency of the "losers" from the policy change is less likely to enjoy bargaining power. Conversely, highly fragmented political systems tend to disperse decision-making power among different actors, so that executives are weaker and characterised by higher turnover. In this context, the different political actors tend to have difficulty agreeing on how to distribute the burden of the policy change, and privatisation will be delayed by a "war of attrition". Political systems with a smaller number of parties and operating under majority electoral rules privatise sooner, while large-scale privatisation is delayed in more fragmented democracies. In this vein, Bortolotti and Pinotti (2008) suggest that political fragmentation, which is related to the number of agents with veto power in a political system, may hamper the implementation of policies with distributional consequences, such as privatisation. This prediction is tested by estimating a statistical duration model with data from a country-level study for 21 advanced OECD economies during the 1977–2002 period. The results are consistent with the empirical implications of the war of attrition theoretical model.

2.3.3 An institutional approach to the explanation of local variations of privatisation policies

Through the lens of the institutional theorising, which we embrace in our work, national policies tend to converge towards isomorphic models under the pressure of globally unfolding cultural processes.

Specifically, word-polity theories postulate that "Many features of the contemporary nation-state derive from worldwide models constructed and propagated through global cultural and associational processes" (Meyer et al., 1997: 144–145) so that "nation-states, are structurally similar in many unexpected dimensions and change in unexpectedly similar ways" (Meyer et al., 1997: 145).

Within this perspective, local variations occur because "…many struggles are over how the forms and rules of wider polities are to be adapted to the exigencies of local setting: how world structures are incorporated into nations, and how world and national rules are incorporated into sub-national contexts" (Jepperson & Meyer, 1991: 229). In this vein, for example, "states are ritualized actors marked by extensive internal decoupling" (Meyer et al., 1997: 173), that is, they formally adopt the requirements of global policies to maintain international legitimacy while informally preserving elements that are idiosyncratic of the local political environment. From the perspective of institutional analysis, traditional explanations of local variations in privatisation policies in economics have two weaknesses.

First, they mainly focus on the administrative features of the political processes and on the interests, and room for manoeuvring, of the political actors that are supposed to initiate and govern privatisations. In other words, economics cannot exploit the concept of *field* to include all the actors that contribute to shaping institutional change. Second, economic explanations almost completely ignore the role of entrenched symbolic and discursive structures, these latter contributing to mould power relations among the actors involved in the privatisation processes.

Instead, in our investigation, first, we assume that the local-specific features of privatisations both reflect the subjugation to globally spreading pressures to isomorphic adaptation and unveil the resilience of local-specific complex tangle of long-seated symbolic, material, and political structures. Second, we maintain that to explain the emergence of local variations of privatisation policies, we need to analyse what Bourdieu labelled a "field of power", which is the interweaved web of power relations among a variety of actors that are differently involved in privatisations.

Therefore, since policies apply to specific areas of a nation's activity, which we label *field* according to our institutional framework, it is necessary to investigate the interaction among field-specific symbolic, material, and political structures. That is, pressures to conform hit specific areas of activity thereby finding their way through field-specific political, discursive, and symbolic structures and influencing the material interests of specific interconnected social groups.

In our case, for example, we study how globally spreading neo-liberal pressures to privatising specifically affected steel privatisation policy in Italy. Therefore, since privatisation policy influences the interests of social actors in the steel industry, understanding the interests of steel producers and other actors in the steel industry is relevant. However, the privatisation of steel not only affects the steel industry but as well impinges on the relations between the state and the private sector and touches the interests of a variety of national and local politicians. Furthermore, the progress of privatisations reinforces or weakens the voice of intellectuals who take different stances towards the beneficial property of neoliberal market reforms. Therefore, to explain local variations of globally spreading policies, we need to consider the power relations among the actors whose interests are primarily influenced by the local application of a policy. In other words, we adopt the already mentioned perspective in the institutional research that suggests that a "field is formed around the issues that become important to the interests and objectives of a specific collective of organizations" (Hoffman, 1999: 352). According to this view, fields form around specific issues, rather than a common product or market, and "become centers of debates in which competing interests negotiate over issue interpretation" (Hoffman, 1999: 351).

Note

1 Decreto legge n° 332 – "Norme per l'accelerazione delle procedure di dismissione di partecipazioni dello Stato e degli enti pubblici in società per azioni".

References

Alesina, A., & Drazen, A. (1991). Why are stabilizations delayed? *American Economic Review*, 81: 1088–1170.
Ansari, S. S., Wijen, F., & Gray, B. (2013). Constructing a climate change logic: An institutional perspective on the "tragedy of the commons." *Organization Science*, 24(4): 1014–1040. 10.1287/orsc.1120.0799
Benford, R., & Snow, D. (2000). Framing processes and social movements: An overview and assessment. *Annual Review of Sociology*, 26 (1): 611–639.
Berger, P. L., & Luckman, T. (1966). *The social construction of reality: A treatise on the sociology of knowledge*. London: Penguin Books.
Biais, B., & Perotti, E. (2002). Machiavellian privatization. *The American Economic Review*, 92(1): 240–258.
Bortolotti, B., Fantini, M., & Siniscalco, D. (2003). Privatisation around the world: Evidence from panel data. *Journal of Public Economics*, 88: 305–332.
Bortolotti, B., & Pinotti, P. (2008). Delayed privatization. *Public Choice*, 136: 331–351.
Boubakri, N., Cosset, J.C., & Guedhami, O. (2005a). Post-privatization corporate governance: The role of ownership structure and investor protection. *Journal of Financial Economics*, 76: 369–399.
Boubakri, N., Cosset, J.C., & Guedhami, O. (2005b). Liberalization, corporate governance and the performance of newly privatized firms. *Journal of Corporate Finance*, 11: 767–790.
Bourdieu, P. (1977). *Outline of a theory of practice*. Trans. Richard Nice. Cambridge: Cambridge University Press.
Bourdieu, P. (1985). The social space and the genesis of groups. *Theory and Society*, 14: 723–744.
Bourdieu, P. (2005). The political field, the social science field and the journalistic field. In R. Benson, & E., Neveu (Eds.), *Bourdieu and the journalistic field* (pp. 29–47). Cambridge, UK: Polity Press.
Brint, S., & Karabel, J. (1991). Institutional origins and transformation: The case of American community colleges. In W. W. Powell, & P. J. DiMaggio (Eds.). *The New institutionalism in organizational analysis* (pp. 337–360). Chicago: University of Chicago Press.
Brune, N., Garrett, G., & Kogut, B. (2004). The International Monetary Fund and the global spread of privatization. *IMF Staff Papers*, 51(2): 195–219.
Clegg, S. (1998). Foucault, power and organizations. In A. McKinlay, & K. Starkey (Eds.), *Foucault, management and organization theory* (pp. 29–48). London: Sage.

Clemens, E., & Cook, J. (1999). Politics and institutionalism: Explaining durability and change. *Annual Review of Sociology*, 25: 441–466.

Commons, J. R. (1924). *The legal foundations of capitalism.* New York: Macmillan.

Commons, J. R. (1932). The problems of correlating law, economics and ethics. *Wisconsin Law Review*, 8(1): 3–26.

Commons, J. R. (1934). *Institutional economics.* Madison: University of Wisconsin Press.

Cornelissen, J. P., & Werner, M. D. (2014). Putting framing in perspective: A review of framing and frame analysis across the management and organizational literature. *The Academy of Management Annals*, 8: 181–235.

Creed, W. E. D., Langstraat, J. A., & Scully, M. A. (2002a). A picture of the frame: Frame analysis as technique and as politics. *Organizational Research Methods*, 5(1): 34–55.

Creed, W. E. D., Scully, M. A., & Austin, J. R. (2002b). Accounts and the social construction of identity clothes make the person? The tailoring of legitimating accounts and the social construction of identity. *Organization Science*, 13(5): 475–496.

Davis, G. F., & Thompson, T. A. (1994). A social movement perspective on corporate control. *Administrative Science Quarterly*, 39(1): 141–173.

Diani, M. (1996). Linking mobilization frames and political opportunities: Insights from regional populism in Italy. *American Sociological Review*, 61(6): 1053–1069.

DiMaggio, P. J. & Powell, W. W. (1983). The iron cage revisited: Institutional isomorpshism and collective rationality in organizational fields. *American Sociological Review*, 48(2): 147–160.

Dinc, I. S., & Gupta, N. (2011). The decision to privatize: Finance and politics. *The Journal of Finance*, 66(1): 241–269.

Elsbach, K., & Sutton, R. I. (1992). Acquiring organizational legitimacy through illegitimate actions: A marriage of institutional and impression management theories. *Academy of Management Journal*, 35: 699–738.

Fligstein, N. (1996). Markets as politics: A political cultural approach to market institutions. *American Sociological Review*, 61: 656–657.

Fligstein, N. (1997). Social skills and institutional theory. *American Behavioral Scientist*, 40(4): 197–405.

Fligstein, N. (2001). Social skill and the theory of fields. *Sociological Theory*, 19: 105–125.

Fligstein, N., & Mara-Drita, I. (1996). How to make a market: Reflections on the attempt to create a single market in the European Union. *American Journal of Sociology*, 102(1): 1–33.

Fligstein, N., & McAdam, D. (2011). Toward a general theory of strategic action fields. *Sociological Theory*, 29(1): 1–26.

Fligstein, N., & McAdam, D. (2012). *A theory of fields.* Oxford: Oxford University Press.

Friedland, R., & Alford, R. (1991). Bringing society back in: Symbols, practices, and institutional contradictions. In W. W. Powell, & P. J. DiMaggio (Eds.), *The new institutionalism in organizational analysis* (pp. 232–263). Chicago: University of Chicago Press.

Garud, R., Jain, S., & Kumaraswamy, A. (2002). Institutional entrepreneurship in the sponsorship of common technological standards: The case of Sun Microsystems and Java. *Academy of Management Journal*, 45: 196–214.

Granqvist, N., & Laurila, J. (2011). Rage against self-replicating machines: Framing science and fiction in the US nanotechnology field. *Organization Studies*, 32(2): 253–280.

Gray, B, Purdy, J. M., & Ansari, S. (2015). From interactions to institutions: Microprocesses of framing and mechanisms for the structuring of institutional fields. *Academy of Management Review*, 40(1): 115–143.

Greenwood, R., & Hinings, C. R. (1996). Understanding radical organizational change: Bringing together the old and the new institutionalism. *Academy of Management Review*, 21(4): 1022–1054.

Greenwood, R., & Suddaby, R. (2006). Institutional entrepreneurship in mature fields: The big five accounting firms. *Academy of Management Journal*, 49(1): 27–48.

Greenwood, R., Suddaby, R., & Hinings, C. R. (2002). Theorizing change: The role of professional associations in the transformation of institutionalized fields. *Academy of Management Journal*, 45(1): 58–80.

Hannan, M. T., & Freeman, J. H. (1977). The population ecology of organizations. *American Journal of Sociology*, 82: 929–964.

Hardy, C., & Maguire, S. (2008). Institutional entrepreneurship. In R. Greenwood, C. Oliver, K. Sahlin, & R. Suddaby (Eds.), *The SAGE handbook of organizational institutionalism* (pp. 651–672). London: Sage.

Hardy, C., & Maguire, S. (2017). Institutional entrepreneurship and change in fields. In R. Greenwood, C. Oliver, T. B. Lawrence, & R. Meyer (Eds.), *The SAGE handbook of organizational institutionalism*, Second edition (pp. 261–281). London: Sage.

Hargrave, T. J., & Van De Ven, A. H. (2006). A collective action model of institutional innovation. *The Academy of Management Review*, 31(4): 864–888.

Henisz, W. J., & Zelner, B. A. (2012). Strategy and competition in the market and nonmarket Arenas. *Academy of Management Perspectives*, 26(3): 40–51.

Henisz, W. J., Zelner, B. A., & Guillén, M. F. (2005). The worldwide diffusion of market-oriented infrastructure reform, 1977-1999. *American Sociological Review*, 70(6): 871–897. 10.2307/4145398

Hensmans, M. (2003). Social movement organizations: A metaphor for strategic actors in institutional fields. *Organization Studies*, 24: 355–381.

Hoffman, A. J. (1999). Institutional evolution and change: Environmentalism and the U.S. chemical industry. *Academy of Management Journal*, 42(4): 351–371.

Ikenberry, G. J. (1990). The international spread of privatization policies: Inducements, learning, and "Policy Bandwagoning". In E. N. Suleiman, & J. Waterbury (Eds), *The political economy of public sector reform and privatization*. Boulder, CO: Westview Press.

Ingram, P., & Clay, K. (2000). The choice-within-constraints new institutionalism and implications for sociology. *Annual Review of Sociology*, 26: 525–546.

Ingram, P., & Rao, H. (2004). Store wars: The enactment and repeal of anti-chain-store legislation in America. *American Journal of Sociology*, 110(2): 446–487.

Jepperson, R. L., & Meyer J. W. (1991). The public order and the construction of formal organizations. In W. W. Powell, & P. J. DiMaggio (Eds.), *The new institutionalism in organizational analysis* (pp. 232–263). Chicago: University of Chicago Press.

Koopmans, R., & Statham, P. (1999). Ethnic and civic conceptions of nationhood and the differential success of the extreme right in Germany and Italy. In M. Giugni, D. McAdam, & C. Tilly (Eds.), *How social movements matter* (pp. 225–251). Minnesota: University of Minnesota Press.

Lawrence, T. B. (1999). Institutional strategy. *Journal of Management*, 25(2): 161–188.

Lawrence, T. B., & Phillips, N. B. (2004). From Moby Dick to Free Willy: Macro-cultural discourse and institutional entrepreneurship in emerging institutional fields. *Organization*, 11(5): 89–711.

Levy, D., & Scully, M. (2007). The institutional entrepreneur as modern prince: The strategic face of power in contested fields. *Organization Studies*, 28: 971–991.

Lounsbury, M., & Glynn, M. A. (2001). Cultural entrepreneurship: Stories, legitimacy, and the acquisition of resources. *Strategic Management Journal*, 22: 545–564.

Maguire, S., & Hardy, C. (2009). Discourse and deinstitutionalization: The decline of DDT. *The Academy of Management Journal*, 52(1): 148–178.

Maguire, S., Hardy, C., & Lawrence, T. B. (2004). Institutional entrepreneurship in emerging fields: HIV/AIDS treatment advocacy in Canada. *The Academy of Management Journal*, 47(5): 657–679.

McAdam, D. (1996). Conceptual origins, current problems, future directions. In D. McAdam, J. D. McCarthy, & M. N. Zald (Eds.), *Comparative perspectives on social movements: Political opportunities, mobilizing structures and cultural framings* (pp. 23–40). New York, NY: Cambridge University Press.

McAdam, D., McCarthy, J. D., & Zald, M. N. (1996). Introduction: Opportunities, mobilizing structures, and framing processes – Toward a synthetic, comparative perspective on social movements. In D. McAdam, J. D. McCarthy, & M. N. Zald (Eds.), *Comparative perspectives on social movements: Political opportunities, mobilizing structures and cultural framings* (pp. 1–20). Cambridge: Cambridge University Press.

McCammon, H. J., Muse, C. S., Newman, H. D., & Terrell, T. M. (2007). Movement framing and discursive opportunity structures: The political successes of the U.S. women's jury movements. *American Sociological Review*, 72(5): 725–749. 10.1177/000312240707200504

Meyer, J. W., Boli, J., Thomas George, M., & Ramirez, F. O. (1997). World society and the nation-state. *American Journal of Sociology*, 103(1): 144–181. 10.1086/231174

Meyer, J. W., & Rowan, B. (1977). Institutionalized organizations: Formal structure as myth and ceremony. *American Journal of Sociology*, 83(2): 340–363.

Meyer, R. E., & Höllerer, M. A. (2010). Meaning structures in a contested issue field: A topographic map of shareholder value in Austria. *Academy of Management Journal*, 53(6): 1241–1262. 10.5465/amj.2010.57317829

Morrill, C., Zald, M. N., & Rao, H. (2003). Covert political conflict in organizations: Challenges from below. *Annual Review of Sociology*, 29: 391–415.

Munir, K. A. (2005). The social construction of events: A study of institutional change in the photographic field. *Organization Studies*, 26(1): 93–112.

North, D. C. (1986). The new institutional economics. *Journal of Institutional and Theoretical Economics*, 142: 230–237.

Phillips, N., Lawrence, T. B., & Hardy, C. (2004). Discourse and institutions. *The Academy of Management Review*, 29(4): 635–652.

Polillo, S., & Guillén, M. F. (2005). Globalization pressures and the state: The worldwide spread of central bank independence. *American Journal of Sociology*, 110(6): 1764–1802.

Rao, H. (1998). Caveat emptor: The construction of nonprofit consumer watchdog organizations. *American Journal of Sociology*, 103(4): 912–961.

Rao, H., & Kenney, M. (2008). New forms as settlements. In R. Greenwood, C. Oliver, K. Sahlin, & R. Suddaby (Eds.), *The SAGE handbook of organizational institutionalism* (pp. 651–672). Sage: London.

Rao, H., Monin, P., & Durand, R. (2003). Institutional change in Toque Ville: Nouvelle cuisine as an identity movement in French gastronomy. *American Journal of Sociology*, 108(4): 795–843.

Rao, H., Morril, C. & Zald, M. N. (2000). Power plays: How social movements and collective action create new organizational forms. *Research in Organizational Behaviour*, 22: 239–282.

Ryan, C. (1991). *Prime Time Activism: Media strategies for grassroots organizing*. Boston, MASS: South End Press.

Schneiberg, M., King, M., & Smith, T. (2008). Social movements and organizational form: Cooperative alternatives to corporations in the American insurance, dairy, and grain industries. *American Sociological Review*, 73: 635–667.

Schneiberg, M., & Lounsbury, M. (2008). Social movements and institutional analysis. In R. Greenwood, C. Oliver, K. Sahlin, & R. Suddaby (Eds.), *The SAGE handbook of organizational institutionalism* (pp. 651–672). London: Sage.

Schneiberg, M., & Soule, S. A. (2005). Institutionalization as a contested, multilevel process. The case of rate regulation in American fire insurance. In G. F. Davis, D. McAdam, W. R. Scott, & M. N. Zald (Eds.), *Social movements and organizational theory*. Cambridge University Press: Cambridge, UK.

Scott, W. R. (1994). Conceptualizing organizational fields: Linking organizations and societal systems. In H. D. Derlien, H. U. Gerhardt, & F. W. Scharpf (Eds.), *Systems rationality and partial interests*, by Baden-Baden, (pp. 203–221). Nomos Verlagsgesselschaft: Germany.

Scott, W. R. (2014). *Institution and organization*. Fourth edition. Thousand Oaks: Sage.

Seo, M. G., & Creed, W. E. D. (2002). Institutional contradictions, Praxis, and institutional change: A dialectical perspective. *The Academy of Management Review*, 27: 222–247.

Snow, D., & Benford, R. (1988). Ideology, frame resonance, and participant mobilization. In B. Klandermans, H. Kriesi, & S. Tarrow (Eds.), *From structure to action: Comparing social movement research across cultures, vol. 1*. JAI press.

Snow, D. A., Rochford, Jr. E. B., Worden, S. K., & Benford, R. D. (1986). Frame alignment processes, micromobilization, and movement participation. *American Sociological Review*, 51: 464–481.

Spolaore, E. (2004). Adjustments in different government systems. *Economics & Politics*, 16(2): 117–146.

Suchman, M. C. (1995). Managing legitimacy: Strategic and institutional approaches. *The Academy of Management Review*, 20(3): 571–610.

Swidler, A. (1986). Culture in action: Symbols and strategies. *American Sociological Review*, 51(2): 273–286.

Tarrow, S. (1994). *Power in movement: Social movements, collective action and politics*. Cambridge, MA: Cambridge University Press.

Tarrow, S. (1996). States and opportunities: The political structuring of social movements. In D. McAdam, J. D. McCarthy, & M. N. Zald (Eds.), *Comparative perspectives on social movements: Political opportunities, mobilizing structures and cultural framings* (pp. 1–20). New York: Cambridge University Press.

Thornton, P. H., Ocasio, W., & Lounsbury, M. (2012). *The institutional logics perspective. A new approach to culture, structure, and process*. Oxford: Oxford University Press.

Tracey, P., Pillips, N., & Jarvis, O. (2011). Bridging institutional entrepreneurship and the creation of new organizational forms: A multilevel model. *Organization Science*, 22(1): 60–80.

Veblen, T. B. (1909). The limitations of marginal utility. *Journal of Political Economy*, 17: 235–245.

Weber, K., Davis, G. F., & Lounsbury, M. (2009). Policy as myth and ceremony? The global spread of stock exchanges. *Academy of Management Journal*, 52(6): 1319–1347.

White, H. (1992). *Identity and control: A structural theory of social interaction*. Princeton, NJ: Princeton University Press.

Willmott, H. (2015). Why institutional theory cannot be critical. *Journal of Management Inquiry*, 24(1): 105–111.

Williamson, O. (1975). *Market and hierarchies: Antitrust implications*. New York: Free Press.

Williamson, O. (1981). The economics of organization: The transaction cost approach. *The American Journal of Sociology*, 87(3): 548–577.

Williamson, O. (1982). The modern corporation: Origins, evolution, attributes. *Journal of Economic Literature*, 19: 1537–1568.

Williamson, O. (1985). *The economic institutions of capitalism*. New York: Free press.

Zelner, B. A., Henisz, W. J., & Holburn, G. L. F. (2009). Contentious implementation and retrenchment in neoliberal policy reform: The global electric power industry, 1989–2001. *Administrative Science Quarterly*, 54(3): 379–412.

3 Gramscian theory of hegemony

3.1 A Gramscian approach to the analysis of local variations of privatisation policies

In this chapter, we introduce the elements of the Gramscian hegemony theory that are paramount to explain our empirical context. Specifically, we propose to bridge the neo-institutional theory and the hegemony theory, as this integration brings about reciprocal advantages that go beyond the specific application of this book.

When addressing the local application of global policy, we are interested in how an old power structure resists by accomodating exogenous pressures or, eventually, makes way to a new power structure that is able to orchestrate the modification of institutions of different nature: bureaucratic, political, cultural, and economic.

To this endeavour, Gramscian hegemony theory examines the idiosyncratic interaction of cultural and political nation-specific forces.

Gramscian hegemony theory examines power relations not only in the realm of economic transactions and in the connected, administrative, legal, and bureaucratic arrangements. Rather, the novelty of Gramsci's theoretical apparatus is to seek out the roots of power relations in ideology as well. In his theoretical apparatus hegemony requires the building of a shared consciousness of common interests and, therefore, has a strong discursive component. According to this narrative, the resilience of hegemonic formations rests in the interplay of economic relations, political-administrative arrangements, and discursive articulations. From this perspective, "some striking parallels are evident between the concept of hegemony and the isomorphic stability of institutional theory" (Scott & Meyer, 1994). In both theories, social order is viewed as contingent on a balance of the coercive pressure of rules and more consensual forces of norms, cognitive frames, and taken-for-granted ideas" (Levy, 2008: 952).

Despite hegemonic processes being predominantly discursive (Burgio, 2014: 218), the role of the material and political forces is not dismissed. As Cornelissen and Werner suggest (2014: 210–211), the analysis of these forces may deepen our knowledge of the relative

DOI: 10.4324/9780429438516-3

difficulty with which different social groups that are divided by political and material tensions can come to shared understandings.

At the same time, however, the fundamental role of cultural processes is recognised so that hegemonic processes may result in a shared consciousness that bonds together, within a historical bloc, social actors with different political and material interests (Gruppi, 1972: 99).

In sum, to explain the peculiar nature of local policies, we propose to employ a Gramscian analysis to unveil how the attempts to locally applying global policies activate "local struggles" (Levy & Scully, 2007: 6) whose unfolding depends on the settlement of field-specific hegemonic formations.

These hegemonic formations develop by intervening on the relations of production (material accommodation, implying a control on material resources), political relations (political accommodation, implying a control on organisational structures and processes), and the construction of a shared consciousness of a group's interests as whole societal interests (cultural accommodation, implying a control on discourse).

Thus, the fundamental role of cultural processes is recognised so that hegemonic processes result in a shared consciousness that bonds together, within a historical bloc, social actors with different political and material interests (Gruppi, 1972: 99).

3.2 Gramsci and hegemony theory

3.2.1 Why Gramsci?

Antonio Gramsci was a Marxist political thinker who focused on the "... relations of human thoughts, feelings, and will to "objective" social process" (Kołakowski, 2008: 969). In his critique of historical materialism, he rejected the idea that cultural superstructures are only a projection of the real and objective aspects of social life, which crystallised into relations of production. Rather, he suggested that superstructures and material forces are in "dialectical tension" (Levy & Egan, 2003: 805; Levy & Scully, 2007: 976) and there is no point in talking about the primacy of material forces.

Born in Italy, Gramsci developed his thought by speculating on the failure of economic determinism. In Russia, the Bolshevik revolution took place when material forces were theoretically not ripe for a revolution. On the contrary, in Italy, where a blue-collar class existed, and where, theoretically, the tensions in the relations of production were mature for a revolution, the hegemony of the bourgeois class thrived into Mussolini's fascist regime (Gramsci, 1916, 1918). In coping with these conundrums, to capture the inertia in socio-political change, Gramsci developed the concept of the historical bloc (Gramsci, 1975: 858). In addition, with the concept of hegemony, Gramsci described the process through which different ideologies struggle for supremacy until one, or a unique combination of ideologies emerges as the winning one (Gramsci, 1975: 457, 1584). Hegemony ensues when an alignment is reached between a winning ideology, political/organisational structures, and economic pressures (Gramsci, 1975: 1583–1585). As suggested by Levy and Scully (2007), despite its influence on social theory, only recently has the theoretical framework developed by Gramsci been mobilised as a Neo-Gramscian approach (Böhm et al., 2008; Contu et al., 2013; Levy, 2008; Levy & Egan, 2003; Levy & Newell, 2002; Levy & Scully, 2007).

3.2.2   The concept of the historical bloc

A historical bloc is made of the complex and contradictory cluster (Gramsci, 1975, p. 1051) of (i) cultural "superstructures", which are shared understandings and meanings, (ii) material forces, or relations of production, and (iii) organisational structures, which wield power through bureaucratic and coercive power. The historical bloc takes shape in the development of power relations within a society. Gramsci (1975: 457–458, 1583–1585) envisages different steps in the formation of hegemony.

After a first step in which relations of production are created, a step follows in which political power relations emerge. This step terminates when a specific social group transforms the self-consciousness of their own specific interests into the shared consciousness of those interests as society-wide interests. Thus, a historical bloc develops when a social group, or an alliance of social groups, attains the moral and intellectual direction of the society so that its own interests expand to become societal interests. As Burgio suggests (2014), in Gramsci, the hegemonic relation is a "sentimental" one; in order to maintain its legitimacy, a hegemonic group needs to be part of the societal body. Thus, hegemony describes a state of relative stability given by the alignment between social groups that share understandings and meaning structures, and that have similar political and material interests. More subtly, hegemonic processes are cultural processes that produce a shared consciousness that bonds together, within a historical bloc, social actors with different political and material interests (Gramsci, 1949; Gruppi, 1972: 99).

Therefore, the concept of *alignment*, on which a historical bloc is built, evokes a subtle work of compromising. Historical blocs, Gruppi recommends, contain different political groups (1972). In this picture, the word "bloc", as a solid entity with clear-cut edges, is deceiving (Contu et al., 2013). The central alignment of the bloc represents a point of reference to define the relative distance among groups thereby describing a complex tangle of power relations.

This endeavour, however, is very different from the simple fight against incumbents and the persuasion of a neutral audience such as, for example, in the social movement theory (Tarrow, 1994; McAdam et al., 1996; Fligstein & McAdam, 2012).

Rather, it is about "building alliances" (Burgio, 2014: 16) and recomposing "fragmented elements" (Filippini, 2017: 67). Each element carries a specific relationship with political and material forces. Thus, political action refers to the "evaluation of homogeneity, self-awareness, and organisation attained by the various social classes" (Filippini, 2017: 102).

3.2.3 The concept of hegemony

In his critique of historical materialism, Gramsci suggested that super-structures and material forces are in "dialectical tension" (Levy & Egan, 2003: 805; Levy & Scully, 2007: 976).

Such a relationship between cultural and political, which are super-structures, and economic structures is at the core of the Gramscian analysis of hegemony; this latter, to materialise, needs to be articulated along with three levels: market, state, and civil society.

Namely, the market is the locus where relations of production produce power relations. The state accommodates the formal political structures (e.g. the State and the public administration) that hold an explicit power of coercion. Hegemony, however, ensues only when these elements are connected to the cultural direction of the civil society. It is only through hegemonic practices, which are cultural processes (Burgio, 2014: 218) that operate through the public discourse (Burgio, 2014: 238), that a shared consciousness is built and alliances among social groups, whose interests are only partially aligned, are created in the civil society.

Hegemony implies the articulation of discourse into a coherent ideology (Levy & Scully, 2007: 977). Through hegemonic practices, residuals of corporatism are abandoned towards the construction of larger alliances and blocs (Burgio, 2014: 16). The concreteness of historical blocs is, therefore, associated with their political form (Gramsci, 1975: 1091). Alliances and blocs clarify how the political opportunity structure is intertwined with a society's cultural repertoire. In this light, we suggest that hegemony is a concept able to integrate discursive and political manoeuvring in an overarching practice.

In its discursive component, hegemonic practice captures available discursive opportunities to create shared consciousness and "intellectual and moral unity" (Gramsci, 1975: 1594) and to develop a "logic of equivalence" (Laclau & Mouffe, 1985). In parallel, in its political component, hegemonic practice captures the penetration of civil society within the institutions (Gramsci, 1975: 859, 1616), and how coalitions are based upon "negotiation and compromise between different interest groups" (Thomas, 2009: 161).

3.2.4 The discursive nature of hegemonic practices

Hegemonic practices are primarily discursive as they regard cultural processes (Burgio, 2014: 218) that operate in the public discourse (Burgio, 2014: 238). Individuals develop their consciousness in ideologies (Gramsci, 1975: 869), which are the battlefield for the conquest of hegemony (Filippini, 2017: 10). Therefore, hegemonic practices move from a critique of past ideologies (Gramsci, 1975: 1053) to realise a "moral and intellectual reform" (1975: 953) aiming at creating a "cultural front" (1975: 1224) unified by a "collective will" (1975: 953). This form of cultural hegemony is obtained in the form of "public opinion" (Thomas, 2009:167).

This discursive practice has been emphasised by Laclau and Mouffe (1985) through the concepts of logics of equivalence and logics of difference. Hegemonic relations emerge when a "logic of equivalence" takes over so that one social actor "assumes the representation of a universality" (2014: 13). Then, a "chain of equivalence" follows (:153), that is, a discursive articulation that enables a set of social actors to recognise their similarity vis-à-vis, for instance, an oppressive force. A "logic of equivalence" is a logic of a simplification of political space (Laclau & Mouffe, 1985: 117) that captures common instances (Laclau & Mouffe, 1985: 113) so as to link contradictory groups (Spicer & Sewell, 2010) in "either you are for us, or you are against us" logic (Hensmans, 2003: 359). A logic of equivalence, Böhm et al. observe (2008: 177), evokes "hegemonic sameness" among actors who build a "united political identity". Challengers employ the logic that everyone who does not antagonise a status quo is considered complicit. For example, local discourse on globalisation linked market-oriented corporations and the interests of those supporting global value (Spicer & Sewell, 2010). In addition, the logic of equivalence may link different social groups that resist change by reducing differences and increasing their collective sense of unity, as was the case of the groups resisting the restructuring of industrial plants reported by Contu et al. (2013).

The stability of a logic of equivalence, however, is always challenged by the potential emergence of a "logic of difference", which tends to increase the complexity of political space by producing "chains of difference", which represent an "alignment where differences are exacerbated because particular interests stay at the forefront" (Contu et al., 2013: 367).

The work of Laclau and Mouffe facilitates the investigation of the discursive side of the alliance among social groups that composes a historical bloc (Contu et al., 2013: 369). However, their approach needs to be handled with care. They advocate the "autonomization of the political" from the economic base (2014: 25) and cannot support the analysis of the political-material dimension of hegemony. In their application of discourse analysis to a general theory of politics and society, Laclau and Mouffe emphasised the role of discourse in Gramscian theory of hegemony and tend to replace the Marxian concept of class identity with the concept of "hegemonic identity" (2014: 11), this latter politically articulated through discourse.

In their view, social actors, defined "particularities" (2014: xiii), occupy differential positions within the discourse. Hegemonic relations emerge when one particularity discursively "assumes the representation of a universality" (2014: xiii).

Thus, hegemony is the product of the discursive dialectic between the logics of equivalence and logics of difference, these latter emphasising the differentiation among particularities.

On the contrary, in our work, we highlight the political and the material components of hegemony and historical blocs. Following Levy, we adopt the concept of the historical bloc as a dominant alliance (Levy, 2008: 951) that ensues from the connection between cultural and political structures in a new ethic-political order that makes sense of and protects the economic structure of society. In this view, the logics of equivalence may support the building of discursive alliances but these latter need to be supported by specific political structures and by a compromise among the material interest of involved actors.

3.2.5 The political dimension of hegemony

In the development of hegemony, a fundamental step is the creation of political and juridical formal institutions that accommodate the shared economic interests of dominant groups (Gramsci, 1975: 1583–1584). Building a historical bloc, Gramsci submits, not only implies building the coercive institutions of the state but also entails the creation of a web of private institutions in the civil society that play a central role in ideological reproduction (Levy & Egan, 2003: 805–806).

In this respect, this political dimension of hegemonic practice regards how, in building a historical bloc, ideologies need to be integrated with the concreteness of both political form and material content (Gramsci, 1975: 1091), which are the institutions of the State, and a web of private institutions in the civil society (Levy & Egan, 2003: 805–806).

These institutions are connected by the efforts of a population of intellectuals that work at the constitution of a *stato integrale* (Gramsci, 1975: 691, 1947), or *extended state* (Levy, 2008: 957), which develops when specific social groups weld alliances between the state bureaucracy and the private institutions of the civil society to operate an "ideological conquer" (Gramsci, 1975: 1516–1518), leading to the formation of the state "in its integral sense" (Jessop, 2005: 432). Actors of the extended state manoeuvre to forge "the organizational structure of the system, comprising alliances and hierarchical relations among various actors"

(Levy, 2008: 952), navigating a web of institutions of civil society that, like "trenches" (Gramsci, 1975: 859–860, 973, 1615–1616), protects the legitimacy of moral and intellectual leadership.

Hegemonic practice thus requires a subtle work of compromising among different political groups to create a connective texture among social actors. Intellectuals manoeuvre to forge "the organizational structure of the system, comprising alliances and hierarchical relations among various actors" (Levy, 2008: 952).

Along these lines, the political organisation refers to both the coercive institutions of the state bureaucracy as well as to the articulation of the web of institutions of civil society that like "trenches" (Gramsci, 1975: 859–860, 973, 1615–1616) protect the legitimacy of moral and intellectual leadership.

These trenches may pair off with the concept of the political opportunity structure, as developed in the social movement theory (Tarrow, 1994, 1996; McAdam, 1996), as they are the constraints and the opportunities that political manoeuvring faces in the extended state (Gramsci, 1975).

Here, however, further clarification is needed. In the work of Gramsci, an apparently clear division of labour assigns to the state the administration of coercive power and to intellectuals in the civil society the creation and maintenance of shared consciousness, the situation is more subtle than the one described. The relationships at work in the civil society may play a role that is not only of intellectual and cultural domestication but of social pressures and coercion as well. Think, for example, of the political pressures that unions, employers' associations, and other interest groups may exert on States and the public administrations. These pressures are not only aimed at cultural control but have an effect on laws and regulations as well. Put simply, intellectuals, who in Gramscian terms are political actors, work in the interstices between state and civil society, not only to influence shared consciousness but to mould formal political administration as well.

Thus, since civil and political societies are tightly interweaved among each other, as Thomas suggests "no ascription of Gramsci's concept of hegemony exclusively to one or the other "terrain", would appear to be legitimate" (2009: 173) and "hegemony is conceived as a practice "traversing" the boundaries between them" (2009: 194).

This attempt to forge political component of hegemonic practices operates in the civil society and occurs "before seizing state power or domination in political society" (Thomas, 2009: 194).

This implies that, in observing the development of a historical bloc, we cannot belittle the purely political content of the hegemonic practices that materialise in the civil society.

3.2.6 Consistency of Gramscian framework with institutional analysis

Gramscian emphasis on the role of discursive articulation and the building, and maintenance, of coherent ideologies in creating hegemony, resonates with the discursive turn that characterised research on social movements beginning from the late 1990s. Shifting the focus from resource endowment and mobilisation, social movement theory concentrated on the capability to frame issues in order to win consensus. More specifically, the literature on framing in social movements looks at the ways social actors produce and maintain *collective action frames*, that is, "action-oriented sets of beliefs and meanings that inspire and legitimate" action (Benford & Snow, 2000: 624) and, more specifically, inspire and legitimate social movement activities and campaigns (Snow & Benford, 1988). The typical components of collective action frames are coherent with the discursive battle that underpins the building of a Gramscian hegemony, at least in the interpretation of Laclau and Mouffe and the subsequent neo-Gramscian literature. As Gamson advises (1992), there are three key components of collective action frames: injustice, agency, and identity. The injustice component implies a political consciousness that crystallises moral indignation. In addition, collective action frames incorporate agency as the consciousness that collective action is able to mobilise a state of the world. In this respect, collective action frames reveal the same discontent that mobilises the action of particular identities collected in a chain of equivalence with the aim to modify institutions. Finally, collective action frames have an identity component that entails the definition of a "we" in opposition to some "they" who have different interests and values" (Gamson, 1992: 7). The same motive animates the articulation of the logics of equivalence in building of political identity, according to Laclau and Mouffe.

In addition, in Gramscian terms, hegemonic practices aim at understanding how previous ideological elements may have "left a deposit in society" (Gramsci, 1975: 34). This practice resonates with the neo-institutional narrative of cultural manoeuvring implying the analysis of fields' "latent meaning structure" (Meyer & Höllerer, 2010) and "multiplicity" of logics (Hoffman, 1999: 2001). Furthermore, hegemony implies the evaluation of the "possibility/impossibility of the inclusion of an ideological element within a given historical bloc" (Filippini, 2017: 10); similarly, the neo-institutional narrative calls for the assessment of the ideological incompatibility (Rao & Kenney, 2008) and "relative incoherence" of fields' logics. Hegemonic practices entail the production of a historical subjectivity ensuing from the transformation of "the ideological elements found to be disjointed within society" (Filippini, 2017: 12). In parallel, the neo-institutional narrative framing activity draws on existing "cultural stocks" (Zald, 1996: 266), "prevalent cultural materials" (Rao,

1998: 916), "shared understandings" (Ingram & Clay, 2000: 541), "broader cultural account" (Creed et al., 2002), and "cognitive schemata" (Helms et al., 2012).

On the other hand, in their political content, hegemonic practices explore the opportunities and constraints that emanate from the coercive institutions of the state that legally enforces discipline (Gramsci, 1975: 1518, 1519). This endeavour pairs the social movement theory narrative in which the political opportunity structure reveals opportunities and constraints crystallised into the "formal legal and institutional structure" (McAdam, 1996: 27) of the field. On the other hand, in Gramscian terms, hegemony requires a subtle political work of compromising among the interests of different social groups (Gramsci, 1975: 458; Burgio, 2014: 214) that requires the mapping of the "complex terrain of parties, movements, institutions, economic forces" (Sanbonmatsu 2004: 135). This work calls for the analysis of opportunities and constraints emanating from the organisations of civil society (Gramsci, 1975: 1518). These organisations constitute the "trenches" for a war of position (Gramsci, 1975: 1567): the idea of "trenches" resembles social movement emphasis on "informal structure of power relations" (McAdam, 1996: 27) at work in the field and, in particular, the presence or absence of elite allies and their stability.

References

Benford, R., & Snow, D. (2000). Framing processes and social movements: An overview and assessment. *Annual Review of Sociology*, 26: 611–639.

Böhm, S., Fleming, P., & Spicer, A. (2008). Infra-political dimensions of resistance to international business: A neo-Gramscian approach. *Scandinavian Journal of Management*, 24(3): 169–182.

Burgio, A. (2014). *Gramsci. Il sistema in movimento*. Roma: DeriveApprodi.

Contu, A., Palpacuer, F., & Balas, N. (2013). Multinational corporations' politics and resistance to plant shutdowns: A comparative case study in the south of France. *Human Relations*, 66: 363–384.

Cornelissen, J. P., & Werner, M. D. (2014). Putting framing in perspective: A review of framing and frame analysis across the management and organizational literature. *The Academy of Management Annals*, 8: 181–235.

Creed, W. E. D., Scully, M. A., & Austin, J. R. (2002). Accounts and the social construction of identity clothes make the person? The tailoring of legitimating accounts and the social construction of identity. *Organization Science*, 13(5): 475–496.

Filippini, M. (2017). *Using Gramsci*. London: PlutoPress.

Fligstein, N., & McAdam, D. (2012). *A theory of fields*. Oxford: Oxford University Press.

Gamson, W. A. (1992). *Talking politics*. Cambridge: Cambridge University Press.

Gramsci, A. (1916). *Socialismo e cultura*. Il Grido del Popolo, 29/01/1916.

Gramsci, A. (1918). La rivoluzione contro il "Capitale". *Avanti!* (edition printed in Milan, Italy) 24/11/1918.

Gramsci, A. (1949). *Il Risorgimento*. Torino: Giulio Einaudi Editore.

Gramsci, A. (1975). *Quaderni dal Carcere*. Torino: Giulio Einaudi Editore.

Gruppi, L. (1972). *Il concetto di egemonia in Gramsci*. Roma: Editori Riuniti.

Helms, W. S., Oliver, C., & Webb, K. (2012). Antecedents of settlement on a new institutional practice: Negotiation of the ISO 26000 standard on social responsibility. *Academy of Management Journal*, 55(5): 1120–1145.

Hensmans, M. (2003). Social movement organizations: A metaphor for strategic actors in institutional fields. *Organization Studies*, 24: 355–381.

Hoffman, A. J. (1999). Institutional evolution and change: Environmentalism and the U.S. chemical industry. *Academy of Management Journal*, 42(4): 351–371.

Ingram, P., & Clay, K. (2000). The choice-within-constraints new institutionalism and implications for sociology. *Annual Review of Sociology*, 26: 525–546.

Jessop, B. (2005). Gramsci as a spatial theorist. *Critical Review of International Social and Political Philosophy*, 8(4): 421–437.

Kołakowski, L. (2008). *Main currents of Marxism*. New York, NJ: W.W. Norton & Co.

Laclau, E., & Mouffe, C. (1985). *Hegemony and socialist strategy: Towards a radical democratic politics*. Second edition. London, UK: Verso.

Levy, D., & Scully, M. (2007). The institutional entrepreneur as modern prince: The strategic face of power in contested fields. *Organization Studies*, 28: 971–991.

Levy, D. L. (2008). Political contestation in global production networks. *Academy of Management Review*, 33(4): 943–963.

Levy, D. L., & Egan, D. (2003). A neo-Gramscian approach to corporate political strategy: Conflict and accommodation in the climate change negotiations. *Journal of Management Studies*, 40: 803–829.

Levy, D. L., & Newell, P. J. (2002). Business strategy and international environmental governance: Toward a neo-Gramscian synthesis. *Global Environmental Politics*, 2: 84–101.

McAdam, D. (1996). Conceptual origins, current problems, future directions. In D. McAdam, J. D. McCarthy, & M. N. Zald (Eds.), *Comparative perspectives on social movements: Political opportunities, mobilizing structures and cultural framings* (pp. 1–20). New York, NY: Cambridge University Press.

McAdam, D., McCarthy, J. D., & Zald, M.N. (1996). Introduction: Opportunities, mobilizing structures, and framing processes – toward a synthetic, comparative perspective on social movements. In D. McAdam, J. D. McCarthy, & M. N. Zald (Eds.), *Comparative perspectives on social movements: Political opportunities, mobilizing structures and cultural framings* (pp. 1–20). Cambridge: Cambridge University Press.

Meyer, R. E., & Höllerer, M. A. (2010). Meaning structures in a contested issue field: A topographic map of shareholder value in Austria. *Academy of Management Journal*, 53(6): 1241–1262.

Rao, H. (1998). Caveat emptor: The construction of nonprofit consumer watchdog organizations. *American Journal of Sociology*, 103(4): 912–961.

Rao, H., & Kenney, M. (2008). New forms as settlements. In R. Greenwood, C. Oliver, K. Sahlin, & R. Suddaby (Eds.), *The SAGE handbook of organizational institutionalism* (pp. 651–672). London: Sage.

Sanbonmatsu, J. (2004). *The postmodern prince: Critical theory, left strategy, and the making of a new political subject.* New York: Monthly Review Press.

Scott, W. R., & Meyer, J. W. (1994). *Institutional environments and organizations.* Thousands Oaks, CA: Sage Publications.

Snow, D., & Benford, R. (1988). Ideology, frame resonance, and participant mobilization. In B. Klandermans, H. Kriesi, & S. Tarrow (Eds.), *From structure to action: Comparing social movement research across cultures*, vol. 1. Greenwich, CT: JAY Press.

Spicer, A., & Sewell, G. (2010). From national service to global player: Transforming the organizational logic of a public broadcaster. *Journal of Management Studies*, 47: 913–943.

Tarrow, S. (1994). *Power in movement: Social movements, collective action and politics.* New York: Cambridge University Press.

Tarrow, S. (1996). States and opportunities: The political structuring of social movements. In D. McAdam, J. D. McCarthy, & M. N. Zald (Eds.), *Comparative perspectives on social movements: Political opportunities, mobilizing structures and cultural framings* (pp. 1–20). New York, NY: Cambridge University Press.

Thomas, P. D. (2009). *The Gramscian moment. Philosophy, Hegemony and Marxism.* Leiden: Brill.

Zald, M. N. (1996). Culture, ideology, and strategic framing. In D. McAdam, J. D. McCarthy, & M. N. Zald (Eds.), *Comparative perspectives on social movements: Political opportunities, mobilizing structures and cultural framings*. New York, NY: Cambridge University Press.

4 Methodology

This chapter presents our methodological choices and the schema of our research. Therefore, we will start by describing our logic of enquiry, which is based on a processual stance. Then we will describe the data sources that we selected and the methods that we used to analyse our data and to elicit the discursive and political structures, on the one hand, and the discursive and the political practices that aggregate into field-level hegemonic practices.

To make sense of the transformation of the field during privatisations, we adopted a processual approach that focuses on evolving phenomena by "incorporating temporal progressions of activities as elements of explanation and understanding" (Langley et al., 2013: 1). Along these lines, we dealt with how processes within the field of steel production emerged, expanded, and modified the field itself over a time span of several years. This analysis is aimed at explaining how forces of different nature fragmented an old historical bloc and then settled again to produce a new historical bloc leading to a new social truce. In particular, coherently with our processual approach, we make sense of this process without delving into correlations among dependent and independent variables (Langley et al., 2009).

Within process studies, we developed what was called by Abdallah et al. (2019) an *evolutionary process story:* we present a process model that explains how and why a historical bloc fragmented and a new historical bloc coalesced around a new institutional arrangement for the Italian steel industry. We adopt an "ontology of being" (Abdallah et al., 2019: 94), as we believe that some properties of the institutions that constitute the world change over time (Langley et al., 2013), and we are specifically interested in explaining these changes. We present our findings mirroring the evolution of the field: we identify some major events that permit us to identify temporal bracketing, and we make wide use of graphical maps to describe the chronological evolution of the field (Langley, 1999). Coherently with our processual stance, we adopt an inductive approach, also because we want to shed light on a phenomenon that is overlooked (Strauss & Corbin, 1990). As there is no

DOI: 10.4324/9780429438516-4

necessary correspondence between the epistemological choices and the methods used, as it is not the method, but its interpretation, that determines the epistemological stance (Maggi, 1988), we stand among those who combine qualitative and quantitative methods (Mohr, 1998; Schneiberg & Clemens, 2006; Meyer & Höllerer, 2010) to disentangle the process under analysis. Specifically, we used content analysis (Krippendorff, 2004), the multivariate technique of multiple correspondence analysis (MCA) (Greenacre & Blasius, 2006), and Topic Modeling (TM) (Blei et al., 2003; DiMaggio et al., 2013). As we focus on processes at different levels (i.e. steel industry, sociopolitical field, but also media sphere), we collected a panoply of data from different sources: official documents from Italian and European institutions, balance sheets, and archival data produced by public and private steel producers, interviews with key actors within the field, and two different samples of newspapers' articles.

To capture the longitudinal unfolding of the privatisation process, we defined two "temporal brackets" that correspond to discontinuities in the longitudinal pattern of observed events (Langley, 1999: 703; Ansari et al., 2013: 1020).

The first period, which we called *fragmentation,* corresponds to 1984–1992, and includes the beginning of the public debate on privatisations, the start of the actual privatisations, and ends with the promulgations of the key laws to guide the privatisation process. Indeed, we assumed that *fragmentation* starts with the issuing of Law 193/1984, aimed at financing the restructuring of the steel industry. The public debate on the privatisation issue reached a peak at the end of 1992 (Figure 4.3), when the law no. 359 transformed large state-owned holding in private companies, making irreversible the ongoing privatisation process.

This law defines the beginning of the second temporal bracket, which we called *settlement:* during 1993–1995, the state steel was completely privatised, and a new historical bloc settled. During *settlement,* the public debate became weaker (Figure 4.3), as in 1994 the decree 332/1994 gave the final push to the privatisation process by removing constraints to direct sale of privatised companies. After 1995, steel production became entirely private. For the sake of completeness, however, we collected data on the discourse that occurred during 1995–2014 as well. During this time, a long period of *stabilisation* started and we wanted to enquire what was left of the privatisation process in the discourse.

4.1 Data collection process

While we mainly work with textual data, which we use to describe the evolution of the discursive opportunity structure (Koopmans & Statham, 1999: 231; McCammon et al., 2007: 745), discourses do not take place in vacuum. Therefore, it is of paramount importance to engage with the description of the political opportunity structure as well (Tarrow, 1994; McAdam, 1996; Mollona & Pareschi, 2020), which accounts for "more comprehensive political struggles" (Meyer & Höllerer, 2010: 1254) and power relations (Rao & Kenney, 2008).

To reconstruct the field's political opportunity structure, we started our data collection process by investigating the social and political context of the years under analysis.

4.1.1 Data regarding the political opportunity structure and the economic structure

First, we scrutinised the Italian and European Laws and Regulations on steel, in order to reconstruct the overall regulation of the steel industry. We analysed the Communications and Decisions of the European Community for Coal and Steel (ECSC), the Minutes of European Community for Coal and Steel Consulting Committee (1985–2002), the *Gazzetta Ufficiale*, which is the official journal of records of the Italian Government and we had access to three important databases: IRI's historical archive, the Prodi[1] archive, and the Gibellieri archive. In our work, we will refer to the two mentioned archives, respectively, as the RP-05 Historical Archive of the European Union (HAEU) and EGI Historical Archive of the European Union (HAEU). In addition, we conducted hours of interviews with leading experts in the steel industry.

Second, we focused on the organisation of the steel industry, which can be defined by the formal and informal agreements and alliances between trade associations, unions, and other key players of the steel industry. For this purpose, we collected data on the industry, balance sheets, and other documents from Finsider, Assider, the World Steel Association, IRI, Italsider, and ILVA.

Third, to understand and describe the economic pressures on field's actors, we analysed the field's economic structure by inquiring about the modes of production, the technology operating in the field, and the allocation of property rights on factors of production in order to describe the evolution of the percentage of public/private steel production (Figures 4.1 and 4.2). We applied the contextual analysis of Contu et al. (2013: 367) and investigated the technology of steel production along with dynamics of profitability and employment in the steel industry. We analysed financial/economic indicators, such as market shares, the production of actors operating in the industry, and macroeconomic data from ISTAT and Bankitalia.

Grounding on this repertoire of information, we produced a "chronological identification of major historical events" (Ansari et al., 2013: 1019), which is our atlas to tease out the field's political opportunity structure. As we strengthened our knowledge of the Italian steel industry

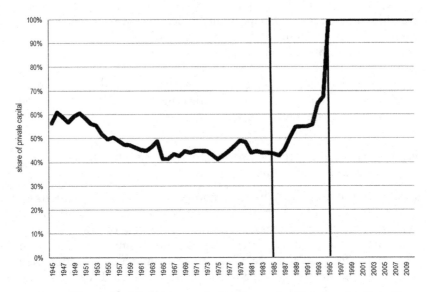

Figure 4.1 Share of public/private capital in the production of steel in Italy since 1945[2]

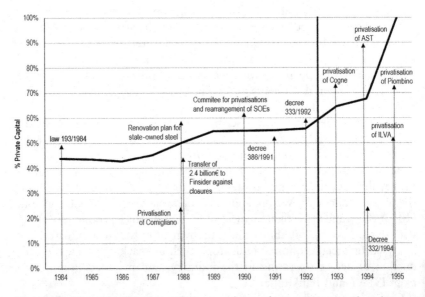

Figure 4.2 Main privatisations and events during fragmentation and settlement (1984–1995)

privatisation through technical and historical publications, balance sheets, and other archival data, also, we were able to identify meaningful keywords, which we used for collecting newspapers' articles in the following data collecting phases.

4.1.2 Data regarding the discursive opportunity structure

As for our textual data, we focused on newspapers' articles for several reasons. Meaning is moulded in the public debate, which is where problems and solutions are discussed (Meyer & Höllerer, 2010): "press coverage both reflects and represents one stream of influence in the formation of elite and public opinion" (DiMaggio et al., 2013; 574), as newspapers "simultaneously act as a stage and a key player" (Meyer & Höllerer, 2010: 1245) within a field. Scholars interested in meanings often used newspapers as a data source, as newspapers' articles provide insights regarding what elites are thinking and doing (DiMaggio et al., 2013); strengthen already existing schemata of interpretations among readers (Iyengar & Kinder, 1987); facilitate the understanding of new issues among those which are not familiar with a theme by helping the development of new mental models (Price & Tewksbury, 1997); integrate new issues within existing broader schemata of representation, such as existing political ideologies (Feldman, 2003); through selective re-telling can be shared by people with strong feelings regarding a certain issue (Bird, 2011), thus facilitating a process of legitimation of such ideas; and fortify the relevance of a certain theme or frame by conveying what opinion leaders think about it (Boczkowski, 2010).

Specifically, we collected two samples of data, which we used for different analytical purposes, and which fed two very different kinds of analysis: the first set of data was used to conduct a qualitative analysis of the frames used by actors during the fragmentation and settlement of the field together with the privatisation models proposed. In our framework, frames represent the structure of meanings, while proposed privatisation models capture the privatisation practices proposed in the public debate. By qualitatively analysing data, we were able to dig deep into articles, describing nuances in the debate, the position towards privatisations, the stances of each category of actors, and how all these issues evolved during fragmentation and settlement. For this purpose, we collected the first set of 524 newspapers' articles published in 1984–1995, specifically dealing with the privatisation of the Italian state steel. We then collected a second sample of newspapers' articles to trace the overarching public debate regarding privatisations in general, in Italy, from 1984 to 2014. This second sample consists of 67,107 articles, a dimension that is not analysable qualitatively, and which fed a semi-automatic analysis. We retrieved both samples from two of the most important Italian daily newspapers: *La Repubblica* and *Il Sole 24 Ore*. The former used to encompass a moderate leftwing vision, while the latter, owned by the General Confederation of Italian Industry (Confindustria), is an economic newspaper and is inspired by a more market-oriented view. In the following paragraphs, we provide more details regarding both samples.

4.1.2.1 Newspapers' articles for the qualitative analysis of the state steel privatisation during fragmentation and settlement (1984–1995)

Based on the knowledge of the field developed through the analysis of secondary data and databases described above, we compiled a list of keywords related to steel privatisation that we used for searching through online newspapers' article databases. This list was composed of (i) the names of the state-owned steel factories, (ii) the names of the cities where plants are (were) based, as these names were often used by journalists for referring to the SOEs, (iii) the most important private entrepreneurs in the steel industry, (iv) the most important steel unions and trade organisations, and (v) the Italian translations for *steel* and *privatisation(s)*. We collected articles from each section of the newspapers, including editorials and letters to the editors, and sampled about 5,000 articles. Then, we read them to select only those articles really dealing with the process of steel privatisation. After discarding the sources that were not relevant, we had 524 articles (239 from *La Repubblica* and 285 from *Il Sole 24 ORE)*: Figure 4.3 shows that we captured the beginning of the Italian debate on privatisations, that follows the British stream of privatisation, as well as its development and conclusion.

From these articles, we then extracted actors' statements on the privatisation issue, which are our first unit of analysis. To be considered as a statement, each fragment had to comply with four properties: (i) it had to be a quote or a direct paraphrase, to clearly attribute it to an agent of the field; (ii) it had to refer to the steel industry privatisation and not privatisations in general; (iii) it had to refer to privatisations in Italy, and (iv) it had to convey an understandable and not too narrow meaning. Specifically, we discarded statements that, while referring to steel privatisations in Italy, did not provide us with enough details as to understand what the actor making the statements was implying, or why. An example of a statement that we did not save was "Lucchini's [buying] proposal is not satisfying", as, while Lucchini was a private entrepreneur in the steel industry, from this kind of statement it is not possible to understand the reasons why such an offer was deemed unsatisfactory. After this process, our first dataset consisted of 2,119 statements.

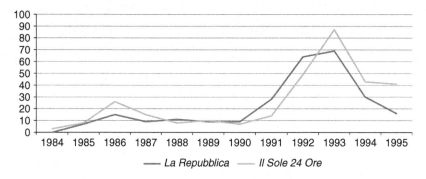

Figure 4.3 Articles per year referring to the privatisation of the steel industry

4.1.2.2 *Newspapers' articles for the semi-automatic analysis of the privatisation issue in Italy during fragmentation, settlement, and stabilisation (1984–2014)*

The qualitative analysis based on the formerly described dataset presents a number of advantages; yet, the depth of analysis is paired with the impossibility of dealing with a massive amount of data, which could be useful for inquiring a longer period, or the privatisation of more industries. Therefore, to complement the qualitative analysis, we also collected a larger amount of textual data to be processed semi-automatically. Specifically, from the archives of the aforementioned newspapers, we selected and extracted each article containing the words "privatization" or "privatizations" and published between 1984 and 2014. We collected 67,107 newspapers' articles; 24,060 articles from *La Repubblica* and 43,047 from *Il Sole 24 Ore*. Figure 4.4 reports the number of articles per year and journal pertaining to this second dataset. This figure shows the evolutions of the debate over time, which was heated for several years after privatisations of the state steel were over, as other industries were being privatised. We will return successively to this issue when describing the analysis of these data.

4.2 Logic of enquiry and methods of analysis

In this section, we describe the techniques that we used to analyse our textual data to understand the Discursive Opportunity Structure (DOS) and its evolution. Before describing the techniques, we recap how we operationalised the DOS. Therefore, we briefly describe how each dataset was analysed, and for which purpose (Table 4.1).

We started our analytical processes by deepening our understanding of the normative, economic, and organisational issues referred to as

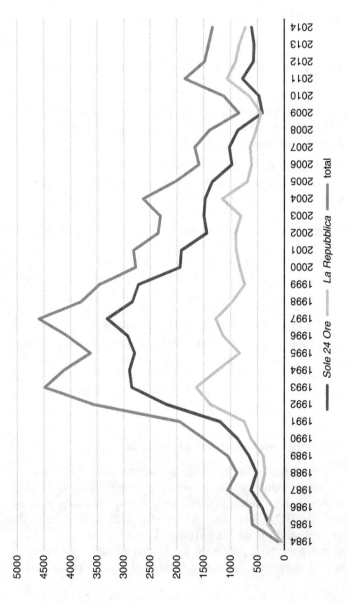

Figure 4.4 Articles per year referring to all privatisations in Italy

Table 4.1 Discursive opportunity structure: data sources, analytical process, and techniques of analysis

	Aim of the Analytical Process	Data Sources	Techniques of Analysis
Discursive Opportunity Structure (DOS)	Ground the interpretation of the DOS and the latent meaning spaces. Define the cultural repertoire and toolkits (Swidler, 1986) available to field's actors.	Communications and Decisions of the European Community for Coal and Steel (ECSC), Minutes of the European Community for Coal and Steel Consulting Committee (1985–2002). *Gazzetta Ufficiale*, the official journal of records of the Italian Government. Prodi's and Gibellieri's archives (respectively, RP-05 Historical Archive of the European Union (HAEU) and EGI Historical Archive of the European Union (HAEU)). Data on the industry, official documents, and balance sheets from Finsider and Assider, and the World Steel Association, IRI, Finsider, Italsider, and ILVA. Data produced by Bankitalia and Istat.	Qualitative analysis
	Identify relevant actors and elicit the frames used by them in the discursive space around the steel privatisation issue. Frames represent the cultural structure where actors are embedded.	Newspaper articles (1984–1995) from *La Repubblica* and *Il Sole 24 ORE*. 1,767 statements from 524 articles	Content analysis
	Identify relevant actors and elicit the proposed privatisation models regarding steel privatisation.	Newspaper articles (1984–1995) from *La Repubblica* and *Il Sole 24 ORE*. 352 statements from 192 articles	Content analysis

(Continued)

Table 4.1 (Continued)

Aim of the Analytical Process	Data Sources	Techniques of Analysis
Privatisation models proposed in the public debate represent the discursive practices.		Multiple correspondence analysis: static analysis for the whole 1984–1995 period; one analysis/map for frames and one for privatisation models
Map the latent meaning spaces, which is mapping the relations between: • Actors/frames/positions toward privatisations • Actors/proposed privatisation models And identify possible discursive alliances and logics of equivalence among actors.	The output of the content analysis	
Describe the evolution of the latent meaning spaces, which is how the support of actors toward frames and models evolves over time. Identify the hegemonic practices.	The output of the content analysis	Multiple correspondence analysis: dynamic analysis (1984–1992 and 1993–1995) for both frames and methods
Describe the evolution of the overarching public debate regarding privatisations in Italy.	Newspaper articles (1984–2014) from *La Repubblica* and *Il Sole 24 ORE*. 67,107 articles	Topic Modeling

privatisations and state steel privatisations. By reading official documents and data, we were able to describe the evolution of the political opportunity structure and to ground our interpretation of the meanings extracted from textual data in a robust understanding of the field. We then used content analysis to reconstruct the meaning space(s): we identified relevant actors and elicited both the frames used by these actors to refer to the privatisation issue and the proposed privatisation models. In our research design, frames represent the more stable cultural and discursive structure, in which actors are embedded. Conversely, proposed privatisation models are the layer where strategic discursive practices take place and actors cluster around policies that mobilise specific meanings to influence the approach to privatisations.

Content analysis is an effective and established methodology for studying human communication and performing analysis of the intentions, attitudes, and values of individuals as crystallised into the meaning of textual messages (Morris, 1994). For this purpose, we analysed the first dataset of articles and statements, which are the 524 articles and 2,119 statements retrieved for *La Repubblica* and *Il Sole 24 Ore* and published during 1984–1995. We then used multiple correspondence analysis to describe two meaning spaces: the first one describes the relations between actors, frames, and positions toward privatisations (positive, negative, ambiguous, and neutral). The second meaning space describes the relations between actors and proposed privatisations models. Such relations describe how actors supported different frames and privatisation models. As we will thoroughly explain when presenting MCA's results, we distinguished between frames and privatisation models because they capture different dimensions of the DOS. Discourses around frames, we argue, are characterised also by ceremonial stances, as actors are not completely free to define their positions, due to political and path dependency reasons. Political parties, for example, are bound by the expectations of their voters, in defining what they think about privatisations. Conversely, discourses around models present less inertia, and this supposedly technical space is where we can observe subtler discursive strategies. As we said, we used MCA to describe the meaning spaces built around frames and models; this technique is particularly suited to relate social agents and the meaning space they enact (Bourdieu, 1984; Meyer & Höllerer, 2010). Also, we did not simply describe these meaning spaces, but we also used MCA to describe their evolution over time, which is how actors change their support to frame and/or models moving from fragmentation to settlement. Leveraging these results, we were able to describe the hegemonic practices at work in the field. Both the static and the dynamic analysis performed through MCA were fed by the output of the content analysis. Finally, we used TM to describe the evolution of the overarching public debate around the privatisation issue in Italy.

TM can be fruitfully used to analyse frames and their usage by social movements, the evolution of meanings, and that of cultural dynamics (Hannigan et al., 2019; Schmiedel et al., 2019; Ferri et al., 2020). Specifically, we used TM to analyse the 67,107 newspaper articles published during 1984–2014 by *La Repubblica* and *Il Sole 24 Ore*, as this sample is too big to be qualitatively analysed. In the remainder of this chapter, we describe content analysis, multiple correspondence analysis, TM, and our methodological choices regarding these techniques.

4.2.1 Content analysis

To elicit frames and proposed privatisation models, we coded each statement according to the category of actors supporting the statement, and the content of the statement. Also, we coded each statement according to the source of the statement, and to the year, in order to conduct the dynamic analysis of the meaning spaces.

We defined the relevant actors as those that have a right to voice in the discursive space around the privatisation issue, as their utterances are legitimate (Bourdieu, 1991). In Gramscian terms, the relevant actors constitute the *extended state* (Gramsci, 1975). Therefore, the actor is anyone who participated in the public debate about privatisation by a direct quote or a paraphrase. We grouped actors into seven categories:

1. *Politicians centre*, composed of the parties that led the government for almost 50 years, the most important being the Christian Democrats party (*Democrazia Cristiana*).
2. *Politicians rightwing*, who aggregate the statements by politicians pertaining to several centre-right neo-liberal parties.
3. *Politicians independent*, who collect all the statements of the Ministers who did not belong to any party before being appointed for such a political role.
4. *Politicians leftwing*, who aggregate statements from non-governmental communist and post-communist parties.
5. *Public managers*, who are the managers of State-Owned Enterprises (SOEs)
6. *Unions.*
7. *Entrepreneurs*, who collects statements from private small and big entrepreneurs, as well as utterances by associations of entrepreneurs (*Confindustria*).
8. *Bankers and Consultants*, aggregating those working for commercial banks and consultancy firms.
9. *Technocrats*, which is composed of elite civil servants not involved in political roles. Specifically, we considered as technocrats those pertaining to the research office of the Central Bank of Italy, the

National Council for Economics and Labour (CNEL), the Italian Securities and Exchange Commission (CONSOB), the Court of Audit (Corte dei Conti), the Stock Exchange Council (Consiglio di Borsa), and the Antitrust Authority.
10. *Journalists.*

As for the content of the statement, we used it to reconstruct both *frames* and *proposed privatisation models*. Indeed, we identified two different kinds of statements: some of them were part of wider narratives, involving a position toward privatisations, and broader ideological content. We used these statements (1,767) to reconstruct frames. Also, in this case, it was possible to code each statement with a position toward privatisations (positive, negative, neutral, and ambivalent). We deem that frames represent the structural component of the discursive opportunity structure. Other statements (352) were devoted to proposing privatisation models. Following the suggestion that supposedly technical statements might reveal subtle discursive strategies (Meyer & Höllerer, 2010), we considered these statements as ontologically different from the former ones, and we deem the discourse about *privatisation models* as the locus where strategies take place, and where the logics of equivalence can emerge.

From the first set of statements, we extracted *frames*, that are collective, interpretive maps that organise experience and guide action (Goffman, 1974). They denote "schemata of interpretation" that enable individuals to locate, perceive, identify, and label occurrences within their life space. Frames provide coherence to a set of idea elements (Gamson & Modigliani, 1989), are "charged" differently with regard to an issue, and bring about different "field positions" for actors (Meyer & Höllerer, 2010). Frames help to render events or occurrences meaningful and thereby function to organise experience and guide action (Snow & Benford, 1988). In particular, media frames organise the world both for journalists and for those who rely on their report (Gitlin, 1980). In other words, frames provide us with a series of mental filters through which we make sense of reality.

Following Meyer and Höllerer (2010), we considered that frames are held together by storylines that link actors, objects, and events in a meaningful way to organise experiences (Gamson, 1992). Frames may be inductively developed or deductively chosen and applied to the case under research (Semetko & Valkenburh, 2000). They may be general or issue-specific (Matthes, 2009).

To capture the richness of the privatisation issue, we inductively developed issue-specific frames through four steps. First, statements were paraphrased to be coded to a claim that represents a basic unit of interpretation and that what we called a *node*. Each of the 126 nodes that we identified collects a set of statements dealing with the same key idea about the privatisation issue. During this step, coding was performed together by the two authors. Second, we iteratively analysed the code-book, which is the collection of nodes, to stabilise it. Third, we in-ductively elicited the frames that mould the public debate. We elicited frames by aggregating nodes held together in storylines that weave them into a meaningful worldview: we casually extracted each node and as-signed it to a developing frame by considering that a claim reveals at least the next or the previous step of the storyline of which it is a part. Claims can thus be analysed to retain not only the explicit but also the implicit meaning. An important assumption of framing theory is indeed that whenever a reasoning device is not explicitly stated in a text, it will nevertheless be evoked by the frame message during the interpretation process of the reader (Van Gorp, 2005). The final product of this third step was the generation of seven frames. In the fourth and last step, we iteratively analysed each frame until reaching a stable nodes-frames matching and a complete agreement. In this respect, to decide whether a set of nodes was a different frame or a side narrative, we applied Snow and Benford's (1988) notion of core framing tasks: diagnostic framing that identifies problems; prognostic framing that involves the articula-tion of a proposed solution to the problem, or at least a plan of attack, and motivational framing that provides a "call to arms" or reason for engaging in action. Following Meyer and Höllerer (2010), we defined separate frames if either the diagnosis or the prognosis was different. In our analysis of the public debate, we elicited frames of different nature. The first group of frames, which we called *systemic frames,* includes broad worldviews: they are rooted in different ideologies, which inform their diagnostic and prognostic characteristics. *Tactical frames* consist of narrower frames, which are the expression of more specific tactics and interests within the sociopolitical field. A third group is constituted of frames supposedly less rooted in ideologies, as they seem to describe practical and technical issues. We labelled them *technical frames.* Our inductive result is confirmed by Feigenbaum and Henig's typology (1994; Feigenbaum et al., 1998) of pragmatic, tactical, and systemic definitions of privatisation. Since a frame implies a range of positions, allowing for controversy among those who share a common frame, and not every disagreement is a frame disagreement (Gamson & Modigliani, 1989), we coded each statement to the positions about the privatisation issue: *positive, negative, neutral* or *ambivalent.*

As for reconstructing the proposed privatisation models, our process mirrored the process described for eliciting frames. In this case, we use the second set of statements to describe the privatisation models. Specifically, we devised 21 nodes and then we inductively reconstructed 4 privatisation models supported by key actors in the discursive space (Hardy & Maguire, 2010). Proposed privatisation models do not explain a worldview toward privatisations; rather, they express the privatisation model that actors would prefer if privatisations were to be performed.

Therefore, they are not characterised by a stance toward privatisations. We deemed proposed models as different if they are characterised by a different desired outcome of the privatisation process (Snow & Benford, 1988). An exemplar case of content analysis used to elicit frames is constituted by the work of Meyer and Höllerer (2010): the authors analyse the meanings associated with the concept of "shareholder value". By analysing newspaper articles, they elicit different frames and examine how the different ways of framing a contested issue – shareholder values – in public discourse are related to the local cultural and sociopolitical context.

4.2.2 *Multiple correspondence analysis*

Multiple correspondence analysis (MCA, Greenacre & Blasius, 2006) is a "descriptive method for examining relationships among categorical variables. It is a close analogue of principal component analysis for quantitative variables" (Le Roux & Rouanet, 2010: 8). This method was widely legitimised by the work of the French sociologist Pierre Bourdieu (i.e. The Distinction, 1984), which extensively used it because Multiple Correspondence Analysis emphasises the relationality among concepts under analysis: "I use Correspondence Analysis very much because I think that it is essentially a relational procedure whose philosophy fully expresses what in my view constitutes social reality. It is a procedure that 'thinks' in relations, as I try to do with the concept of field" (Bourdieu et al., 1991: preface to the German edition of "Le métier de sociologue", quoted by Le Roux & Rouanet, 2010). MCA is often used by scholars to elicit latent meaning structures (Breiger, 2009), and to relate meanings to the social space in which they were created (Meyer & Höllerer, 2010; Anheier et al., 1995).

The input of MCA is a contingency table, where each row is a unit of analysis, and each column is a categorical variable. For example, Pareschi and Lusiani (2020) used MCA to analyse the relations between discourses used by acquisition editors working for Italian publishers, and the organisational characteristics of the publishers and the field (i.e. size of the publisher and geographical location). In their work, each unit of analysis is an interview; therefore, each row corresponds to an interview to an editor, and each column defines these characteristics (i.e. column 1: size; column 2: location, and so on). MCA proceeds inductively from contingency tables, matching rows (unit of analysis) and columns (categorical variables), and draws a bi-dimensional map, which is the projection of the multi-dimensional space created by categorical variables (Greenacre & Blasius, 2006; Le Roux & Rouanet, 2010). Categories that frequently co-occur in the same row in the contingency table are plotted close together, while those that do not co-occur are plotted apart. This map allows the understanding of the relationships between variables and categories that are depicted in the same field. Following our example, Figure 4.5 is the graphical output of an MCA relating discourses used by editors, and geographic location of their publishing house, and the dimension of the publisher (Pareschi & Lusiani, 2020). Discourses (topics) are pinpointed by square indicators, the size of the publisher by round indicators, and the geographic location by triangular indicators. For example, and simplifying for a first understanding, Figure 4.5 highlights that a market discourse (references to market) is used only by acquisition editors working for small publishers in cities different from Milan, Turin, and Rome, as "location other", "size small", and "market" are all in the upper-left quadrant.

This graphical output of the MCA is a bi-dimensional (Euclidean) representation of a multi-dimensional space; which dimension depends on the number of categories and variables. As such, it is only partially able to represent the complex multi-dimensional structure. The quality of the bi-dimensional approximation is measured by the inertia of the model, which is the total amount of inertia explained by the two axes that define the bi-dimensional space. These values are provided by a statistical output of the algorithm. The higher the percentage of inertia explained by the model, the higher its quality.

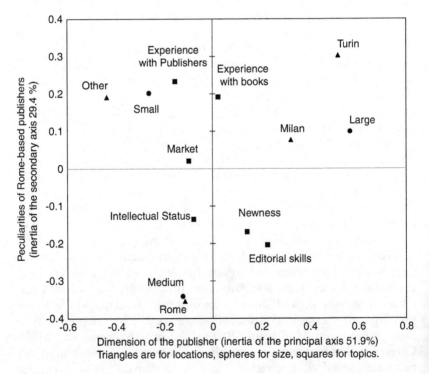

Figure 4.5 Example of MCA. Adapted from Pareschi and Lusiani (2020)

The graphical output of MCA is complemented by a statistical output that provides the researcher with data regarding the quality of the model, the quality of depiction of each category, the contribution of each category in explaining each of the axes and the overall model, and other data that are paramount to interpreting the graphical output. In particular, some categories weigh more than others in the definition of the Euclidean space, contribute more to explain the total inertia of the model, and, conversely, their variance is better explained by the space. These categories are those that are crucial in assigning the meaning to the axis. Indeed, the meaning of each axis is induced by the researcher based on these data. Also, the quality of the plot of each category is assessed and is useful to interpret categories' positions. Indeed, interpreting the relationship of dimensions and points is somehow recursive: the position of certain categories is used to induce the meaning of the axis, which is then used to understand the position of other categories.

Thus, assuming that the system of meanings competing in the field can be related to the actors through MCA (Meyer & Höllerer, 2010), we used the analyses to map the latent meaning spaces that capture the relations between (i) actors, frames, and positions toward privatisations, and between (ii) actors and proposed privatisation models.

Both for frames and privatisation models, we realised a static analysis, which serves to describe each meaning space in the whole 1984–1995 period. Then we also conducted a dynamic analysis, where we considered the positions of actors during fragmentation and settlement as supplementary variables (we will provide technical details about this step in the next chapter). The dynamic analysis made available a picture of the evolution of the latent meaning spaces over time thereby providing an account of how the support of actors towards frame and/or methods changed.

In the next chapter, we will present the latent meaning structures for the whole period; while when we will describe the fragmentation and the settlement phases, we will make use of the maps that depict the evolution of the latent meaning spaces during 1984–1992 and during 1993–1995. Overall, we will present six maps, which are based on the qualitative coding performed through content analysis. Since MCA depicts the relative positions of frames/models and actors, and their evolution over time, we grounded on this technique to identify discursive alliances among categories of actors. These discursive alliances might be used to investigate possible logics of equivalence that underpin the emergence of political identities that glue together social groups (Laclau & Mouffe, 1985). Based on these logics, and the evolution of the political opportunity structure, we identified the hegemonic practices at work during fragmentation and settlement, which we will describe in the chapters devoted to these temporal brackets.

4.2.2.1   *Technical details on multiple correspondence analysis*

For those readers willing to dig further into the technicalities of the MCA, in the remainder of this chapter, we will provide more technical information. As we said, the input for the MCA is a contingency table where each row represents a statement and each column a categorical variable. Data in each row detail the categories to which that statement is coded. From a geometrical point of view, the categorical variables used for the MCA create a multi-dimensional space, where categories are near each other if they often co-occur in the same rows. This multi-dimensional space has a dimension (L) which is a function of the overall number of categories, K, and variable, Q, and does not depend on the number of rows. Technically, the dimension of the L-dimensional space depends on the formula: $L \leq K - Q$. In this L-dimensional space, each row is a point, and all the rows represent a cloud of points. Categories are also represented by points, in this multi-dimensional cloud. Also, the total variance of the cloud is a function of the number of variables and categories and does not depend on the number of rows. The aim of the MCA is to find the best possible bi-dimensional projection of this L-dimensional space. In other words, given this distribution of points and categories in a multi-dimensional space, MCA finds the axes that explain most part of the variance of the cloud. Indeed, the L-dimensional space is composed of l (where $L = l$) orthogonal axes. Each axis contributes to the model by explaining a percentage of the overall variance, which is also called *eigenvalue* (λ). The sum of the inertias of the l axes is equal to the overall variance ($\sum_l \lambda_l = V_{cloud}$). The two principal axes chosen by the algorithm are the ones that explain more inertia. In this context, it is important to point out that the terms *inertia* (borrowed from mechanics) and *variance* are synonymous while dealing with MCA (Le Roux & Rouanet, 2010: 18). In the case of Figure 4.5, the first axis explains 51.8% of the total variance of the L-dimensional space, while the second axis accounts for another 29.4%. Thus, the two-dimensional space created by the first two axes explains 81.3% of the overall inertia.

The graphical representation of the MCA is a bi-dimensional approximation of an L-dimensional space. Therefore, as the cloud of points is flattened on a Euclidean space, the distribution of points will be distorted. As for the whole model, the percentage of explained inertia measures how much information we lose by flattening the L-dimensional space: for example, a 90% explained inertia means that in the bi-dimensional space we lose only 10% of the understanding that we could have grasped if keeping a multi-dimensional representation. A similar index, which measures the quality of the bi-dimensional representation, can be obtained also for each point, and the position of each category of each variable. From a geometrical point of view, the quality of representation of each point measures the ratio between the segment connecting the origin of the axis in the bi-dimensional space, and the same segment in the L-dimensional space. For each category, this index measures the correlation between the representation of a category in the bi-dimensional space and its representation in the L-dimensional space. Imagine a segment connecting the point where the principal axes cross (origin of the space) and the point representing the category in the L-dimensional space. The projection of this segment in the bi-dimensional space will be shorter than the original segment: the quality of representation is this. Being a ratio, this value ranges from 0 to 1. A value of 1 means that the segment between a point and the origin of the axis lies in the bi-dimensional space and is completely defined by it. Conversely, a value of 0 means that the segment in the L-dimensional space is orthogonal to the Euclidean space, which is not able to describe it. For most points, the value of the quality of representation will be a value between 0 and 1. As such value represents the projection (correlation) of the segment connecting the origin of the space with the point representing a category in the L-dimensional space, it can be defined by a component on each of the axes.

There are other statistical data that are provided by the algorithm and that help to interpret the map. One of these values regards the mass of each frequency, which is the normalised frequency of the occurrence of a category in all of the rows of the database. Table 4.2 reports this information for the MCA in the above-mentioned paper (Pareschi & Lusiani, 2020): for example, 36.78% of the sources were interviews with editors working for publishers based in Milan. For each variable, the sum of the frequencies of all categories is 100%.

Table 4.2 Frequency of each category

Variable	*Category*	*Frequency*	*%*
Discourse	Newness	38	14.56
	Market	42	16.09
	Experience with books	45	17.24
	Experience with publishers	49	18.77
	Intellactual status	47	18.01
	Editorial skills	40	15.33
Location	Location Milan	96	36.78
	Location Other	72	27.59
	Location Rome	75	28.74
	Location Turin	18	6.90
Size	Size big	69	26.44
	Size medium	84	32.18
	Size small	108	41.38

Source: Adapted from Pareschi and Lusiani (2020).

More than the mass, a very relevant value is the contribution of each category to the variance of the L-dimensional space. As if they were planets, categories are represented in the L-dimensional space by points that have a mass, a gravity attraction, and relation with other points that depend on how often they co-occur in the contingency table. Points with very high mass can determine the shape of the cloud of points. But also, smaller points can determine this distribution if they are far from the origin of the space. The value called contribution measures how much each category is relevant in determining the distribution of points in the whole space. For this reason, it is very relevant for interpreting the map. For each variable, the sum of the contribution of all its categories measures its total contribution to the inertia of the L-dimensional space. From a mathematical point of view, the contribution of variable Q is $Ctr_q = (K_q - 1)/(K - Q)$, where K_q is the number of categories of variable Q, K is the total number of categories, and Q is the number of variables. The contribution of each variable to overall inertia is a geometrical property of the space created by variables: it depends on the number of categories for each variable and the total number of categories. It does not depend on the rows, that is to say on the cloud of individual statements.

There are actually two kinds of variables: active categories and passive (or supplementary ones). Active categories are used to create the L-dimensional space, whereas passive (or supplementary) categories are present in the database but are just projected into the resulting space. The difference is theoretical: the researcher chooses as active categories the ones that she thinks have a meaning in explaining the discursive space. Passive categories can be projected on the Euclidean-generated map to enquire how they behave in the space created. In our case, as we will describe, after several attempts, we came to the conclusion that our discursive space is determined by actors, frames, and positions toward privatisations (or actors and proposed privatisation models), so we used them as active variables. We just projected the variable source (i.e. *La Repubblica* and *Il Sole 24 Ore*) on the maps to enquire whether there were differences in the statements from different newspapers.

Another important index is the contribution of a point (category) to an axis. The index captures the proportion of normalised variance of each axis due to a point (Le Roux & Rouanet, 2010: 41) and is used to induce the meaning of each of the axes. For example Table 4.3 reports the contribution of each category to the principal and secondary axes X and Y. Deciding how many categories are considered for interpreting the meaning of an axis is somehow an arbitrary task; yet, the *baseline criterion* suggests selecting all the categories whose contribution exceeds the average contribution (Le Roux & Rouanet, 2010: 52), where the average contribution is the total contributions divided by the number of active categories (in the example of Table 4.3, that is 100/13 = 7.7).

Table 4.3 Contribution of categories to each axis

Variable	Category	X	Y
Discourse	Newness	1.18	2.92
	Market	0.63	0.05
	Experience with books	0.04	4.46
	Experience with publishers	1.83	**7.20**
	Intellactual status	0.45	2.32
	Editorial skills	3.14	4.50
Location	Location Milan	**15.31**	1.52
	Location Other	**21.17**	7.10
	Location Rome	1.55	**25.40**
	Location Turin	**7.34**	4.45
Size	Size big	**33.83**	1.82
	Size medium	2.02	**26.36**
	Size small	**11.53**	**11.90**
		100.00	100.00

Source: Adapted from Pareschi and Lusiani (2020).

Nonetheless, it is still possible to consider more categories if (i) their contribution is close to the baseline criterion and/or if (ii) adding the interpretation of more variables improves the inductive process. Once the researcher has selected the most informative categories based on their contribution, she can use those categories to induce the meaning of each axis. In our examples, categories used for inducing the meaning of each axis are reported in bold. Then, the meaning of the axes is used to induce the general meaning of the map and of the disposition of different categories. Finally, it is possible to calculate how much of the inertia of one axis is explained by the selected categories by adding their contribution values.

Other ways for interpreting MCA's topographic map exist, which primarily focus on the interpretation of the angles that categories form with respect to the origin of the bi-dimensional space. The idea is that if the angle between two categories and the origin is acute, these categories are positively correlated. If the angle is obtuse, categories are negatively correlated; if the angle is 90° categories do not interact and are independent. Anyway, while considering cluster of categories, one may take into account relative differences in distances among categories, as "a cloud of points is not just simply a 'graphical display', like a temperature chart; a cloud of points is like a geographic map with the same distance scale in all direction. A geometric diagram cannot be stretched or shrunk among one particular direction" (Le Roux & Rouanet, 2010: 7).

4.2.3 *Topic Modeling*

TM is a technique based on Bayesian Statistics (Blei et al., 2003) that is able to analyse big corpora of textual data to extract meanings from them (Mohr & Bogdanov, 2013). Through an algorithm called Latent Dirilecht Annotation (LDA, Blei et al., 2003), TM analyses texts and creates *topics,* which are sets of meaningful words (Mohr & Bogdanov, 2013), which often co-occur in the same texts. Then the meaning of topics must be induced by researchers. In other words, TM combines an automatic phase, where a corpus (or corpora) of texts is coded into a set of "topics", and an inductive phase, where the researcher has to interpret the meaning of topics based on the output of the algorithm (Grimmer & Stewart, 2013). The idea at the basis of TM is that texts pertaining to the corpora are generated based on underlying topics: each document is thus constituted by those topics in a certain mixture. We cannot directly observe these topics, but the aim of TM is to re-construct topics starting from the documents that are supposedly generated by those topics, in a sort of reverse engineering of the lan-guage. Clearly, there is no way of defining an exact result, but based on the documents, thorough an iterative process, TM searches for a sound solution. With a more technical language, we can say that textual sources are a probability distribution over a set of topics. For the same reason, topics are probability distribution of words over a fixed vo-cabulary (Schmiedel et al., 2019).

TM algorithm combines different useful characteristics: first of all, the automatic feature permits the algorithm to deal with big corpora, non-analysable by a human being. Nonetheless, the automatic step is followed by a qualitative one, which preserves the inductive approach, while at the same time making easier the reproducibility of results (DiMaggio et al., 2013). Second, most or all the topics are often in-terpretable by a human being, which makes them particularly useful, although interpretability is not required by the approach (Blei et al., 2003: 996). TM can also deal with *polysemy*, which means that TM is able to disambiguate the different meanings that a certain word can have in different contexts. This feature depends on the fact that the meaning of a word depends on the surrounding words (Mohr, 1998). Also, as documents are constituted by different topics, TM can manage *heteroglossia*, which is the fact that texts can be composed by "com-peting 'voices' – perspectives or styles of expression – within a single text" (DiMaggio et al., 2013: 578). Because of its scalability and the reproducibility of the analyses, TM is an appealing tool for researchers, for analysing large collections of qualitative data (Schmiedel et al., 2019).

TM made its way to social sciences through the sociology of culture, where this algorithm was used to analyse newspapers' coverage of arts funding (DiMaggio et al., 2013), the different use of language in Academia (McFarland et al., 2013), the meanings regarding the nature of violence during the Qing Dynasty in China (Miller, 2013), the media and public attention to a terrorist alert (Bonilla & Grimmer, 2013), the "grammar of motives" in national security strategic texts (Mohr & Bogdanov, 2013), the comparison of cross-national disciplinary evolutions of themes in texts (Marshall, 2013), the application of TM to humanities (Tangherlini & Leonard, 2013), and the analysis of the themes of about 3,200 novels in 19th-century novels (Jockers & Mimno, 2013).

In management and organisational research, TM is increasingly legitimised (Hannigan et al., 2019), as it is used more and more in those contexts where researchers are interested in re-constructing meanings by analysing words, as the language used in a document represents its cognitive content (Whorf, 1956), and the meaning is conveyed by vocabularies (Loewenstein et al., 2012). This is, for example, the case of scholars working with the impact of cultural meanings on institutional logics working at the field level (Thornton et al., 2012): the cultural impact of logics embedded in the text is apparent, but it is hard to empirically measure these meanings (Hannigan et al., 2019).

TM within management and organisational literature was used for a variety of purposes (Hannigan et al., 2019). First, it was used to detect novelties and emergencies: Toubia and Netzer (2017) used TM to understand innovation, while Kaplan and Vakili (2015) analysed shifts in patent citations. Second, TM was used to develop inductive classification systems, such as how categories affect competitive dynamics (Haans, 2019), how scientific journals evolve over time (Antons et al., 2016; Ferri et al., 2018), or how theory is used to account for empirical narratives (Ferri et al., 2020). Third, TM was used to understand online audiences and products, such as understanding the online customers' evaluations (Wang & Chaudhry, 2018). Fourth, TM was used to understand cultural dynamics as, for example, understanding the professionalisation of a field (Croidieu & Kim, 2018; Pareschi & Lusiani, 2020). Fifth, TM was also recently used for analysing frames and social movements, as "many topics may be viewed as frames [...] and employed accordingly" (DiMaggio et al., 2013: 578). For example, Levy and Franklin (2014) used TM to elicit frames characterising a regulatory debate regarding the U.S. truck industry, while Fligstein and McAdam (2011) used TM to analyse the decision-making process of the Federal Open Market Committee.

Notes

1 Romano Prodi was the President of IRI during 1982–1989 and 1993–1994; has been president of the European Commission in the period 1999–2004 and Italian Prime Minister twice. Enrico Gibellieri was the last President of the ECSC (European Community for Steel and Coal) Consultative Committee, and he is Co-President of the Consultative Commission on Industrial Change within the EESC (European Economic and Social Committee). Since March 2006, he has been elected as Deputy Vice-President of the Steering Committee of the European Steel Technology Platform (ESTEP).
2 For calculating the aggregate production of raw steel of privately and state-owned firms in each year in the period 1945–2010, we defined as state-owned a firm when more than 50% of the equity is owned by the state.

References

Abdallah, C., Lusiani, M., & Langley, A. (2019). Performing process research. In *Standing on the shoulders of giants* (Vol. 11, pp. 91–113). Emerald Publishing Limited. 10.1108/S1479-838720190000011008

Anheier, H., Gerhards, J., & Romo, F. (1995). Forms of capital and social structure in cultural fields: Examining Bourdieu's social topography. *American Journal of Sociology*, 100(4): 859–903. http://www.jstor.org/stable/2782154

Ansari, S. S., Wijen, F., & Gray, B. (2013). Constructing a climate change logic: An institutional perspective on the "tragedy of the commons." *Organization Science*, 24(4): 1014–1040. 10.1287/orsc.1120.0799

Antons, D., Kleer, R., & Salge, T. O. (2016). Mapping the topic landscape of JPIM, 1984--2013: In search of hidden structures and development trajectories. *Journal of Product Innovation Management*, 33(6): 726–749.

Bird, S. E. (2011). Seeking the audience for news: Response, news talk, and everyday practices. In *The handbook of media audiences* (pp. 489–508). Wiley-Blackwell. 10.1002/9781444340525.ch25

Blei, D., Ng, A., & Jordan, M. (2003). Latent Dirichlet allocation. *Journal of Machine Learning Research*, 3(4–5): 993–1022.

Boczkowski, P. J. (2010). *News at work: Imitation in an age of information abundance*. University of Chicago Press.

Bonilla, T., & Grimmer, J. (2013). Elevated threat levels and decreased expectations: How democracy handles terrorist threats. *Poetics*, 41(6): 650–669. 10.1016/j.poetic.2013.06.003

Bourdieu, P. (1984). *Distinction: A social critique of the judgement of taste*. Cambridge, MA: Harvard University Press. http://books.google.it/books/about/Distinction.html?id=nVaS6gS9Jz4C&pgis=1

Bourdieu, P. (1991). *Language and symbolic power*. Harvard University Press.

Bourdieu, P., Chamborderon, J.-C., & Passeron, J.-C. (1991). *Soziologie als Beruf* Berlin: D. Gruyter.

Breiger, R. L. (2009). On the duality of cases and variables: Correspondence analysis (CA) and qualitative comparative analysis (QCA). In D. Byrne, & C. C. Ragin (Eds.), *The SAGE handbook of case-based methods* (pp. 243–259). SAGE.

Contu, A., Palpacuer, F., & Balas, N. (2013). Multinational corporations' politics and resistance to plant shutdowns: A comparative case study in the south of France. *Human Relations*, 66: 363–384.

Croidieu, G., & Kim, P. H. (2018). Labor of love: Amateurs and lay-expertise legitimation in the early US radio field. *Administrative Science Quarterly*, 63(1): 1–42.

DiMaggio, P., Nag, M., & Blei, D. (2013). Exploiting affinities between topic modeling and the sociological perspective on culture: Application to newspaper coverage of U.S. government arts funding. *Poetics*, 41(6): 570–606. 10.1 016/j.poetic.2013.08.004

Feigenbaum, H., Henig, J., & Hamnett, C. (1998). *Shrinking the state: The political underpinnings of privatization*. Cambridge University Press.

Feigenbaum, H. B., & Henig, J. R. (1994). The political underpinnings of privatization: A typology. *World Politics*, 46(2): 185–208. http://www.jstor.org/ stable/10.2307/2950672

Feldman, S. (2003). Enforcing social conformity: A theory of authoritarianism. *Political Psychology*, 24(1): 41–74. 10.1111/0162-895X.00316

Ferri, P., Lusiani, M., & Pareschi, L. (2018). Accounting for accounting history: A topic modeling approach (1996–2015). *Accounting History*, 23(1–2). 10.11 77/1032373217740707

Ferri, P., Lusiani, M., & Pareschi, L. (2020). Shades of theory: A topic modelling of ways of theorizing in accounting history research. *Accounting History*, 26(3): 484–519.10.1177/1032373220964271.

Fligstein, N., & McAdam, D. (2011). Toward a general theory of strategic action fields. *Sociological Theory*, 29(1): 1–26.

Gamson, W., & Modigliani, A. (1989). Media discourse and public opinion on nuclear power: A constructionist approach. *American Journal of Sociology*, 95(1): 1–37. http://www.jstor.org/stable/10.2307/2780405

Gamson, W. A. (1992). *Talking politics*. Cambridge University Press.

Gitlin, T. (1980). *The whole world is watching: Mass media in the making and unmaking of the new left*. University of California Press.

Goffman, E. (1974). *Frame analysis: An essay on the organization of experience*. Harper & Row.

Gramsci, A. (1975). *Quaderni dal carcere* (G. E. Editore (Ed.)). International Publishers.

Greenacre, M., & Blasius, J. (Eds.). (2006). *Correspondence analysis in the social sciences: Recent developments and applications*. Academic Press.

Grimmer, J., & Stewart, B. M. (2013). Text as data: The promise and pitfalls of automatic content analysis methods for political texts. *Political Analysis*, 21(3): 267–297. 10.1093/pan/mps028

Haans, R. F. J. (2019). What's the value of being different when everyone is? The effects of distinctiveness on performance in homogeneous versus heterogeneous categories. *Strategic Management Journal*, 40(1): 3–27.

Hannigan, T. R., Haan, R. F. J., Vakili, K., Tchalian, H., Glaser, V. L., Wang, M. S., Kaplan, S., & Jennings, P. D. (2019). Topic modeling in management research: Rendering new theory from textual data. *Academy of Management Annals*, 13(2): 586–632. 10.5465/annals.2017.0099

Hardy, C., & Maguire, S. (2010). Discourse, field-configuring events, and change in organizations and institutional fields: Narratives of DDT and the Stockholm Convention. *Academy of Management Journal*, 53(6): 1365–1392.

Iyengar, S., & Kinder, D. R. (1987). *News that matters: Agenda-setting and priming in a television age*. University of Chicago Press.

Jockers, M. L., & Mimno, D. (2013). Significant themes in 19th-century literature. *Poetics*, 41(6): 750–769. 10.1016/j.poetic.2013.08.005

Kaplan, S., & Vakili, K. (2015). The double-edged sword of recombination in breakthrough innovation. *Strategic Management Journal*, 36(10): 1435–1457. 10.1002/smj.2294

Koopmans, R., & Statham, P. (1999). Ethnic and civic conceptions of nationhood and the differential success of the extreme right in Germany and Italy. In M. Giugni, D. McAdam, & C. Tilly (Eds.), *How social movements matter* (pp. 225–251). University of Minnesota Press.

Krippendorff, K. (2004). *Content analysis: An introduction to its methodology*. Second edition. Sage.

Laclau, E., & Mouffe, C. (1985). *Hegemony and socialist strategy: Towards a radical democratic politics*. Second edition. London, UK: Verso.

Langley, A. (1999). Strategies for theorizing from process data. *Academy of Management Review*, 24(4): 691–710. 10.5465/AMR.1999.2553248

Langley, A., Smallman, C., Tsoukas, H., & Van de Ven, A. (2009). Call for papers: Special research forum on process studies of change in organization and management. *Academy of Management Journal*, 52: 629–630.

Langley, A., Smallman, C., Tsoukas, H., & Van De Ven, A. H. (2013). Process studies of change in organization and management: Unveiling temporality, activity, and flow. *Academy of Management Journal*, 56(1): 1–13. 10.5465/amj.2013.4001

Le Roux, B., & Rouanet, H. (2010). *Multiple correspondence analysis*. 10.4135/9781412993906

Levy, K. E. C., & Franklin, M. (2014). Driving regulation: Using topic models to examine political contention in the US trucking industry. *Social Science Computer Review*, 32(2): 182–194.

Loewenstein, J., Ocasio, W., & Jones, C. (2012). Vocabularies and vocabulary structure: A new approach linking categories, practices, and institutions. *Academy of Management Annals*, 6(1): 41–86. 10.5465/19416520.2012.660763

Maggi, B. (1988). L'azione organizzativa in Thompson e oltre. In *Introduzione a "L'azione organizzativa" di James D. Thompson* (pp. 1–58). Isedi.

Marshall, E. A. (2013). Defining population problems: Using topic models for cross-national comparison of disciplinary development. *Poetics*, 41(6): 701–724. 10.1016/j.poetic.2013.08.001

Matthes, J. (2009). What's in a frame? a content analysis of media framing studies in the world's leading communication journals, 1990–2005. *Journalism & Mass Communication Quarterly*, 86(2): 349–367. 10.1177/107769900908600206

McAdam, D. (1996). Conceptual origins, current problems, future directions. In D. McAdam, J. D. McCarthy, & M. N. Zald (Eds.), *Comparative perspectives* on *social movements: Political opportunities, mobilizing structures and cultural framings* (pp. 23–40). Cambridge: Cambridge University Press.

McCammon, H. J., Muse, C. S., Newman, H. D., & Terrell, T. M. (2007). Movement framing and discursive opportunity structures: The political successes of the U.S. women's jury movements. *American Sociological Review*, 72(5): 725–749. 10.1177/000312240707200504

McFarland, D. A., Ramage, D., Chuang, J., Heer, J., Manning, C. D., & Jurafsky, D. (2013). Differentiating language usage through topic models. *Poetics*, 41(6): 607–625. 10.1016/j.poetic.2013.06.004

Meyer, R. E., & Höllerer, M. A. (2010). Meaning structures in a contested issue field: A topographic map of shareholder value in Austria. *Academy of Management Journal*, 53(6): 1241–1262. 10.5465/amj.2010.57317829

Miller, I. M. (2013). Rebellion, crime and violence in Qing China, 1722-1911: A topic modeling approach. *Poetics*, 41(6): 626–649. 10.1016/j.poetic.2013.06.005

Mohr, J. W. (1998). Measuring meaning structures. *Annual Review of Sociology*, 24: 345–370. 10.2307/223485

Mohr, J. W., & Bogdanov, P. (2013). Introduction-topic models: What they are and why they matter. In *Poetics* (Vol. 41, Issue 6, pp. 545–569). Elsevier B.V. 10.1016/j.poetic.2013.10.001

Mollona, E., & Pareschi, L. (2020). A Gramscian perspective on field dynamics. The case of the privatization of Italian steel industry. *Scandinavian Journal of Management*, 36(4): 101128. 10.1016/j.scaman.2020.101128

Morris, R. (1994). Computerized content analysis in management research: A demonstration of advantages & limitations. *Journal of Management*, 20(4): 903–931. 10.1177/014920639402000410

Pareschi, L., & Lusiani, M. (2020). What editors talk about when they talk about editors? A public discourse analysis of market and aesthetic logics. *Poetics*, 81: 101444. 10.1016/j.poetic.2020.101444

Price, V., & Tewksbury, D. (1997). News values and public opinion: a theoretical account of media priming and framing. In G. Barnett, & F. J. Boster (Eds.), *Progress in communication science* (pp. 173–212). Ables.

Rao, H., & Kenney, M. (2008). New forms as settlements. In R. Greenwood, C. Oliver, K. Sahlin, & R. Suddaby (Eds.), *The SAGE handbook of organizational institutionalism* (pp. 651–672). Sage.

Schmiedel, T., Müller, O., & vom Brocke, J. (2019). Topic modeling as a strategy of inquiry in organizational research: A tutorial with an application example on organizational culture. *Organizational Research Methods*, 22(4): 941–968. 10.1177/1094428118773858

Schneiberg, M., & Clemens, E. S. (2006). The typical tools for the Job: Research strategies in institutional analysis*. *Sociological Theory*, 24(3): 195–227. 10.1111/j.1467-9558.2006.00288.x

Semetko, H., & Valkenburg, P. (2000). Framing European politics: A content analysis of press and television news. *Journal of Communication*, 93–109. http://onlinelibrary.wiley.com/doi/10.1111/j.1460-2466.2000.tb02843.x/abstract

Snow, D., & Benford, R. (1988). Ideology, frame resonance, and participant mobilization. In B. Klandermans, H. Kriesi, & S. Tarrow (Eds.), *From structure to action: Comparing social movement research across cultures*, vol. 1. JAI press.

Strauss, A., & Corbin, J. (1990). *Basics of qualitative research: techniques and procedures for developing grounded theory*. Sage.

Swidler, A. (1986). Culture in action: Symbols and strategies. *American Sociological Review*, 51(2): 273–286. 10.2307/2095521

Tangherlini, T. R., & Leonard, P. (2013). Trawling in the Sea of the Great Unread: Sub-corpus topic modeling and Humanities research. *Poetics*, 41(6): 725–749. 10.1016/j.poetic.2013.08.002

Tarrow, S. (1994). *Power in movement: Social movements, collective action and politics*. Cambridge University Press.

Thornton, P. H., Ocasio, W., & Lounsbury, M. (2012). *The institutional logics perspective: A new approach to culture, structure, and process*. Oxford: Oxford University Press.

Toubia, O., & Netzer, O. (2017). Idea generation, creativity, and prototypicality. *Marketing Science*, 36(1): 1–20.

Van Gorp, B. (2005). Where is the frame?: Victims and Intruders in the Belgian press coverage of the asylum issue. *European Journal of Communication*, 20(4): 484–507. 10.1177/0267323105058253

Wang, Y., & Chaudhry, A. (2018). When and how managers' responses to online reviews affect subsequent reviews. *Journal of Marketing Research*, 55(2): 163–177.

Whorf, B. L. (1956). Language, thought, and reality: Selected writings of…. (Edited by John B. Carroll). Technology Press of MIT.

5 Latent meaning spaces

5.1 Framing of the privatisation issue

Our analysis of the discursive struggles that developed around the issue of privatising steel in Italy lead to the identification of seven frames used by social actors around the privatisation issue. We leverage the distinction among *systemic, tactical,* and *technical* frames to assign meaning to privatisations, proposed by Feigenbaum and Henig (1994) and Feigenbaum et al. (1998), and in the next part of the chapter, we describe them. Table 5.1 reports, for each frame, the diagnosis and prognosis for the privatisation process in Italy, together with some exemplary quotes.

5.1.1 Systemic frames

1. *Labour versus Capital (LVSC).* This frame aims at developing a political identity that is built around two dimensions. The first dimension is the logic of difference that opposes the system of private firms owned by private capital, this latter is described as only inspired by individualistic aims, and the system of state-owned enterprises that, on the contrary, are not only profit-seeking but aim as well at preserving public goods. The second logic of difference focuses, specifically, on the opposition between the owners of the means of production and the workers, and the need to protect the interests of the latter. The idea that underpins the frame *Labour versus Capital* is that the state must be involved in economic life to protect jobs and state-owned firms should provide employment and a stable working life to employees. Privatisations are thus evil, as they both imply mass layoffs and point at overturning the system of state-owned firms. By taking the side of the workers, this frame is used to warn against the hidden stakes that allegedly drive the privatisation process; namely, selling state-owned enterprises at a very reduced price for the benefit of large powerful industrial firms. In addition, the frame *Labour versus Capital* takes issue with the discourse that ascribes the need to privatise to external constraints

DOI: 10.4324/9780429438516-5

Table 5.1 Frames moulding the public debate

	Frame	Diagnosis	Prognosis	Quotes
Systemic Frames	Labour versus Capital (LVSC)	Privatisations will create mass layoffs	Privatisations must be avoided	*The privatization of Piombino can transform this city into a border town, with social and institutional dangers* [Union] *Any privatization hypothesis must prejudicially completely safeguard employment* [Union] *Private entrepreneurs cannot pretend to receive Taranto's plant without any risk or duty. The State cannot donate Taranto* [Union]
	Developmental State (DS)	The State must have an entrepreneurial role	Privatise only if it is not avoidable	*Public Managers are attacked through a campaign that is defamatory, unfair, slanderous, and also counterproductive for Italian economics and the image of the Country* [Public Manager] *Managerial culture in SOEs has nothing less than in private firms. Moreover, public managers need to show a strong willingness to reach industrial goals, as they have to face pressures from the social and political environment* [Public Manager] *Historically, we have no proof that private forms perform better than SOEs* [Public Manager]
	Continental Capitalism (CC)	Privatisations are one of the available industrial policy tools	SOEs and private firms can co-exist, specialised in different market niches	*I think that a mixed economy is the right path for the future. The point is that the firm must be managed like a private one. It must be transparent, professional, and oriented to profit* [Public Manager] *Public enterprises must create a joint venture with private ones to better compete in international markets, redefine "strategic industries", and reduce losses. If compared to privatisations, private-public alliances are more realistic and effective* [Technocrat]

Neo-Liberalism (NL)	Privatisations are a cultural shift that is able to improve the economy of the country	Privatise as much and as fast as possible	*IRI wants to sell activities that are not strategic* [Public Manager] *Obstacles to competition depend only on bureaucracy, administrative obstacles, and on the dirigistic approach of politicians* [Technocrat] *There is nothing that is strategic and cannot be privatised* [Independent Politician] *Privatizing is not a choice, but a necessary requirement for economic development. The State has to sell most of its SOEs* [Entrepreneur]
Tactical Frames Stigma Entrenched Powers (SEP)	The entrenched power system guiding Italian SOEs is responsible for the poor results	Privatise to dismantle this entrenched power structure	*There is the risk that the privatisation plan remains just an issue for an eternal debate. Several actors push in this direction: Boiardi, seeking revenge, and parties, which are worried to lose a power that they thought to be eternal, up to a few months ago* [Journalist] *The point is that it is necessary a will to really perform privatisations. Then we have to manage the market accordingly* [Public Manager] *Whatever the end of the story will be, it is clear that the rules for privatizing are dramatically inadequate, as Public Managers are at the mercy of politicians' desires* [Banker and Consultant]
Technical Frames Pragmatic Legitimising Approach (PLA)	Privatisations are not good or bad, they are just a technical tool	If privatisations are to be performed, they must be carefully planned	*I did not take any ideological decision regarding privatisations. We just need to perform them, or the economic system will die* [Public Manager] *Technicalities may change, but no politician seems to be against privatisations* [Public Manager] *Regarding privatisations, we must proceed "full speed ahead"* [Independent Minister]

(Continued)

Table 5.1 (Continued)

Frame	Diagnosis	Prognosis	Quotes
European Forces (EF)	Privatisations are imposed by an external Constraint due to the European Union	It's not possible to avoid privatisation.	*At the end of the day, the State is privatizing because Europe impose us the same rules that they impose on other States* [Independent Minister] *European choices will affect the future of private synergy, as well as the plan to relaunch Finsider* [Journalist] *The European constraint and the burden of the debt make the privatisation decision a no-turning back road* [Journalist]

imposed by the European Union, which is the theory crystallised in the frame *European Forces* (which we will describe in the following). This theory of the external European constraints is rather described as a rhetoric strategy used by Italian firms that want privatisations to occur in order to support their interests. Finally, *Labour versus Capital* warns against the threat of privatising SOE's profits through privatisations, while at the same time socialising their losses in the process.

2. *Developmental State (DS)*. The frame supports the idea that the state and politics may play an important role in guiding the development of the economy. The specific historical economic development of the country, in which the state traditionally substituted for the weak private sector in developing large investments in fixed capital and infrastructures, provided a base to root and legitimise the role of the state as an entrepreneur. Therefore, SOEs' system is considered as a natural and effective means to develop the economy. This frame is used to emphasise the good results of state-owned enterprises, while their apparent failure in financial management is explained by reference to exogenous disturbances rather than specifically to the form of ownership.

3. *Continental Capitalism (CC)*. The frame calls for "mobile borders" between the systems of privately and state-owned enterprises. According to this frame, the role of the state in an economy is central for redistributing wealth, and industries exist in which the presence of the state is strategic and non-questionable. Nonetheless, other industries may be partially or completely privatised, as privatisations can be an opportunity to develop a better economy, where the state and private companies co-exist without wars, specialising and focusing in different niches. Privatisations are neither good nor bad, but as times are changing, formerly state-owned enterprises can be sold to create a better industrial system. In this context, privatisations must be planned to avoid the shift from State monopolies to private ones, as they are just a tool of industrial policy. In particular, the frame *Continental Capitalism* is used with reference to the Renan model.[1]

4. *Neo-Liberalism (NL)*. The frame assigns a symbolic meaning to state-owned companies' privatisations: privatisations will represent the cultural shift that is a prerequisite to creating an improved economic system. This frame describes Italian state-owned enterprises as an anomaly and urges the country to quickly moving to a market economy to unleashing the invisible hand of the market. Neo-liberalism pretends to derive its strength from being rooted in economic science and not in political discourse: economic logic is considered as decoupled from, and often above, the political one. Advocates of this frame envision a radical reform that includes the

most extensive privatisation plan. Large-scale privatisations, according to this perspective, would remove power from parties, destroy corporatism, create more robust and efficient stock markets and job markets, create the conditions for better capitals' movements, and create better enterprises that would be emancipated from the rigid bureaucracy, slowness, and lack of result that are typical of state-owned companies. Statements using this frame explicitly define the profit as the only aim of enterprises: there is no stakeholder view. "Stalinism" and "catholic solidarity" are described as degenerations, as they tend to justify managerial conducts that do not pursue the maximisation of profits. A corollary of this frame is that market superiority (compared to state economics) will create a better industry system through popular capitalism.

5.1.2 Tactical frames

5. *Stigma Entrenched Powers (SEP)*. In the analysed discourse on privatisations, this frame is used to blame those social actors who oppose privatisations to preserve existing power structures. Among the actors who are blamed as being responsible for a sort of hidden sabotage are unions, "communists" and leftwing parties, and even conservative rightwing parties. A category of actors especially blamed is the one that includes bureaucrats who work for state-owned enterprises. These latter are called *Boiardi* (*Boiardi* is an Italian word that indicates the members of the very high Russian aristocracy. This feudal aristocracy was often deemed even more powerful than the monarch himself.). According to this frame, *Boiardi* are the bureaucrats who are not willing to cope with free-market forces but, to take refuge under the shelter of political belonging, comply with the requests of politicians rather than aiming at financial and economic targets. Governmental parties are blamed as well, as they are defined as too weak to conceive of a serious privatisation plan and to impose privatisations. Also, this frame is used to blame *lottizzazione,* which is an Italian neologism typically referring to the pathological allotment of power among political parties in state-owned holdings. *Lottizzazione* is blamed as a burden that must be removed from Italian enterprises if they are to perform well.

5.1.3 Technical frames

6. *Pragmatic Legitimising Approach (PLA)*. Users of this frame adopt a technical language for describing privatisations as a technical means to reform the Italian industrial system. With apparently no

ideological flavour, the frame considers privatisations as a technical problem. As an example, the allocation of property rights of privatised enterprises must be decided on a case-by-case basis, and appropriate institutions and laws must be set to perform privatisations in a clear and transparent way. Privatisations must be performed quickly to preserve the market's trust; all the trustworthy available buyers are suitable, both foreigners and Italians. Measures to cope with resulting unemployment must be taken into consideration. Before starting the process of privatisation, it is important to decide whether the aim is maximising profits, reducing the public debt, or adopting underpricing techniques to push the diffusion of stocks, thereby rapidly changing the structure of the Italian capital market. The reductions in production capacity that are imposed by the European Commission, as well as the difficult financial conditions that several state-owned enterprises experience, are considered among the key problems the government has to deal with. Overall, this frame is used to problematise the privatisation issue and to identify possible technical solutions. Yet, this discourse problematises *how* to privatise, and not the *what*, thereby subtly implying that the idea that privatisations will improve the Italian economic system is taken for granted. Indeed, this frame is used also to refer to other successful privatisation processes in other Western economies and to legitimise the support of the privatisation process in Italy.

7. *European Forces (EF)* is a frame that is used to ascribe the need to privatise state-owned enterprises to an external constraint exogenously imposed by European Commission. Therefore, privatisations cannot be avoided. Indeed, the European Coal and Steel Community (ECSC) imposed the suppression of State financial aids to steel firms in trouble. State financial aids to state-owned enterprises were allowed only in exchange for production capacity reduction.

5.2 Proposed privatisation models

Frames describe the structural part of the discursive opportunity structure, which defines the cultural milieu in which actors are embedded. The statements that constitute frames are more ideologically charged and suggest an implicit or explicit position towards privatisations. Conversely, statements describing proposed privatisation models are about practices, techniques, and approaches to perform privatisations. Such models represent the tools for building discursive alliances, or logics of equivalence among actors. Indeed, supposedly technical arguments serve to perform subtle discursive strategies (Meyer & Höllerer, 2010: 1257), and we deem these proposed models as very relevant to describe the power struggles at work. Different privatisation models have a different impact on the selling process, on its outcome, and on the final distribution of property rights. The technical knowledge, which is brandished to support proposed methods, is, therefore, to be interpreted as the symbolic capital that is leveraged to conduct the struggle that takes place among actors who aim at legitimating a specific idea of the social world (Bourdieu, 1991).

By analysing statements that referred to how to perform privatisations, if they had to be performed, we inductively reconstructed four privatisation models proposed by the key actors in the discursive space (Hardy & Maguire, 2010). These models (Table 5.2) differ according to the privatisations process, and the desired outcome (Snow & Benford, 1988):

1. *Government Controlled.* This model asks for strong governmental control on the privatisation process and privatised firms. The control on the process can be obtained by using instruments such as golden shares, while the control over the outcome can be achieved by conglomerating SOEs in undifferentiated financial holdings to sell minority shares, as explained in a quote by Giuseppe Guarino, the Ministry of Industry: "we must conglomerate all the SOEs in three big holdings. Then, we offer shares of these holdings to the market". During 1992–1993, the privatisation plan of Giuseppe Guarino clearly embodied this model, as it advised to gather companies to be privatised in two state-owned holdings owned by both a hard core of Italian entrepreneurs and by the Ministry of Finance.
2. *Market Driven.* The model mobilises statements that support a market approach to privatisations and vehemently encourages a dismissal of government control over SOEs to be implemented as rapidly as possible. Sponsors of this approach recommend to sell SOEs' majority share and, eventually, breaking up large state-owned enterprises and selling the most valuable assets. Also, this model wants privatisations to be fast: "privatizing does not mean selling minority shares but completely entrusting the enterprises to the care of national or foreign shareholders" [Bankers and Consultants]. In the period 1992–1993, the privatisation plan conceived of by the Ministry of Treasure embodied traits of this approach: the idea was for the Ministry to be assigned the power to direct selling or dismissing SOEs with the support of national and international financial advisors. A subtle implication that emerges by the analysis of the statements coded as associated with this approach is that, in order to avoid politicians' interferences, proponents of the approach ask for the direct control of SOEs managers over the privatisation process. In other words, the lack of confidence in the ability, and the will, of the government to rapidly privatise made it more palatable

Table 5.2 Proposed models for privatisations

Model	The Desired Outcome of the Privatisation Process	The Desired Features of the Privatisation Process	Quotes
Government Controlled	Safeguard the role of the State in the economy through golden shares or the control of the majority share.	The conglomeration of SOEs in undifferentiated financial holdings to sell minority shares	*We must conglomerate all the SOEs into three big holdings. Then, we offer shares of these holdings to the market* [Politician] *The Party of Communist Re-foundation […] asks to make the golden shares permanent.* [Politician]
Market-Driven	Sell the more enterprises and the faster to exclude the State from the economy.	Neo-liberal ideas: breaking up the large holdings; selling majority shares; selling all the companies that can possibly be sold.	*Privatizing does not mean selling minority shares but completely entrusting the enterprises to the care of national or foreign shareholders* [Banker and Consultant] *The market does not like undifferentiated holdings and does not like Russian dolls: chains of controlled enterprises in which a controlling shareholder can have an influence are far wider than their share* [Banker and Consultant] *It may be hard to explain to foreign analysts, but during electoral campaigns, the privatization process may speed up, as the parties' interference loses strength, and management may benefit from greater autonomy* [Journalist] *We demand autonomy for the holding company's management in making decisions on privatizations* [Public Manager]

(Continued)

Table 5.2 (Continued)

Model	The Desired Outcome of the Privatisation Process	The Desired Features of the Privatisation Process	Quotes
Public Company	Privatise firms to redistribute wealth to small investors, including workers (popular capitalism).	Create public companies through a transparent and democratic sales process in the stock market.	*Real privatizations are those in which enterprises are sold from the State to a public of small shareholders, using serious laws* [Public Manager] *Unions have an American dream: to reproduce the "made in USA"* [Union]
Noyaux Durs	The Government controls the process through protectionism against new foreign entrants in the Italian steel industry.	The government exits the industry but selects the consortium of enterprises that will buy privatised firms.	*In order to sell major enterprises [...] a hard kernel of trustworthy shareholders will be created.* [Politician] *Government should create the so called "noyaux durs": control structures capable of creating collaborations in order to provide enterprises with resources and to defend them from hostile takeovers.* [Technocracy]

for "market-driven" advocates to concede to the top management the power to lead their companies towards privatisation. This was especially true for those state-owned companies whose top managers, rather than coming from political parties, were recruited from the ranks of technocracy and academia.

3. *Public Company.* In the context of Italian privatisations, the idea of Public Companies represents a subtle compromise between government control and market incentives. Of course, the suggestion to transform SOEs into public companies appeals to a market approach when it involves the sale of shares to investors. In particular, some statements suggest that a population of small shareholders could be created, and shares could be transferred to workers through a transparent and democratic sales process in the stock market. Indeed, often, the adoption of public companies aims at including workers in the equity.[2] Yet, in the Italian case, privatisations through public companies wink at a well-balanced distribution of shares among shareholders, financial and industrial groups, employees, and the government. As illustrated by a union member: "Unions have an American dream: to reproduce the "made in USA" experience of distributed share ownership among workers. [Union]". As suggested, in 1992, by Piero Barucci, at the time Ministry of Finance, the creation of public companies aims at finding a compromise between diffused shareholders and a stable core of investors in which the government is still likely to play a central role.[3] For example, ENI[4] and ENEL, two large state-owned holdings, were privatised by creating two public companies in which the government was the controlling shareholder (nowadays, the government still is the controlling shareholder in the two companies, holding about one-quarter of the equity).

4. *Noyaux Durs.* The cluster of statements associated with this model is labelled after a French word that refers to the creation of block holders in privatised firms. Typically, with reference to the French case, the use of noyaux durs manifests the will of a state to transfer the control of privatised firms to specific large firms or groups of large firms (Suleiman, 1990; Feigenbaum et al., 1998: 99). To detractors, the approach allows politicians to maintain and reward political friends (Feigenbaum et al., 1998: 106). In the Italian context, the concept of noyeaux durs describes privatisations in which, as in the French case, the government creates a stable group of investors. For example, a technocrat suggests that "[noyeaux durs are] control structures capable of creating collaborations [between politicians and entrepreneurs] in order to provide enterprises with resources and to defend them from hostile takeovers".

5.3 Latent meaning spaces

In the next paragraphs, we will describe how we used the multiple correspondence analysis (Greenacre & Blasius, 2006) to explain how actors are embedded in latent meaning spaces. Specifically, we present two MCAs relating (i) actors, frames, positions, and (ii) actors and proposed privatisation models. The first analysis uses maps and statistics to describe the relative positions of actors, frames, and positions towards privatisations in the discursive space and is aimed at presenting the structural aspects of the discursive opportunity structure. The second analysis adopts the same method but describes the relationship among actors and proposed privatisation models, which is where discursive alliances can be built. Both MCAs refer to the whole 1984–1995 period, as in this chapter we describe the overarching latent meaning spaces. In the next two chapters, we will present other analyses aimed at describing the changes in the meaning spaces during fragmentation and settlement, respectively.

5.3.1 MCA *relating actors, frames, and positions toward privatisations: structure*

As we explained in chapter 4, when introducing the multiple correspondence analysis, MCA creates a bi-dimensional map in which variables that often co-occur are plotted close together, while variables that never co-occur are plotted apart. Figure 5.1 presents the MCA relating actors, frames, and position towards privatisations: its general meaning is that if an actor is depicted close to a certain frame, that actor used that frame often in her statements. If two actors are depicted near each other, they often voiced the same frames. If a frame is near to a certain position towards privatisations, that position describes the attitude of that frame. Therefore, Figure 5.1 depicts the average relationship between actors, frames, and positions toward privatisations during the 1984–1995 period.

Technically, each MCA is the projection on two dimensions of a multidimensional space, which number of dimensions depends on the number of variables and categories for each variable. Therefore, the model is characterised by an explained inertia, which is an index of how well the bi-dimensional space approximates the multi-dimensional one. Also, the bi-dimensional space is characterised by two axes, which are called "principal" and "secondary", and which meaning must be induced by the researcher. The graphical output is complemented by statistical results, which we present in Table 5.3. These data describe the contribution of each category of the variables in defining the space and describe how well a category is represented in the bi-dimensional space. The researcher interprets the meaning of the axes based on the statistical

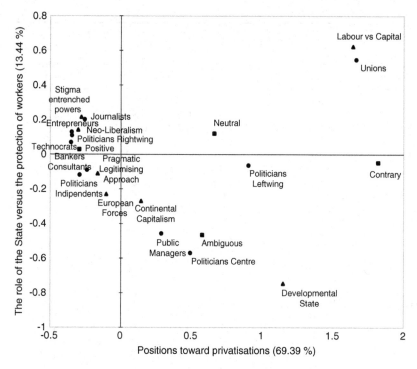

Figure 5.1 MCA relating frames, actors, and positions – 1984–1995

output, and the categories' positions on the map. Indeed, the inter-pretation of the map is inductive and recursive: the researcher induces the meaning of each axis based on the categories with higher contribu-tion and employs the induced meaning to interpret the relative positions of the other categories (Meyer & Höllerer, 2010).

We performed the MCA with the software XLSTAT, which we used for generating the maps (see Greenacre & Blasius, 2006: 76). Figure 5.1 explains 82.8% of the total inertia, which is a very good approximation of the multi-dimensional space. The first and most important dimension (the x-axis) is highly explanatory and accounts for 69.4% of the inertia, while the second dimension (the y-axis) adds another 13.4%. All the categories are well represented by the two dimensions (see Table 5.3), with the only exception of the category *European Forces*, which, in any case, does not contribute to explaining the model. In particular, all the most important categories for inducing the meaning of the axes are very well represented in the model.

The most relevant categories for defining the principal axis are, on the right camp of the map, the categories *Contrary*, *Labour versus Capital*,

Table 5.3 Statistical output for the MCA relating frames, actors, and positions in 1984–1995

Variables	Categories	Contribution		Quality of Depiction		
		X	Y	X	Y	Overall (X+Y)
Positions	Ambiguous	2.6%	8.8%	0.532	0.345	0.878
	Contrary	18.1%	0.1%	0.893	0.001	0.893
	Neutral	5.9%	1.0%	0.864	0.029	0.893
	Positive	6.9%	0.3%	0.947	0.009	0.956
Actors	Bankers Consultants	0.5%	0.4%	0.427	0.061	0.488
	Entrepreneurs	1.9%	1.4%	0.656	0.090	0.746
	Journalists	1.2%	3.8%	0.293	0.181	0.474
	Politicians Centre	1.6%	11.2%	0.351	0.472	0.824
	Politicians Independents	0.7%	0.6%	0.313	0.052	0.365
	Politicians Leftwing	2.4%	0.1%	0.697	0.003	0.700
	Politicians Rightwing	0.7%	0.8%	0.532	0.117	0.649
	Public Managers	1.1%	14.8%	0.222	0.563	0.785
	Technocrats	1.9%	0.4%	0.887	0.034	0.921
	Unions	21.4%	11.9%	0.821	0.089	0.910
Frames	Continental Capitalism	0.3%	5.3%	0.144	0.519	0.663
	Developmental State	7.1%	15.3%	0.590	0.248	0.838
	European Forces	0.0%	1.2%	0.031	0.157	0.188
	Labour versus Capital	20.0%	14.9%	0.804	0.116	0.920
	Neo-Liberalism	3.6%	1.9%	0.827	0.082	0.909
	Pragmatic Legitimising Approach	0.7%	1.7%	0.382	0.179	0.560
	Stigma Entrenched Powers	1.4%	4.2%	0.263	0.155	0.418

Developmental State, *Unions*, and *Neutral*, while the most relevant categories on the left camp of the map are the categories *Neo-Liberalism* and *Positive*. Therefore, we called the principal axis *Position towards privatisations*, as it depicts a clear opposition between actors and frames supporting privatisations, in the left camp of the map, and actors and frames opposing them, in the right camp of the map.

The distinction between the upper and the lower camps of the map, which characterises the secondary axis, is more subtle. Indeed, the categories that define the secondary axis Y are, in the upper part of the map, the actor *Unions*, and the frames *Labours versus Capital* and *Stigma Entrenched Powers*. Taken together, these categories identify a stance towards the privatisation issue that puts first the safeguarding of employment and that blames politicians and public managers for the poor results of SOEs. Conversely, in the lower part of the map, the most relevant categories are *Politicians Centre, Public Managers*, the frame *Developmental State*, and the *Ambiguous* position towards privatisations. The groups of social actors who are clustered in these categories are the politicians who had been at the heart of the governments that run the country for the former 40 years and that appointed public managers. Thus, the cluster represents an entrenched power structure that adopts an ambiguous attitude toward privatisations to preserve the traditional role of the State in the economy. After the inspection of the opposite logics, we labelled this axis: *The role of the State versus the protection of workers*.

Table 5.3 reports MCA's statistical output referred to the principal variables, which are the ones used to elicit the latent meaning space. Each row represents a category (i.e. the variable "actors" is composed of ten categories, such as *Unions* and *Entrepreneurs*). The column "contribution" describes the percentual contribution of each category to determining the meaning of the principal and secondary axis, respectively. This is the most important value for understanding the meaning of the axis[5] (Le Roux & Rouanet, 2010: 41): the positions of the categories with a higher contribution in explaining the variance associated with an axis are used to induce the meaning of that axis. The *baseline criterion* suggests inducing the meaning of an axis by relying on those categories whose contribution exceeds the average contribution (Le Roux & Rouanet, 2010: 52). In this case, we have 21 categories, so the average contributions would be 4.7%, although other categories can be used to induce the meaning if their average contribution is around the average contribution and adding them improves the interpretation of the map (Le Roux & Rouanet, 2010: 52). We report in bold the contribution of the categories used to induce the meaning of the map. The last three columns detail the quality of depiction of each category in the bi-dimensional space: the overall quality represents the projection in the bi-dimensional space of categories' position in the multi-dimensional space. Therefore, it varies from 0 (not represented at all) to 1 (perfectly represented). The *horizontal axis* of our map reveals the cohabitation of a repertoire of institutional logics in framing privatisations in reference to models of state intervention. In the left camp of the map are those frames that explicitly support privatisation policy. This position is centred on the systemic frame that captures neo-liberalist positions that advocate a model of limited state intervention. The frame is associated with the idea that privatisation is to be considered a panacea to a wide repertoire of weaknesses and malaises of the Italian economy and that Italy is late in adopting the globally spreading market discipline. Thus, in the map, *Neo-Liberalism* is close to *Stigma Entrenched Powers* that blames the pathological allotment of power among political parties in state-owned holdings and the delays to the privatisation process as an underhanded attempt by public managers to impede the systemic transformation.

Close to these frames, we find the actors *journalists, entrepreneurs, bankers and consultants, technocrats, independent politicians,* and *rightwing politicians*. Rightwing politicians traditionally hailed the market as the most efficient mechanism to organise economic activity. This group of actors includes also the cast of politicians that came to power after the ruinous and adventurous demise of *pentapartito,* the five-party coalition that had led the country in the period 1983–1993. These parties, namely Forza Italia and Lega Nord, legitimised themselves as a new force that proposed critical changes in established institutions. In this light, the positioning in the left-hand side of the map describes the attempt to gain status by demising an old institutional logic.

As well in the left section of the map, another frame, the *Pragmatic Legitimising Approach,* includes the utterances that refer to privatisation as an accepted and undisputable destiny for the Italian steel industry and portrays the outcome of the institutionalisation process in the discourse on privatisation. This frame crystallises the global pressures to isomorphism at work that push the worldwide spreading of neo-liberal policy adoption (Jepperson & Meyer, 1991; Meyer et al., 1997; Polillo & Guillén, 2005; Weber et al., 2009). The working of institutionalisation pressures as well emerges, in the same frame, in the articulation of a typical technical discourse that sees privatisation as a necessary and accepted policy. Close to this pragmatic frame are the *Independent Politicians* who are skilled experts that have been called from time to time to serve in the government. Coercion pressures as well are fundamental to capturing the spread of privatisation policies (Brune et al., 2004; Henisz et al., 2005). These coercion pressures to isomorphism are as well described by the pragmatic frame *European Forces* that refers to the coercive pressures exerted by the European Commission.

On the right side of the map are those frames that either are connected to a strong refusal of privatisation or maintain an ambiguous or neutral view towards privatisation. In the far right of the map is the systemic *Labour versus Capital* frame that, as expected, clearly opposes privatisation policies. According to this view, state policies are evaluated in their ability to create employment and is therefore not surprising that *Unions* are the principal supporters of this frame. In the middle of the map is located the *Developmental State* systemic frame that is close to an ambiguous position towards the privatisation process. This frame is positioned in the middle between the neo-liberal logic of state intervention and a logic of conflict between labour and capital. Indeed, the developmental state frame does not necessarily oppose privatisation in principle, yet it advocates the fundamental role to be played by the state in the economy. As expected, the actors that are close to this frame are the *Centre Politicians,* and namely the Socialist and the Christian

Democratic parties. These politicians, in most cases, have been the engineers, the paladins and the guardians of the developmental state, and the warrantors of the corporatist pact that constituted the truce among the members of the historical bloc that materialised after WWII. In this respect, they cannot entirely share with the neo-liberal frame the clear-cut support to privatisation. Another interesting frame refers to the tradition of *Continental Capitalism* (CC): this frame is clearly separated from the cluster of actors and frames that support privatisation as a taken-for-granted remedy or as the product of a globally institutionalised neo-liberal point of view. Yet, the frame reveals an attitude towards privatisation that differs from a typical developmental state logic and that is more prone to accept privatisation as a mechanism of industrial policy. Associated to the frame are the *Public Managers*, who are both conscious of the unsustainable inefficiency of state steel but are culturally part of the state-owned enterprises system and have often been part of the technocracy that managed the system. In a number of speeches, the role of specific interests is well visible and suggests that not only cultural embeddedness but the interest as well triggers opposition or support to privatisation.

In the middle of the map are also *Leftwing Politicians*, mostly from the communist and post-communist parties. This is a group of politicians that, in most cases, grew up together in the former PCI (Italian Communist Party). Interestingly, they are in the middle between neutral, ambiguous, and contrary positions towards privatisations. This position reveals the cohabitation of those that maintained a conflict-based view of the state and those that followed the gradual transition of the PCI away from communism towards social democracy. Another perspective to interpret this neutral stance towards privatisations, and the equidistance between, *Labour versus Capital* and *Developmental State*, reveals the entrenched tradition of the PCI that contributed to building up the Italian state and has been a key piece of the ruling political class in the post-WWII reconstruction, despite never directly taking part in governments. When the decision to maintain IRI was to be taken in the late 1940s, the PCI kept an ambiguous position not opposing the revival of IRI but considering this choice a second best in respect to the preferred idea of nationalising large firms (Castronovo, 2011: 60).

The *vertical* dimension is particularly useful to disentangle the differences between actors and frames not supporting privatisations. Politicians representing the *Centre, Leftwing Politicians, Public Managers,* and *Unions* belong to the preexisting historical bloc that had learned how to coexist. Deep differences, however, remain, and along the horizontal axis are distributed the forces and the logics that underpin a truce that lasted for decades and that is now threatened by the violent burst of the privatisation issue. Yet, these actors who are located along the vertical axis are embedded in asymmetric power relations. In the lower part of the map is the political elite that ruled the country in the post-WWII period, together with *Public Managers*. Especially through the frame *Developmental State* they show an ambiguous position towards privatisations, as they want to preserve the entrenched power system and the role of the State in the economy.

In the upper part of the map, there are those forces that subscribed to the truce but maintained a conflict-based dialectical interaction with the elite. Namely, *Unions,* that support the frame *Labour versus Capital* and that clearly communicate that their primary interest lies with the protection of workers. The *Leftwing Parties* are once again in the middle, since, as explained before, they are part of the ruling elite without being part of the government. Interestingly the axis makes explicit a dialectic tension that occurs within the camp of those social actors who are not supporters of privatisations. From another perspective, this tension unveils a fracture that cracks the surface of a long-standing corporatist pact among workers, unions, and the post-WWII political establishment.

Interestingly, Meyer and Höllerer (2010), in their study of the diffusion of the shareholder value concept in Austria, obtained a very similar map and confirmed that the MCA analysis of discourse is effective in unpacking the composition of the corporatist alliances that resist policies to preserve a historical bloc. In their work, the alliance that opposes the diffusion of shareholder value concept includes politicians, trade unions, and employers. These actors, Meyer and Hollerer suggest, embody the corporatist pact at work in the last decades in Austria. In their map, the vertical alignment of actors that take a negative stance towards the shareholder value concept is opposed to a cluster of actors and frames supporting the concept on the right-hand side to form a "triangle" (2010: 1253). We, as well, observe that the alliance of actors that resisted privatisation can be unpacked into the members of a threatened corporatist pact. Yet, in our map, this alliance does apparently not include employers. This is an interesting variation that captures a feature peculiar to the Italian political system. In many respects, Austria and Italy are a similar expression of European continental capitalism (Gourevitch and Shinn, 2020: 53). However, Italy has been characterised by ambiguous and changeable relationships between the state and the association of large industrial entrepreneurs, Confindustria. Rather than a pure corporatist or associative state, in which interaction between governments and business takes place through consultation of social partners and business associations, Italy is characterised by a "party state" (Wilson & Grant, 2010: 201) in which the business-government relationship takes place through the "factions of dominant political party" and political power was unbalanced in favour of political parties (Lanza & Lavdas, 2000: 207). More subtly, we suggest, and we will demonstrate, that entrepreneurs took the opportunity to strategically mobilise the rhetoric on the virtues of the market to gain power in respect to the ruling political class.

5.3.2 MCA relating actors and proposed privatisation models: discursive strategising

A second MCA contributes to the understanding of how actors strategised within the constraints provided by the meanings crystallised within the DOS. Namely, we report a map relating actors and the proposed privatisation models. Exactly as we did before, we present a general map, describing the meaning space during the whole 1984–1995 period, and the statistical output that is necessary to induce the meaning of the map.

Figure 5.2 is the overall latent meaning space, referring to the 1984–1995 period, where we see the average positions of actors and privatisation models. This model accounts for 93% of explained inertia, which is a very high result. In particular, the principal axis accounts for 60.2, while the secondary axis adds 32.8% more. The graphical output is complemented by statistical results, which we present in Table 5.4, and that, exactly as before, describe the contribution of each category of the variables in defining the bi-dimensional space and describe how well a category is represented.

In our case, all the categories are well depicted, with the only exception of *Leftwing Politicians*. Regarding the interpretation of axes, the categories that describe the principal axis are, on the right of the map, the actors *Bankers and Consultants*, and *Journalists*, together with the model *Market Driven*. On the left of the map, the defining categories are the actors *Politicians Independents, Unions*, and the model *Public Company*. We thus labelled the principal X-axis *Market versus Controlled Privatisation Process*, as it describes an opposition between an approach demanding privatisations and freedom from state's intervention (on the right) and an opposite approach supporting a sort of control on privatisations (on the left of the map) and a distribution of shares among shareholders, financial and industrial groups, government, and also employees, as highlighted by the support of unions.

The secondary axis is defined by the models *Government Controlled* and *Noyeaux Durs*, in the upper part of the map, together with *Independent Politicians*, while in the lower part of the map the defining actors are interestingly *Entrepreneurs* and *Unions*, together with the model *Public Company*. This axis captures the discursive antagonisms between actors belonging to the productive core of the industry, located in the lower part of the map, who want to loosen the political control on privatised firms, and actors who are willing to retain control on the privatisation process by virtue of their political legitimisation, in the upper part of the map. Therefore, we labelled this axis *Productive Core of the Industry versus the Unproductive Class*.

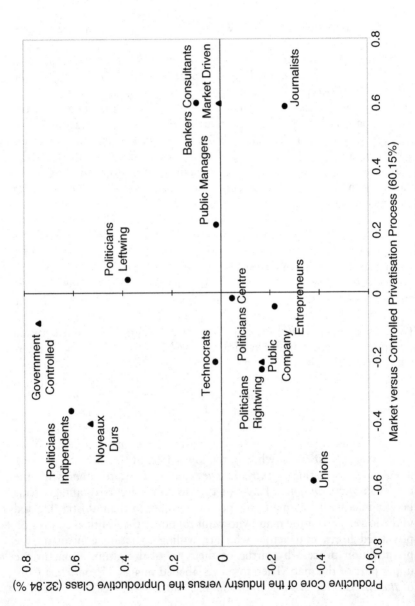

Figure 5.2 MCA relating actors and proposed privatisation models – 1984–1995

Table 5.4 Statistical output for the MCA relating actors and proposed privatisations models 1984–1995[6]

Variables	Categories	Contribution		Quality of Depiction		
		X	Y	X	Y	Overall (X+Y)
Actors	Bankers	**20.3%**	1.0%	0.954	0.026	0.980
	Consultants					
	Entrepreneurs	0.1%	**5.8%**	0.037	0.904	0.941
	Journalists	**5.9%**	2.2%	0.825	0.167	0.992
	Politicians Centre	0.0%	0.1%	0.101	0.654	0.755
	Politicians Indipendents	**6.0%**	**29.7%**	0.268	0.726	0.993
	Politicians Leftwing	0.0%	1.4%	0.003	0.261	0.264
	Politicians Rightwing	1.2%	1.1%	0.393	0.184	0.577
	Public Managers	2.2%	0.0%	0.837	0.007	0.843
	Technocrats	2.1%	0.0%	0.927	0.012	0.938
	Unions	**12.1%**	8.8%	0.679	0.269	0.947
Privatisation Models	Government Controlled	0.2%	**25.3%**	0.014	0.839	0.852
	Market Driven	**35.2%**	0.0%	0.997	0.000	0.997
	Noyeaux Durs	4.7%	**14.4%**	0.299	0.500	0.799
	Public Company	**9.9%**	**10.3%**	0.634	0.358	0.992

Overall, the map identifies three main positions. On the right part of the map, the *market-driven model* proposes practices free from state intervention, where the invisible hand of the market is deemed able to orient the privatisation process. In the left camp of the map we find two different models of intervention that are able to drive the process in different ways: in the upper part of the map, *Noyaux Durs* and *Government Controlled* define a position where the political power should drive the privatisation process. In the lower-left camp of the map, we find the *Public Company* model, which prioritises the distribution of wealth among a large population of shareholders. In the next two chapters, we will describe how actors changed their positions in reference to these methods during fragmentation and settlement, respectively.

Notes

1 In this case, the model is used to appropriately refer to a model of mixed economy, rather than to the governance system typical of Renan model, with the co-presence of workers and managers in boards.
2 Deliberation of CIPE 30/12/1992.
3 Sole 24 ORE, 17-11-1992.

4 ENI (Ente Nazionale Idrocarburi) and ENEL (Ente nazionale per l'energia elettrica) are diversified energy companies that managed, respectively, the state operations in gas and oil search and extraction, and delivery of electricity.
5 From a geometrical point of view, these contributions are the proportion of normalised variance of each axis due to a category.
6 Categories which contribute more to each axis and that were used to induce axes' meaning are indicated in bold.

References

Bourdieu, P. (1991). *Language and symbolic power*. Harverd University Press.

Brune, N., Garrett, G., & Kogut, B. (2004). The International Monetary Fund and the global spread of privatization. *IMF Staff Papers*, 51(2): 195–219.

Castronovo, V. (2011). Un profilo d'insieme. In V. Castronovo (Ed.), *Storia dell'IRI. Dalle orogini al dopoguerra: 1933–1948* (pp. 162–268). Editori Laterza.

Feigenbaum, H., Henig, J., & Hamnett, C. (1998). *Shrinking the state: The political underpinnings of privatization*. Cambridge University Press.

Feigenbaum, H. B., & Henig, J. R. (1994). The political underpinnings of privatization: A typology. *World Politics*, 46(2): 185–208. http://www.jstor.org/stable/10.2307/2950672

Gourevitch, P. A., & Shinn, J. (2010). *Political power and corporate control: The new global politics of corporate governance*. Princeton University Press.

Greenacre, M., & Blasius, J. (Eds.). (2006). *Correspondence analysis in the social sciences: Recent developments and applications*. Academic Press.

Hardy, C., & Maguire, S. (2010). Discourse, field-configuring events, and change in organizations and institutional fields: Narratives of DDT and the Stockholm Convention. *Academy of Management Journal*, 53(6): 1365–1392.

Henisz, W. J., Zelner, B. A., & Guillén, M. F. (2005). The worldwide diffusion of market-oriented infrastructure reform, 1977-1999. *American Sociological Review*, 70(6): 871–897. 10.2307/4145398

Jepperson, R. L., & Meyer, J. W. (1991). The public order and the construction of formal organizations. In W. W. Powell, & P. J. DiMaggio (Eds.), *The new institutionalism in organizational analysis*. The University of Chicago Press.

Lanza, O., & Lavdas, K. (2000). The disentanglement of interest politics: Business associability, the parties and policy in Italy and Greece. *European Journal of Political Research*, 37(2): 203–235. LA-English. 10.1023/A:100701 7624486

Le Roux, B. & Rouanet, H. (2010). *Quantitative applications in the social sciences: Multiple correspondence analysis.*Thousand Oaks, CA: SAGE Publications.

Meyer, J. W., Boli, J., Thomas George, M., & Ramirez, F. O. (1997). World society and the nation-state. *American Journal of Sociology*, 103(1): 144–181. 10.1086/231174

Meyer, R. E., & Höllerer, M. A. (2010). Meaning structures in a contested issue field: A topographic map of shareholder value in Austria. *Academy of Management Journal*, 53(6): 1241–1262. 10.5465/amj.2010.57317829

Polillo, S., & Guillén, M. F. (2005). Globalization pressures and the state: The worldwide spread of central bank independence. *American Journal of Sociology*, 110(6): 1764–1802.

Snow, D., & Benford, R. (1988). Ideology, frame resonance, and participant mobilization. In B. Klandermans, H. Kriesi, & S. Tarrow (Eds.), *From structure to action: Comparing social movement research across cultures*, vol. 1. JAI press.

Suleiman, E. (1990). The politics of privatization in Britain and France. *The Political Economy of Public Sector Reform*, 1: 113–136.

Weber, K., Davis, G. F., & Lounsbury, M. (2009). Policy as myth and ceremony? The global spread of stock exchanges. *Academy of Management Journal*, 52(6): 1319–1347.

Wilson, G., & Grant, W. (2010). Business and political parties. In D. Coen, W. Grant, & G. Wilson (Eds.), *The Oxford handbook of Business and Government*. Oxford Univerity Press.

6 Fragmentation of the historical bloc

6.1 The state of the field before the fragmentation phase

6.1.1 IRI and the birth of the state economy in the post Second World War Italy

Within a tradition of continental capitalism, in the period that spans from the WWII to mid-1990s, in a number of European countries the state maintained a central role in the economy. In particular, in Italy, the prominent role played by governments to contribute to the accumulation of fixed capital is coherent with a model of developmental state (Johnson, 1982) that pursues objectives of development through direct employment and capital accumulation by substituting for a weak private initiative. Also, the developmental state promotes import substitution industrialisation to reduce the dependence of domestic production on imports. The pervasive role of the state in Italy is well captured in the history of IRI, the largest state-owned corporation funded by Mussolini in 1933. As its name suggests – Istituto di Ricostruzione Industriale (Institute for Industrial Reconstruction) – IRI was initially created with temporary status to salvage and reorganise the Italian banking system during the crisis of the 1930s. Once the banking system was restructured, however, Mussolini foresaw in IRI a key mechanism to control strategic levers of industrial policy and to achieve three objectives: supporting an autarchic policy, contributing to the national defence, and supporting the intervention in the African colonies (Castronovo, 2011: 34). Thus, with royal decree no. 905 on the 24 of July 1937, IRI became a permanent state-owned holding controlling the equity of the most important banks and a large portion of the industrial production.

Notwithstanding the mires of Mussolini, IRI remained a relatively independent organism led by Alberto Beneduce, who was not affiliated to the Fascist Party, rather was appreciated by Mussolini for his technical skills despite his previous sympathy for the socialist party and his anti-fascist mood. Under the leadership of Beneduce, IRI raised a group of

DOI: 10.4324/9780429438516-6

skilled technocrats and, in the late 1930s, expanded its activity from financial engineering to the restructuring and management of firms.

At the end of the Second World War, a debate opened concerning the destiny of IRI. Suspects arose from the most liberalist side of the Italian political array that feared a statist turn in the newly born Italian Republic and from those international partners, such as the United States, that looked at IRI as both the incarnation of expansionistic mires previously awakened by the Fascist Party and of socialist aspirations towards the nationalisation of the economy. Despite these suspicions, IRI survived this delicate new turn in Italian history to represent an interesting compromise among the aim of the left side of catholic political representation to reduce poverty and redistribute income, the sympathy of the socialist and communist party for state control in the economy, the enthusiasm of laic progressivism for moderate engineering of the economy, the pressures to corporatism inherited from the revolutionary unionism that permeated the Fascist Party and the aspiration to the survival of a highly skilled group of technocrats (Castronovo, 2011: 38–39, 54, 60).

6.1.2 IRI and the state steel

At the end of 1933, IRI directly owned the entire military and 40% of the civil steel industry and in 1938 a company was created, Finsider, directly controlled by IRI, to organise all the state-owned steel producers: ILVA, SIAC, TERNI, and DALMINE. These firms used to be privately owned but they had to be salvaged by IRI in the 1930s. In 1938, Finsider produced 66% of national pig iron and 45% of national raw steel and was one of the key centres of the autarchic political economy of the Fascist Party as stated in the National Autarchic Plan announced on the 25th of March 1936. In the plan, the design of the steel industry was aimed at increasing the production of raw steel through pig iron, thereby reducing the dependence on imported scraps, and at providing flat steel products for the nascent automotive industry (D'Antone, 2011: 225). The autarchic plan for the steel aimed at producing internally 93% of the 2,500,000 tons/year of raw steel domestically needed by 1941. Also, the plan stated that half of the raw steel had to be produced by a state-owned system from pig iron through an integrated process and half had to be produced by private steel makers through electric furnaces (Doria, 2011: 393) thereby giving rise to that specialisation, which survived in the Italian steel industry until its privatisation, that associates state steel mainly to the production of flat products through integrated processes (Balconi, 1991: 220). To capture this robust trend, which describes a characteristic trait of the Italian economy, in Figure 4.1, in chapter 4, we reported data on state and private raw steel production. As shown in the figure, after WWII, state initiatives came again to play a central role in the attempt to rebuild damaged industrial infrastructures. In particular, the Sinigaglia Plan was initiated in 1949 (Oscar Sinigaglia was Finsider President after the end of WWII). The plan was aimed at rebuilding the pre-war Italian steel production capacity with an investment of 300 billion Italian liras (Balconi, 1991). The plan, completed in 1956, brought the production of ILVA, the major state-owned steel producer, from 482,760 tonnes/year in 1949 to 1,391,849 tonnes/year in 1956. This implied a 250% increase in the production of the state-owned holding in the steel production, Finsider, whose production jumped from 833,415 tonnes/year in 1949 to 2,934,177 tonnes/year in 1956. In the same period, Italian production of raw steel increased 188%, from 2,050,000 to 5,907,631 tonnes/year, thus explaining the slight proportional increase in the role of state production in Figure 4.1 in chapter 4.

In the 1960s, a remarkable trend in private steel production was the upsurge of minimills in the north of Italy, and especially in the area surrounding the town of Brescia. More specifically, in the period 1959–1970, aggregate minimills' production capacity increased by 700% from 465,000 to 3,750,000 tonnes/year whereas raw steel produced by large traditional private firms (Falck, Fiat Ferriere, and others) increased by nearly 60% from 2,823,000 to 4,475,000 tonnes/year (Balconi, 1991: 163–166). In the same period, however, the production of Finsider, the holding that aggregated most of the state-owned steel producers, increased by 170% from 3,573,143 to 9,685,800 tonnes/ year. Given that in 1970 the Italian national production of steel was 17,277,000 tonnes/year, notwithstanding the growth of minimills, the proportion of private raw steel production remained just above 40% over the entire national production.

State intervention, with some oscillations, returned around 1975–1979. The doubling of a plant for integrated steel production located in Taranto was completed in that period. The plant was owned by Italsider, a state-owned steel company that was part of Finsider. The aim of the doubling of the Taranto plant was to reach an installed capacity able to produce 12.5 million tonnes/year of raw steel. Furthermore, the effects of the industrial recession of 1973–1974 encouraged state intervention. On the verge of an economic slowdown, many private firms collapsed and the state acquired portions of the equity to salvage these firms.

Thus, from the end of the Second World War to the 1990s, when the privatisation process started, state ownership oscillated around 50% of the entire national installed capacity and the national production of raw steel. Retrospectively, the state contributed to placing Italy among the leading steel producers in Europe. In 1900, Italy produced only 135,000 tonnes/year, whereas Germany, Great Britain, and France produced, respectively, 6,177,000, 4,979,000, and 1,565,000 tonnes/year (Doria, 2011: 359). Even though during the Second World War a large part of the

Italian installed capacity was either destroyed or disassembled, in 1974, Italy produced nearly 24 million tonnes/year and Great Britain, France and Germany produced, respectively, 22, 27, and 53 million tonnes/year.

6.1.3 A historical bloc

The steel field was organised around a historical bloc. As said, a pivotal role in this organisation was played by the SOE system. From a political point of view, after WWII, the Christian Democratic Party (Democrazia Cristiana, DC) was the centre around which the SOE system was built. Thus, this party played a central role both in the nomination of state-owned enterprises' managers and in guiding their industrial policy. The SOE system, however, had been built in coordination with large private companies pertaining to the General Confederation of Italian Industry (Confindustria). Not only, as reported above, coordination between state and private steel producers was conceived in the Fascist National Autarchic Plan issued in 1936, but, after the Second World War, the funds allocated by the European Recovery Fund to the investments in the Italian steel industry were shared among Finsider and two large private companies, FIAT and Falck.

In general, strong ties resisted that interwove the SOE system and private producers in the steel industry. Private firms often benefited from state support, as when IRI accepted to bail out inefficient private steel producers as was the case of Teksid, a large private producer nationa-lised in 1982. Teksid was a steel producer owned by the private car-maker FIAT. The company was in deep crisis due to excessive workforce, mistaken investments, and obsolete technology (Balconi, 1991: 419). Willing to focus on the core business, FIAT relied on state intervention to overcome the barriers to exit the steel industry. First, FIAT took advantage of 20% of the funds made available through article 20 of law no. 46 issued on 17/02/1982[1] to close two electric furnaces for a total installed capacity of 150 tonnes of crude steel. Then, the government bought Teksid using a method to determine the selling price that was strictly linked to the equity. Thus, FIAT was not required to pay the future stream of losses. Balconi, in her report of the deal (1991: 420–423), calculated that the Teksid sale cost the state a sum within 450 and 500 billion liras.

In addition, the state-holding company Finsider was at the centre of a web of participations in the equity of private producers and often co-ordinated its production plans with these latter. For example, in 1952, FIAT and Finsider agreed not to duplicate investments in rolling mills. Specifically, FIAT did not install its own rolling capacity and Finsider committed to supplying rolled coils at cost-plus price (Balconi, 1991).

Thus, this agreement between IRI, state steel, and private producers builds up the "historical bloc" (Gramsci, 1975: 1051) that exercised hegemony in Italy after the Second World War. Of course, the bloc was far from homogeneous; unions and the Communist Party looked at the post WWII governments as truces to which they opposed a more dialectical interpretation of labour-capital relationships. When the decision to maintain IRI was to be taken in the late 1940s, the Communist Party kept an ambiguous position not opposing the revival of IRI but considering this choice a second-best in respect to the preferred idea of nationalising large firms (Castronovo, 2011: 60). On the other hand, however, rather than pursuing economic profit only, SOEs had also societal goals, for example fighting unemployment and, therefore, had the support of unions.

Yet, the historical bloc was probably consolidated around a more nuanced model of state intervention. Specifically, a widely agreed upon armistice accepted an ambiguous compromise between two main cultural models.

First, as in a number of European countries, in Italy, a tradition of continental capitalism was embraced according to which the state played an important role in regulating the economy. In this respect, Italy is an expression of European continental capitalism so that Gourevitch and Shinn (2010: 53) position Austria, Germany, and Italy, on the one hand, and the United States, on the other extreme, in a coordination index that measures institutional complementarity among 20 countries.

Second, as anticipated in the foregoing, in Italy, in the post WWII period, the prominent role played by governments in the accumulation of fixed capital is coherent with a model of developmental state (Johnson, 1982).

An ambiguous blend of these two models of state intervention has dominated the scene in the post-war Italian economy.

In 1990s, power was balanced, a coalition of political parties tightly held power over a series of succeeding governments in the previous 40 years; the communist party held many regional administrations and maintained a large share of the members of parliament. Large firms, represented by Confindustria, held economic capital, often supported by protectionist policies and strategic devaluation of the national currency. Symbolic capital, as Bourdieu labelled the legitimisation to speak (1991), was evenly distributed as well. Ruling politicians had been the constituents of the post WWII political institutions and had ruled the country without real political competition for 40 years; on the other hand, large entrepreneurs were considered the backbone of the Italian post-war renaissance. More importantly, until that moment, both ruling political and economic elites had no reasons to reciprocally weaken their legitimisation. In this light, our analysis confirms Silva's description (2013) of the pre-privatisation state of affairs in Italy where *de facto* and *de iure* power, that is, the elites holding economic and political power, reinforced each other (Acemoglu & Robinson, 2006).

In this light, some political scientists suggest that rather than a pure corporatist or associative state, in which interaction between governments and business takes place through consultation of social partners and business associations, Italy is characterised by a "party state" (Wilson & Grant, 2010: 201) in which a business-government relationship takes place through the "factions of dominant political party" and political power was unbalanced in favour of political parties (Lanza & Lavdas, 2000: 207).

In sum, the SOE system, repeatedly stigmatised for its inefficiency, resisted because it was a central element of a power system, or a historical bloc. If, as many observers suggest, IRI and the state intervention in the Italian economy were inefficient, this was a typical case of an inefficient institution that persisted "because they favour particular actors who have the power to defend them" (Ingram & Clay, 2000: 526).

With a number of laws, the government repeatedly supported private producers. For example, in 1981, with law no. 155, the government provided funds to encourage early retirements; in 1982, as noted before, the article 20 of the law no. 46 created a fund[2] to finance the closure of plants; and, in 1984, the law no. 193 assured further funds to finance restructuring and closures of plants of private producers (Balconi, 1991: 425). The logic underpinning the law was that that state acquired plants and machines of private producers to abate the barrier to exit to the industry for private producers. Along similar lines, the state-owned holding operating in the steel industry used to acquire minority stakes in Italian private steel producers with the aim of protecting their equities from aggressive acquisitions by foreign steel producers.[3]

6.2 The fragmentation phase

6.2.1 Material pressures and the misalignment of economic interests during fragmentation

6.2.1.1 The crisis of the Italian state-owned steel production system

With a bleak landscape in the global and European steel markets, in the passage from the 1970s to the 1980s, the crisis of the state-owned Italsider established its roots. The origins of the crisis of Italian state steel originates from a combination of weaknesses in the holding's corporate and competitive strategies along with skyrocketing costs of labour. Despite a number of investments in new technology, the company proved unable to vertically integrate production and coordinating operations within the group. Another problematic area was distribution and marketing strategy.

According to Balconi (1991: 256), in 1980, Italsider, one of the key companies of Finsider, was one of the most technologically advanced companies in Europe. The proportion of blast furnaces with a diameter greater than 10 metres was 71% compared to 55% in France and 42% in Germany. Converters less than 8 years old were 70% in Italsider and 15% in the other European countries and, in 1980, the old Martin-Siemens technology was completely dismissed. Whereas in the other European countries only 15% of operating rolling mills were acquired after 1970, in Italsider this percentage reached 50%. Another area of excellence for Finsider was in the production of seamless pipes where Dalmine, a pipe producer of the group, developed innovative mandrel technology to pierce steel pipes. Yet, the investment in new technologies was plagued by two problems.

First, investments focused mainly on the upward stages of production, blast furnaces, and converters, whereas, in the downstream stage of production, the investments in continuous casting were still lacking. For example, in 1981, in the Italsider's plant in Taranto only 35% of production was obtained through continuous casting whereas, for example, the plant of French company Usinor in Dunkerque was able to produce more than 90% through continuous casting (Balconi, 1991: 263). This situation created bottlenecks and impeded an effective vertical integration of the production process. The same issue plagued the Italsider's plant in Bagnoli that was in direct competition with minimills; minimills, on the contrary, had all adopted continuous casting.

Second, technological investments were often not properly co-ordinated. For example, in the plant of Cornigliano, in the northwest of Italy, new investments focused on both continuous casting and converters. Yet, converters had a production capacity of 2.4 million tonnes/year, whereas continuous casting, downstream, had a production capacity of 1 million tonnes/year. Thus, the investment in converters could be utilised only by 50% of its installed production capacity. In addition, technology was unfit to face global competition. For example, the plant located in Terni, in the centre of Italy, produced magnetic metal sheets that were too narrow compared to market needs (Balconi, 1991: 269).

Furthermore, a number of incongruous choices characterised the holding's corporate strategy. For example, in the business of large forged products, the plant based in Terni was in direct competition with another plant of the group located in Campi, in the northwest of Italy (Balconi, 1991: 269).

Finally, Finsider was unable to capture a key trend of the market. In the 1970s, the demand for steel products became increasingly advanced. Precisely, steel products were not commodities, rather clients' value was connected to the number of downstream rework and finishing, and the timing and logistics of delivery. A need emerged to change the traditional logic of steelmaking that hinged on economies of scale and large batches. Large steelmakers faced the challenge to harmonise economy of scale and product differentiation being able to offer different batch sizes and flexibly managing the variety of downstream reworking of the products. Large European competitors followed this trend. They integrated the distribution channels and offered a number of services in-house. Finsider, on the other hand, was unable to adapt to the evolving competition dynamics and was forced into the segment of commoditised products, whose demand was very elastic to prices (Balconi, 1991: 275–280). Finsider's competitive strategy was therefore squashed between the high cost of production and the need to maintain low prices. To make things worse, the company suffered from difficulties in managing industrial relations. At least until 1977, the conflict between unionised workers and the company was very violent. As Balconi reports (1991: 293), between 1969 and 1980, 10 million tonnes of raw steel production was lost due to strikes. In general, however, it was very difficult to cut, or even to move from one site to another. This rigidity in the management of the workforce inhibited the effort to integrate and coordinate production processes in the group and curtailed productivity.

In sum, as Balconi advocates (1991), the origin of the crisis of Finsider was not in the lack of investments, or pathological financial management, but in flawed strategic choices, in the lack of vertical integration, in the lack of coordination in the technological investments, and the management of industrial relations. These elements eroded the productivity of operations and curbed the rate of utilisation of production capacity, thereby inhibiting the capability to control average costs of production.

Of course, the weaknesses in the management of operations and the corporate strategy, associated with large investments in the decade 1970–1980, weakened as well the financial structure of Finsider, the state-owned holding in the steel industry. As reported in Figure 6.1, investments accelerated in the mid-1970s along with both short- and long-term debt, thereby increasing financial costs. As shown in Figure 6.2, the return on investments initially grew to sharply decrease in the period 1973–1977 when investments accelerated and became negative in 1980. Thus, investments were structurally unable to generate enough income but resulted in the weakening of both the economic and the financial structure of the company. Specifically, economically, Figure 6.3 shows the financial costs of debt grew in the proportion of sales and, as reported in Figure 6.4, as well in the proportion of operating income pushing net income to negative value since 1975. As for the structure of the capital, as reported in Figure 6.5, the weight of the debt grew in proportion to the equity.

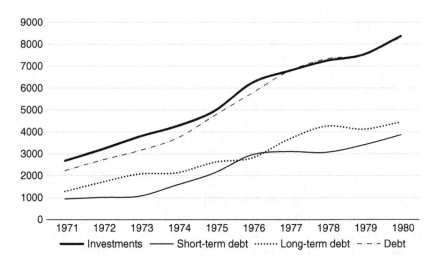

Figure 6.1 Financial figures of Finsider: debts and investments
Source: Elaboration on IRI Annual Report. Figures in billions of Italian liras.

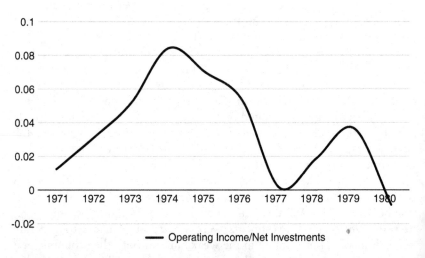

Figure 6.2 Financial figures of Finsider: operating incomes and investments
Source: Elaboration on IRI Annual Report.

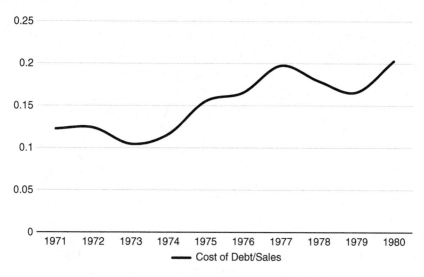

Figure 6.3 Financial figures of Finsider: cost of debt and sales
Source: Elaboration on IRI Annual Report.

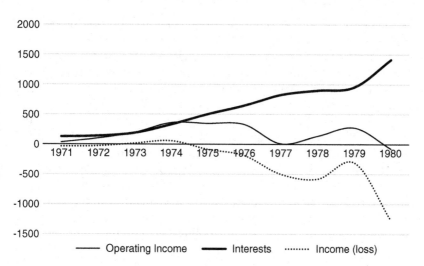

Figure 6.4 Financial figures of Finsider: operating income, cost of debt and
income

Source: Elaboration on IRI Annual Report. Figures in billions of Italian liras.

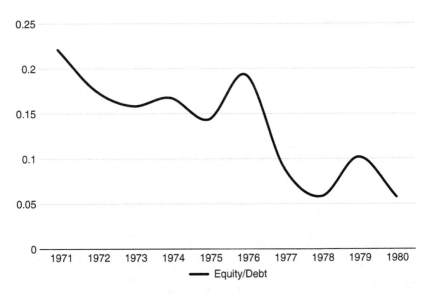

Figure 6.5 Financial figures of IRI: equity and debt
Source: Elaboration on IRI Annual Report.

6.2.1.2 Privatisation and the economic interests of elites

The interests of the key actors regarding the privatisation process revealed several misalignments. Privatisation was both a guarantee for the
European Union that the Italian government would end its involvement
in the financially burdensome steel industry and the way to make
available installed capacity and market share for private producers.
These producers, however, showed a nuanced collection of contradicting
interests; efficient private entrepreneurs foresaw in privatisations the
opportunity of buying the equity of state-owned competitors (Mucchetti,
2013: 585), or to see powerful competitors excluded from the market;
from this perspective, "large private steel producers had the interest to
force the European Union and the Italian government to privatize and
sell AST to take out of the market a strong competitor in the long steel
products". Moreover, in general, by supporting privatisations, private
entrepreneurs hoped to weaken the political grip on the economy.

Yet, in many respects, private producers depended on the government's
intervention. First, they feared the opening of the equity of privatised firms to
foreign investors. In 1985, for example, Mr. Arvedi, owner of one of the
largest private producers, called for the help of SOEs to protect Italian steel
from foreigners' supremacy. Second, private producers lobbied the government to lower barriers to industry exit by making funds available to encourage the dismissal of inefficient producers (Balconi, 1991: 419–420) and

guaranteeing a financially backed exit option. This relationship required a continuous political dialogue with the government and suggested a cautious approach to privatisation. Other actors had strong incentives to support privatisations. For example, bankers and consultancy firms saw in the privatisation process the chance for getting large commissions, playing the role of intermediaries (Cavazzuti, 2013: 99, 116).

A general expectation that privatisations would improve the Italian economy motivated technocrats to support privatisations. As reported by Curli (2013: 192), an *elite consensus* had developed in Italy among members of the technocracy that the stringent economic constraints set by the inclusion in the European Union, and the connected pressures to privatisations, were painful but necessary steps towards the modernisation of the Italian economy. Such a technocratic elite enjoyed the support of an across-the-board political coalition that included members of the Parliament belonging to parties of the right, the centre, and the Communist Party as well. This elite consensus was well testified by the journalists who wrote for mainstream newspapers and who largely shared such an enthusiast perspective toward privatisations.

Yet, if a number of politicians championed privatisations, for others privatisations represented an unavoidable peril threatening consolidated interests. For example, some of the politicians who were members of the government feared losing their control on the top management of the SOEs, which were diffusely used to create jobs and to gain consensus, while unions feared privatisations, as they reasonably expected mass layoffs.

The top management of the SOEs, also, was a composite group: along with the managers typically appointed by political parties, in the 1980s, forced by worrying economic performances, the Italian government started to appoint academicians known for their skills. For example, in 1982, Romano Prodi became president of IRI and, during his tenure, the so-called "Protocollo IRI" ("IRI protocol") was created. The protocol was a restructuring plan aimed at reducing costs through rationalisation, privatisations, and workforce reduction in accordance with unions (Balconi, 1991: 403). Therefore, for such a group of managers, privatisations posed the challenge to navigate among the grip of political parties, the mandate to restructure the financially wrecked companies, and a genuine credo in the possibility to unleash market incentives by preserving a role for the state in domesticating market forces.

6.2.2 Political opportunity structure during fragmentation

6.2.2.1 The issue of plant closure and state aid in the steel industry: a trigger for privatising

The regulation of state aids to their national economies is a central economic institution of the European Union and a key determinant of the fate of the European steel industry. Article 4 of the Treaty of Paris, which in 1951 instituted the European Community of Coal and Steel, forbids state aids to private enterprise. The Treaty of Rome, which institutes the European Economic Community in 1957, in article 92, provides the first articulation of the principle. The article asserts that state aids are incompatible with the common European market when they distort competition by favouring specific companies. The Treaty of Maastricht, which institutes the European Union,[4] reprises the issue of state aid in articles 87, 88, and 89. Namely, article 87 confirms the principle of incompatibility of state aids, except for specific waivers.[5]

Despite since the Treaty of Paris in 1951 state aids were banned, but tolerated, a clear direction was undertaken only with the Davignon plan. Specifically, the pressing need to reduce installed production capacity in Europe contributed to the strengthening of the state aids discipline reinforcing the link between state aids and closures of plants. The rationale was to bargain with member states the relax of constraints on state aid in exchange for the reduction of installed production capacity.

Excess capacity was estimated at around 50 million tonnes (Howell et al., 1988), in the 1980s. In 1979, the European Commission had issued "The General Objective Steel 1980–1985" that articulated the commitment to stimulate and support national re-conversion of national steel industries. Overall, the Commission asked European steel producers for 26.7 million tonnes of capacity reduction in exchange for the permission to national governments to grant 36.4 billion ECU of state aids (Balconi, 1991: 390).

Italy was among those countries that needed to reduce its installed production capacity by closing either SOEs or private producers. In 1983, the Commission initially asked the Italian government for closures of plants corresponding to 5.8 million tonnes of which 2.4 million were requested to private producers (Balconi, 1991: 389–390). Yet, in 1985, the Commission in response to an increase of state aids asked for further reductions so that the total amount of the reduction of installed capacity was 7.3 million tonnes for Italy.

In exchange, in the period 1980–1985, the Commission had authorised the Italian government to financially support Finsider with the aim of restructuring the steel industry. Precisely, with decisions 257/80/CECA and 2320/81/CECA, the Commission allowed state aids to Finsider but required that the holding reduced installed hot rolling capacity by 4,604,000 tonnes, equal to 23.6% of total installed capacity, and to cut employment by 43,200 units, equal to 32% of the workforce in 1980.

The quarrel between the Italian government and the Commission concerning state aids burst out at the end of the 1980s when Peter Sutherland became EC Commissioner for Competition.

The market-oriented spirit of the white paper of the president of the Commission, Jacques Delors, in 1985, gave a further push to grease the wheel of competition and placed the Directorate General for Competition (DG IV), the department in the Commission that supervises competitions dynamics, at the centre of the regulation of the European Union. Thus, in the second half of the 1980s and the first half of the 1990s, the three commissioners who headed the DG IV, Peter Sutherland, Leon Brittan, and Karel Van Miert, interpreted the state aid discipline strictly and applied it with determination (Curli, 2013: 205).

Sutherland and Brittan, in particular, published in 1989 a report on state aids in the European Community. The report showed that Italy, in 1986, accounted for 55% of the whole amount of state aids in the Community.[6] For this reason, Italy, particularly, was under the scrutiny of the Commission.

Following such a political temper, in 1988, the Commission noted that, despite the aid aimed at restructuring competitiveness, the 1987 economic report of Finsider reported an increase in losses for 1,700 billion of Italian liras (about 1 billion euros) of which 1,000 billion of liras referred to Italsider, the main state-owned steel producer in the holding.

The dramatic financial conditions required the state-owned banking system to support Finsider with a loan of 1,155 billion Liras despite the holding, with a debt that was higher than the holding's sales,[7] was clearly incapable of supporting its operations with the equity. The Commission interpreted this loan as a violation of the state aid discipline and, therefore, initiated a violation procedure against Italy on the 4th of May 1988.

On the 10th of May 1988, the Finsider's shareholder general assembly approved the voluntary liquidation of the holding. Thus, IRI, which was the single shareholder of Finsider with 99.8 % of the equity, guaranteed liabilities for the holding towards the creditors. As a consequence, the Commission, on the 15th of June 1988, extended the violation procedure to the IRI's guarantee.

As a response to the procedure, IRI conferred profitable activities of Finsider to a new company, ILVA, and proposed to the Commission to allow further state aids for 7,670 billion liras for supporting an articulated plan for the restructuring of the Italian state steel system. The plan included closures and privatisation of state-owned plants. The agreement reached with the Commission with decision 89/218[8] implied the extension of state aids for 2/3 of the original request from the Italian government. The Italian government, on its side, was requested by the 31st of March 1988 to close production capacity for raw materials (pig iron for 2,350,000 and crude steel for 3,425,000 tonnes) and finished product (1,180,000 hot rolling and 708,000 cold rolling) and to privatise production capacity of raw materials (590,000 pig iron and 385,000 crude steel) and finished products (hot rolling 510,000 tonnes). In this context, with the law no. 181/1989,[9] the Italian government facilitated 29,000 early retirements in the SOE system (Balconi, 1991: 414).

What emerges from the analysis of the quarrel between the Commission and the Italian government is that the enforcement of the discipline on state aids and the issue of privatisations were tightly intertwined.

Specifically, Curli advocates, the Italian government asked a softer application of the discipline on state aids in exchange for the promise of the structural reform of the Italian economy grounded on a diffused program of privatisations (2013: 218–220).

More generally, the neo-liberal creed that inspired the action of the Commission strongly moulded the way in which formal political and legal institutions were mobilised. In particular, the Commission often brandished the discipline on state aids as a club to impose privatisations. In other words, legally, article 222 of the Treaty of the EC assigns to the member States the decision to privatise. This latter, therefore, is a fundamental prerogative of member states. The Commission cannot intervene to force member states to privatise. Yet, the European Council and Commission have been entangled into the contradiction between the Treaty legal framework and the political-ideological torsion, and the hegemonic attempt that inspired the interpretation of the law.

In particular, Verhoeven argues (1996: 862), "the European Council and Commission have openly encouraged privatisations as a means to establish a more competitive internal market" and they "have advocated privatisation as a counterpart of liberalisation". Yet, legally, article 222 of the Treaty clearly invokes the "principle of subsidiarity, which call for a careful division of powers between the Member States and the European Union" (1996: 862). In resolving this tension, rather than playing the role of a "neutral" guardian of the EC Treaty, the Commission applied its supervisory powers with respect to privatisations in a way that furthers an agenda of liberalisation of the member States' economies (Verhoeven, 1996: 862).

The argument that Verhoeven puts forward is that the Commission too often made the approval of aid to companies in difficult conditions conditional on a commitment to privatise. More specifically, Verhoeven takes issue with the guidelines that the Commission drafted for applying article 92, which regulates state aids, to cases of privatisations. The guidelines ask member states to communicate to the Commission cases in which privatisations of a state-owned company are preceded by a debt write-off by the State enterprises or by conversions of debt into capital. This rationale is that capital injections, debt write-offs, or State guarantees of borrowings to companies to be privatised may, in the Commission's opinion, favour "the buyer of the privatised company over its competitors and thus distort competition" (Verhoeven, 1996: 871).

The conjecture articulated by Verhoeven is that the Commission, in facing cases of privatisations, behaved inconsistently. On the one hand, with reference to article 222, the Commission states that "aid which facilitates privatization may not as such benefit from a derogation from the basic principle of incompatibility of State aid with the common market" (2009: 877). On the other hand, "The Commission's official position that privatisation is no 'excuse' for granting aid to companies at the time of their privatisation may not always be applied in a strict manner" (1996: 877). In sum, according to Verhoeven, "Aid is declared compatible with the common market 'provided that' privatization is achieved" (1996: 877).

6.2.3 Discursive opportunity structure during fragmentation

In the previous chapter, we illustrated the latent meaning spaces built around frames to capture the structural elements of discourse on privatisations: the discursive opportunity structure. In the following, we ground on the description of the latent meaning structure of chapter 5 and we specifically address the features of the discursive opportunity structure during fragmentation.

When actors occupy close positions in the graphical output of an MCA, the analysis of discourse suggests that these actors support similar frames or propose similar privatisation practices. Indeed, in our study, if an actor and a frame are near each other, that actor very often proposed that frame in the observed period in the public debate. Yet, actors may change their statements over time. For example, a category of actors may support a specific privatisation model during fragmentation and another one during settlement, as the political and discursive opportunity structures change. These repositionings pave the way for new alliances among actors. Nonetheless, when analysing frames and proposed privatisation models, we found a striking difference in the behaviour of actors. When analysing the frames employed to talk about the privatisation issue, actors seem to support these frames in a quasi-ritual way. There are no substantial differences in the association between the positions of actors and frames in the whole period, and shifting from fragmentation to settlement, as we will see in the next chapter. Actors seem bonded to support only certain frames. Therefore, we think that this association is part of the discursive structure. Actors are embedded in such a structure and find it difficult to abandon specific frames. Conversely, when we move to the layer of practice, which is represented by the association of actors and proposed privatisation models, we notice that actors effectively change their positions in the period under analysis. Therefore, we argue that privatisation models are the locus where actors perform discursive strategies while frames are the structural elements of discourse.

To go beyond a static description of the latent meaning spaces, we conducted specific MCAs referred to as 1984–1992 (fragmentation) and 1993–1995 (settlement). In Figure 6.6, we report the position of actors with reference only to the fragmentation period (1984–1992).[10] We can compare this map with Figure 5.1, which reported the overall meaning space. From a graphical point of view, the position of actors in the first period is identified by a "1" near each label. If we compare Figures 5.1 and 6.6, we see that they resemble each other very much, with the horizontal axis portraying an opposition between actors and frames opposing privatisations – on the right – and privatisations supporters – on the left. Also, the vertical dimension portrays an opposition among actors and frames mainly focusing on the role of workers – in the upper part of the map – and frames and actors mainly aiming to preserve the role of the state in economics. The only difference between this map and the general one is that during fragmentation actors' positions are slightly more polarised, as *Unions, Politicians Centre*, and *Public Managers* are positioned a bit more on the right, in this map, if compared to the general map in Figure 5.1.

6.3 Strategic manoeuvring in the field

6.3.1 Political manoeuvring: search of alternative alignments

Between 1983 and 1993, with very short interruptions, the Italian government was held by a coalition labelled that included Partito Socialista Italiano (PSI) along with Democrazia Cristiana (DC), Partito Socialdemocratico (PSDI), Partito Liberale (PLI), and Partito Repubblicano (PRI). This coalition of parties was challenged by the privatisation issue and the first steps to steel privatisation were moved during the Craxi government. Yet, the privatisation issue emerged in its whole urgency and saliency during the X° Legislature, between 1987 and 1992.

The debate concerning privatisation put forward differences in opinions between not only the government and the opposition but also within the government itself. In the government coalition, PLI and PRI, typical expressions of laic liberal thought, inclined to principles of the free market, coexisted with PSI and DC, these latter more prone to buttress a statist approach.

A further push toward privatisations occurred in 1991 and 1992, during the two governments led by Giulio Andreotti. In these governments, Guido Carli was the Minister of Treasury, who appointed Mario Draghi as the director of the Ministry. Carli, a member of the DC and a former governor of the Bank of Italy, strongly believed that privatisations and liberalisations were fundamental steps toward the modernisation of the Italian economy. He was the expression of a politically

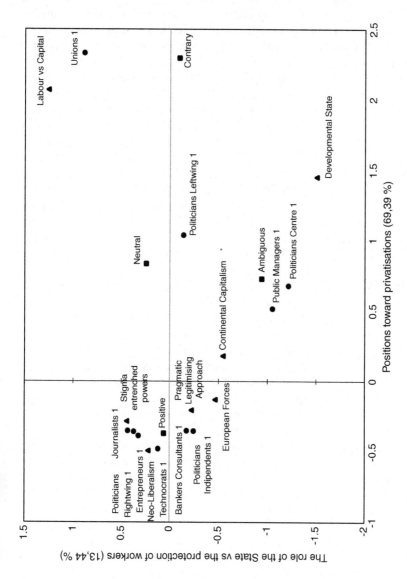

Figure 6.6 Frames, actors, and positions – detail of actors' positions in 1984–1992

mixed coalition   of interests, Curli suggests (2013: 202), including members not only of DC, PLI, and PRI but of the Communist Party (PCI) as well.

In 1990, Guido Carli created a Committee for the restructuring of the public asset and for the analysis of privatisation policies. The Committee listed the assets and the participations owned by the state, conceived of a proposal for the transformation of the state-owned company into limited companies, and proposed a number of guidelines for the dismissal of state-owned assets. Following the activity of the Carli Committee, the government led by Giulio Andreotti issued decrees no. 309 on the 3rd of October 1991 and no. 386 on the 5th of December 1991. The decrees allowed state-owned companies to be transformed into limited liability companies. Under the pressure of Guido Carli, the government passed as well law no. 218 issued on 30/07/1990 that applied to state-owned banks. The transformation, however, was discretionary and, therefore, did not produce tangible effects (Cavazzuti, 2013).

The debate on privatisations unfolded in parallel to the restructuring of the state-owned steel producers. The before mentioned "General Objective Steel 1980–1985" plan issued in 1979 by the European Commission forced Italy to restructure national steel industries and reduce installed production capacity.

In 1987, the intertwined disciplines of state aids and capacity reduction forced the Italian government to address the financial crisis of Finsider. When the European Commission allowed a softer application of the discipline on state aids after the promise of the government to deal with the dramatic financial conditions of Finsider, the Italian state-owned holding was defined "*caso unico*", a case to be addressed singularly by the European Commission since the company was the sole among the other large European state-owned steel producers that was still experiencing dramatic financial and economic tensions.

Consequently, in the second half of the 1980s, the political pressures pending on the Italian government motivated the sharp discontinuity that occurred in the state involvement in the steel industry. Under the political pressures by the European Union, the government issued a plan to restructure the steel industry; as anticipated, in 1988 Finsider was liquidated, and its assets were conferred to a newly created company: ILVA. The restructuring plan envisioned 20,000 layoffs. By presenting this plan, the Italian government obtained by the European Commission the permission to transfer further 5,170 billons liras of state aids.

Within the restructuring plan, beginning in 1988, the government envisioned as well a programme to sell assets belonging to the Finsider to private producers through auctions. The programme led to the sale to private producers of rolling mills, furnaces, and even electric power plants. In addition, the government decided to close a large plant located in Bagnoli, a suburb close to the city of Naples in the region of

Campania. The plant was specialised in the production of flat steel coils. The closure of the plant was accompanied by strong contestations and criticisms. In the second half of the 80s, in Italy, the demand for steel coils was growing. According to Balconi (1991: 445), the quality of the coils produced in Bagnoli was high. Nevertheless, in June 1988, the government developed a plan to restructure state-owned steel production that included the closure of Bagnoli plant. The plan was presented to the European Commission and this latter issued decision no. 89/1988[11] that dictated the closure of Bagnoli by the 30th of June 1989 (the deadline for closure was postponed to the 31st of December of 1990).

To have an idea of the intricate knot of interests surrounding the closure of the plant, Balconi reports that Arvedi, a large private Italian producer, in meeting the members of the Italian government, raised the issue that the plant was necessary for the supply of coils to Italian producers and suggested a privatisation project led by private Italian producers supported by unions. Reportedly, Giovanni Gambardella, the CEO of ILVA, refused the project since this would have created an internal competitor to the state-owned production of coils (Balconi, 1991: 449).[12]

The case of Bagnoli illuminates another perspective to interpret political manoeuvring that occurred in the course of steel privatisation. In the tormented sequence of events occurring in Bagnoli, the interests of unions and private producers were somehow aligned, whereas, on the other hand, the top managers of state-owned steel producers were perceived as lined up in the enemy camp.

Top managers of state-owned companies were often genuinely aimed at protecting a productive system that had been a heroic fortress of Italian post-war economic renaissance and was now seriously endangered by both its dramatic financial situations as well as neo-liberal rhetoric, and connected political pressures. As Petrini reports, (2013: 151), the case of Franco Nobili, chairman of IRI in the period 1989–1993, was symptomatic. Franco Nobili was a typical product of the post-war anti-fascist, and Catholic technocracy that contributed to the management of Italian state-owned companies and economic institutions. During the privatisations, Nobili opposed the hegemonic neo-liberal rhetoric that advocated the inevitability of privatisations and strongly tried to maintain the privatisations processes in the hands of IRI by limiting the intrusion of the government. He represented a group of managers and technocrats whose political interests were in opposition to the fraction of the government that pushed for privatisations. In this light, the relationships among government, technocrats, private producers, and unions were complex and articulated.

Unions, furthermore, were forced to manage the political alliance with both state-owned top management, with which, since the time of "protocollo IRI", an agreement existed to cooperatively address emerging issues, and the private producers, who emerged as a possible ally in the preservation of Bagnoli production site.

This tension was reflected in the fracture within unions with the national representatives, more willing to diplomatic solutions, pitted against more militant local representatives.

To face the situation, the government was in the thorny situation to respond to the requests of the European Union and to face internal mounting political pressures. To accommodate the tensions arising in the private sector, the government issued the mentioned laws no. 46[13] and no. 193[14] that provided financial aid to private producers willing to close their plants, including incentives for workers' retirement.

The financial support provided by the law no. 193 was used in 1984 to restructure the Cornigliano plant, a large productive site located in the north of Italy close to Genova. The plant was in the assets of COGEA, a state-owned company. The existing rolling mills were closed but the blast furnaces were enlarged and the continuous casting area survived.

The plan was aimed at promoting cooperation between private and state-owned producers. Specifically, private producers, largely using electric furnaces, were dependent on scraps, whose cost was increasing.[15] The availability, thus, of an alternative to producing steel semi-finished products was appealing for private producers. Thus, in 1986, Finsider opened the equity of COGEA to private shareholders. Private steel producers such as Leali, Riva, and Lucchini became shareholders of COGEA. Two years later, COGEA became entirely private thereby producing the first relevant privatisation in the steel industry.

On the other hand, to sustain the restructuring of the SOE system, the government issued the law no. 189 on 15/05/1989 that outlined policy interventions in the geographical areas in which reduction in state-owned installed capacity was planned. The law included the possibility for workers receiving payroll subsidies to have 36 anticipated monthly payments to start up new ventures and the financing of training programmes for workers. In addition, the law created a fund for re-industrialisation to be used to invest in the areas that experienced industrial crises related to the dismissal of steel production. In connection with the law, in these areas, specifically, the CIPI (Inter-Ministry Committee for the Industrial Policy) planned investments in fixed assets for 1,716 billion lira producing 7,190 new jobs.[16]

In 1989, steel producers decided to eliminate previously separated associations (ISA and Assider) to join forces in a new association, Federacciai, which represents the alliance between large and smaller private producers.

In the described circumstances, unions pursued the aim of containing layoffs. The endeavour was not an easy one, considering both the financial conditions of both state-owned and private producers and the impending menace of privatisations. In the first half of the 1980s, unions had been able to mobilise their belonging to a corporatist agreement to discuss with the government and the top management of IRI, the destiny of the 26,500 employees in the state-owned steel sector that were considered redundant.

The result of this bargaining process was that the law no. 193, issued in 1984, to support the restructuring of the steel industry, including lowering to 50 years the age to access early retirements. By the means of this norm, unions were able to support 70% of redundant employees in the state-owned steel industry.

In addition, in December 1984, unions completed an agreement with IRI, the previously mentioned "Protocollo IRI", that conceived of mechanisms for monitoring and guiding the restructuring of state-owned companies and cooperatively managing layoffs.

The agreement provided for the formation of consulting committees (Comitati Consultivi Paritetici) equally composed of representatives of state-owned companies and unions. The committees met quarterly and were supposed to contribute to the definition of strategic options regarding economic and industrial policy, alternative restructuring plans, and employment strategies. The committees were as well involved in the monitoring of the fulfilment of the stages of restructuring plans. Consultation of the committees was obligatory but not constraining.

The agreement included as well a mechanism for dispute settlement that reflected the reciprocal commitment of both the management and the unions to address controversies regulating and limiting the adoption of industrial actions and work stoppages.

In general, as reported by Barca and Magnani (1989: 17–18), in the 1980s, the government and private producers revived a corporatist pact to orchestrate a response to the pressures to reduce employment. The cooperation, however, brought about a deceleration in the growth of real salaries and increased flexibility in the use of labour.

6.3.2 Discursive manoeuvring: awakening of discursive battles

In the map that depicts the association between actors and the proposed privatisation model, we can see how the meaning space changes, moving from fragmentation to settlement. While actors supported roughly the same frames during the fragmentation phase and in the whole period under analysis, we notice in Figure 6.7 that their support to different privatisation models is different during fragmentation and in the whole period (Figure 5.2).

During fragmentation, *Independent Politicians* are in the upper-left quadrant of the map. In the same quadrant, we find *Noyaux Durs*: "Following the French example, we mean by Noyaux Durs the creation of a consortium of shareholders defined by the government" [Public Manager].[17] In addition, we find in the same quadrant the model labelled

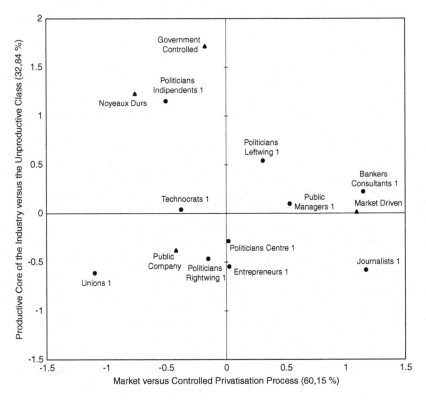

Figure 6.7 Actors and proposed privatisation model – detail of actors' positions in 1984–1992

Government Controlled: "The Ministry of Treasury may own a 'golden share', that is, a powerful share, conferring to the State the possibility of avoiding assault by foreign enterprises [Public Manager]". Also, very near to the horizontal axis, we find the *Technocrats*.

In the lower-left quadrant of the map, we interestingly find the *Rightwing Politicians* and the *Unions* who support the *Public Company* model: "we cannot follow the French model, as it assumes a state that is rich, strong, and efficient. But we need to privatize as the Italian State is weak, inefficient and with a very high public debt [Technocracy]". *Unions* look at a public company as a way to redistribute wealth: "the union wants the workers to buy shares of the enterprises. We want a population of small investors [Union]".

The right quadrant of the map is characterised by the model *Market Driven*: several actors share a logic of equivalence built upon the opposition to the hypertrophy of state intervention in the economy. A dormant discourse is revived against the "party state" that characterises the Italian political system (Wilson & Grant, 2010). Here we find actors both in the lower quadrant – where there are those that we defined as the "productive core of the industry" – and in the upper quadrant – which is nearer to the political management of the industry. In the upper-right quadrant, we find the discursive alliance among *Bankers and Consultants*, and *Public Managers:* "the main objective is to prevent political power from interfering with privatised firms. To do so, control must be transferred to private capital [Technocracy]". It is interesting to note that during fragmentation, *Leftwing Politicians* are in this quadrant. In the lower quadrant, we find *Journalists.* Interestingly, in the first period, the *Entrepreneurs* and *Politicians Centre* are in the lower-right quadrant, which is the same as the *Market Driven* model. This position oscillates between two discursive alliances. On the horizontal dimension, the right camp of the map signals the antagonism toward state interventionism. However, on the vertical dimension, they are aligned with *Unions.* In the case of *Entrepreneurs,* this position can signify a revival of the "Pact of Producers" (Berta, 2001), a rhetoric that is well entrenched in the Italian industrial relations, and particularly in the steel industry, and that emphasises the value of productive work as the backbone of the Italian manufacturing-based economy and the fuel for the Italian post-war renaissance.

6.4 Weaving together political and discursive manoeuvring: formation of competing hegemonic practices

Overall, research suggests that the 1980s (Barca & Magnani, 1989; Balconi, 1991: 412) was a period in which social actors attempted to brush up a deep-rooted corporatist agreement. On the other hand, we suggest that in the 1980s the seeds of the fragmentation of historical bloc were established. Despite participating in a general process of dialogue, social actors were as well testing different opportunities for strategising, exploring different political alliances.

Hegemonic practices acted as a bridge between discursive opportunity structure, and political opportunity structure and they worked by creating alliances that are viable in both dimensions (Mollona & Pareschi, 2020). In their discursive component, hegemonic practices selected logics of equivalence (Laclau & Mouffe, 2014), which are a simplification of the discursive space, which captures common instances among different categories of actors. In their political component, hegemonic practices worked on the commonality of interests among different groups of actors (Gramsci, 1975). Bridging logics of equivalence, and commonality of interests, hegemonic practices wove together alliances that are both discursive and political. In this section, we discuss the different hegemonic practices emerging during fragmentation.

As for the discursive dimension of hegemonic practices, we described two latent meaning spaces, which, taken together, form the discursive opportunity structure: both involve actors, but while the first one is built around frames and positions toward privatisations, the latter involves proposed privatisation models: it is now relevant to focus on both spaces. Figure 5.1, which shows the relative position of actors, frames, and position, is not surprising: *Unions* oppose privatisations and try to safeguard employment; *Public Managers* and *Politicians* representing the centrist parties that ruled the country for decades adopt an ambiguous position, supporting the role of the State in the economy, without overtly opposing privatisations; *Leftwing Parties* are not in favour of privatisations, but at the same time are not able to propose a counter-narrative. All of the other agents are grouped around the neo-liberal frame, showing clear support for privatisations. In a context where the privatisation wave defined what is sayable and what is not sayable regarding privatisations, agents are bounded to a predefined script in public utterances regarding the issue at stance: in this context, actors adopt a quasi-ritual virtue-signalling stance. All the agents that have nothing to lose from the privatisation process enthusiastically support it; conversely, agents that fear the privatisations wave cannot embrace the privatisation policy, but at the same time just opposing privatisations seems a losing strategy. The fact that the association between actors and frames is ritual is confirmed by the fact that there is not any substantial difference in the association between the positions of actors and frames in the whole period (Figure 5.1), during fragmentation (Figure 6.6), and also during settlement, as we will see in the next chapter. The world changes, privatisations are timidly started and then completed, but actors keep supporting the same frames. This is exactly the reason why we focused also on proposed privatisation models, which are discourses around practices. The debate around how privatisations will be performed, if they have to be performed, is characterised by supposedly technical arguments (Meyer & Höllerer, 2010: 1257), around which subtle discursive strategies can be put in place (Mollona & Pareschi, 2020). Indeed, the technical knowledge involved in the discourses around *how to perform privatisations* is at the same time the basis for the symbolic struggles that take place among actors (Bourdieu, 1991) for designing a legitimate idea of the Italian economic system, but also a shield to perform more subtle strategising: *Unions*, for example, cannot embrace privatisations, but at the same time it is clear that only opposing it does not pay, as *Unions* would risk remaining alone against an unstoppable process. Conversely, while for *Unions* it is possible to keep opposing privatisations, joining discourses on about how to perform one, if it eventually had to be performed, permit *Unions* to join a space where unexpected logics of equivalence can be deployed among supposedly competing agents, as we will see in the remainder of this chapter and the next one. Specifically, we need to analyse the map that relates actors and proposed privatisation models during fragmentation to describe three hegemonic practices competing during the first temporal bracket, which we also synthesise in Figure 6.8:

1. *The Party State.* Independent politicians, a group of Ministries who were appointed after the election because of their competencies, during fragmentation spearheaded a first hegemonic practice, whose supporting logic of equivalence was to recognise the importance of State economy for the post-war renaissance, that had built one of the largest European economies. As it was not possible to simply oppose privatisations, this discursive alliance emphasised the role of the government in guiding the privatisation process, and in selecting a stable core of investors for the SOEs to be sold. Indeed, discursively, the practice was based upon the models of Government Controlled and Noyeaux Durs, with the latter model aimed at softening the approach of the former, at shielding privatisation from free-market forces, and at leveraging the competencies of technocrats in reigning the privatisation process. As explained in the foregoing, this situation can be defined by the concept of "party state" (Wilson & Grant, 2010), a situation in which a "dominant political party" defines business-government relationships (Lanza & Lavdas, 2000: 207). It is interesting to note that at the core of these hegemonic practices are politicians that did not have to pass through elections: consequently, they are more free to support unpopular positions regarding the role of the State in the economy. To strengthen the political dimension of the alliance, these politicians tried to attract the actors that had some interest against the privatisation process: first, the government facilitated an agreement between the Unions and the state holding company. Also, to involve the entrepreneurs in the logic of equivalence, the government tested a sort of co-management of privatisations in 1986 when a group of private producers became shareholders with 67% of the equity of COGEA. By relying as well on the support of unions,[18] the COGEA agreement represented an attempt to mobilise a typical corporatist approach. In addition, it is important to notice that, in the first half of the 1980s, private steel producers had enjoyed large financial support from the government. Article 20 of the law no. 46 issued in 1983 transferred 484 billion liras to private entrepreneurs to support the closures of electric steel furnaces and the law 193, issued in 1984 to continue the financial support of the law no. 46, transferred to private producers 660 billons liras (Balconi, 1991: 433). Adding the financial support provided by other laws to private producers, Balconi calculates that the government transferred to the private

EMERGENCE OF COMPETING HEGEMONIC PRACTICES

PARTY STATE

KEY ACTORS: Politicians and Technocracy.

DISCURSIVE STRATEGY: The rhetoric on the role of the state as the actor that made available the post-war economic renaissance is associated with the emphasis on technocratic competencies.

MODEL OF PRIVATISATION: *Government Controlled and Public Company* .

POLITICAL STRATEGY:
- The co-managing of privatisations in COGEA is an example of the attempt to build a typical corporatist alliance. The government maintains a central role and Entrepreneurs envision in the agreement the possibility to enlarge production capacity in flat products and to protect Italian steel from foreign producers. At the same time, the government promotes the dialogue between unions and SOEs' holdings.
- Definition of the "Protocollo IRI".

PACT OF PRODUCERS

KEY ACTORS: *Unions* and (partly) Entrepreneurs.

DISCURSIVE STRATEGY:
The rhetoric that focuses on the right to voice of the actors who are central in the steel industry in opposition to "parasitic forces," such as Politicians and Consultants and Bankers, is mobilised to smoothen the conflict between labour and capital and to justify an alliance between Entrepreneurs and Employees.

MODEL OF PRIVATISATION: *Public Company.*

POLITICAL STRATEGY:
Mobilisation of *Unions'* to promote strikes and protests in state-owned producers describes *Unions'* interest is to soften privatisation. On the other hand, *Entrepreneurs* aim at shielding privatisations from foreign investors

AGAINST THE PARTY STATE

KEY ACTORS: Bankers and Consultants, Journalists, and (partly) Entrepreneurs and Public Managers

DISCURSIVE STRATEGY:
The rhetoric stigmatises politicians' intrusion in the economy. This latter is associated with inefficiency, bribery, and corruption. This logic assigns market freedom benefic properties to modernise the Italian economy.

MODEL OF PRIVATISATION: *Market Driven.*

POLITICAL STRATEGY:
Bankers and Consultants seek rents as intermediaries. Entrepreneurs fight the intrusiveness of the government into the economy. For example, large private steel producers wrote a letter to the European Commission to warn against the Italian government's delay in reducing SOEs' installed capacity

Discursive opportunity structure

Political opportunity structure

Figure 6.8 Hegemonic practices in fragmentation phase

steel industry approximately 250 billions liras (1991: 433) along with the sale cost of Teksid within 450 and 500 billion liras. In sum, laws no. 46 and no. 193 are the instruments that the government used to support its hegemony practice and to maintain its pivotal role in the maintenance of a corporatist pact.

2. *The Pact of Producers.* A second hegemonic practice is mobilised by actors in the lower-left quadrants of Figure 6.7, the most important being *Unions* and *Entrepreneurs.* From a discursive point of view, this practice is built around the model *Public Company,* but it is also anchored in the rhetorical argument of the "Pact of Producers" (Berta, 2001), which is well entrenched in the Italian industrial relations, and particularly in the steel industry, as it emphasises the value of manufacturing as the backbone of Italian economy that fuelled Italian post-war economic renaissance. This hegemonic practice emphasises the converging interests of blue-collar workers and employers (Trentin,[19] 1977: LXXII) and leveraged a political identity that associates the direct involvement in steel production to the concept of technical knowledgeability of the industry and the right to voice. By stimulating a sense of proudness, suggesting a commonality of interest, and implying a right to speak about the destiny of the industry, this logic unites actors within the industry in opposition to "parasitic forces" (Trentin, 1977: LXXII). For example, one of our informant reported that "Unions felt that the situation in which steel production was driven by public managers offended their dignity. Workers knew that their productivity was equal to that of foreign steelworkers and were annoyed by the overall performance of the companies in which they worked". It is interesting to note that during fragmentation this logic is joined also by some rightwing politicians, and politicians representing the centre that run the country for decades: while these actors and *Unions* are fiercely opposing each other at the frame level, they end up supporting the same practices, in a very peculiar decoupling between ideas and practices. Indeed, in the political arena, *Unions* were fiercely fighting against privatisations: the number of strikes and protests was 625 in 1985 and grew to an average of 840 between 1986 and 1988 (Balconi, 1991: 484). Yet, the "Pact of Producers" was viable also in the POS, as all the actors linked by this hegemonic practice shared an interest in shielding the privatisation process from the free market. *Unions'* political objective was to soften the privatisation process, fearing mass layoffs; entrepreneurs foresaw the opportunity to shield privatisations from foreign investors. This alliance was as well glued by the need to protect a supposedly mature manufacturing industry against a post-manufacturing ideology that, as suggested by Balconi (1991: 405–406), influenced the economic policy of the government and emphasised the opportunities emerging in more innovative industries.

3. *Against the Party State.* A third hegemonic practice is mobilised by *Bankers and Consultants, Journalists,* and *Public Managers.* Discursively, this hegemonic practice speaks to those who want to remove power from parties and politicians: they want to leave the process to the market, shielding it from the intrusiveness of politicians. The hegemonic practice is built around the *Market Driven* model and associates the concept of the market economy to the ones of freedom, the modern development of the economy, and the struggle against corruption. Journalists join the climate of widespread enthusiasm for neo-liberal policies, and this hegemonic practice pairs well with the interests of a number of public managers: as the president of IRI explained in 1991, for example, downgrading the role of the management of the SOE, by letting the government determine the lists of companies to be privatised each year, would contradict the needs of market logic thereby subjugating decision-making to political pressures.[20] Another source argues "we demand autonomy for the [...] company's management in making decisions on privatizations. [Public Manager]". Perhaps surprisingly, we find leftwing politicians associated with this hegemonic practice, although not very near to market driven: this position signals a lack of discursive space for leftwing parties. Indeed, they cannot openly support a government-controlled process, at least in this phase, but at the same time all the other options are not really better: *market driven* is at odds with the traditional position of leftwing parties, but also public company, with its emphasis on popular capitalism of workers, is not embraced by leftwing politicians, which do not find a clear and effective stance. Once again, the case of entrepreneurs is ambiguous: while they were at the core of the hegemonic practice "Pact of Producers", supporting a corporatist agreement grounding on *Public Company,* they are also in the right camp of the map, where *Market Driven* model is located, to express their distrust of politicians' intrusiveness in the privatisation process. Indeed, this stance is confirmed by a political act by entrepreneurs in 1998, when the European Commission allowed the Italian government to waive the constraints that forbade governments from bailing SOEs out,[21] including the transfer of about 2.4 billion euros to Finsider in exchange for the closure of several plants. A group of large private steel producers wrote a letter to the Commission to express their fear that behind the promise of the Italian government to close those state-owned plants was the intent to waste further public money without a real intention to proceed with the planned closures.[22]

Notes

1 The law created a fund to support the closure of production capacity.
2 "Fondo per la razionalizzazione aziendale ed interaziendale degli impianti siderurgici" (Art. 20)
3 "Valutazione della ACCIAI SPECIALI TERNI", report developed by IMI (Istituto Mobiliare Italiano) for IRI (Istituto Ricostruzione Industriale), page 5, 25/08/1993. The report was submitted to the Meeting of the Board of Directors of IRI on the 31st of August 1993.
4 Official Journal of the European Union, 191/1, 29 July 1992. See also the consolidated version of the European Community: Official Journal of the European Union, C321 E/37, 29 December 2006.
5 The principle was further reported in the article 107 of the Treaty of Lisbon, on the Functioning of the European Union, in 2007, that states that "*Save as otherwise provided in the Treaties, any aid granted by a Member State or through State resources in any form whatsoever which distorts or threatens to distort competition by favouring certain undertakings or the production of certain goods shall, in so far as it affects trade between Member States, be incompatible with the internal market*" (Official Journal of the European Union, C 306/1, 17 December 2007).
6 "First Survey on State Aids in the European Community", Office for Official Publications of the European Communities, Catalogue number: CB-55–89-455-EN-C, 1989.
7 At the end of 1987, the debt of Finsider reached 1003 billion liras that is 104% of the sales.
8 Official Journal of the European Communities, 86/76, 31 March 1989.
9 Official Journal of the European Communities, 86/76, 31 March 1989.
10 From a technical point of view, in Figure 6.6 we plotted the positions of *Actors* in the first temporal bracket as supplementary variables. We did the same also for other variables depicted in the figures that we present in this and in the next chapter. Technically, after calculating a map with the entire data covering all time periods (Figure 5.1), and inferring the meaning of the two structuring dimensions "bottom-up" using the statistical output, we used this general statistical model, and plotted the variables for each period as supplementary variables into this space. In practice, data for actors for the first period only were projected in the overall meaning space. Also, we needed to perform one more adjustment for a technical reason: among the possible techniques for performing MCA, we adopted the *adjusted inertia* method, as it is the "one to be used as a matter of course in all (graphical) MCA application" (Greenacre & Blasius, 2006: 75). Yet, "adjusted inertia" creates different scaling for active and passive (supplementary) variables: "the adjustment [...] simply changes the scale on each dimension of the map to best approximate the two tables of association between pairs of variables, leaving everything else in the solution intact" (Greenacre & Blasius, 2006: 75). Indeed, "In the case of the adjusted analysis, [...] it is only a-posteriori that we adjust the eigenvalues, and this adjustment affects only the positions of the principal coordinates of the active category points, not the supplementary categories" (Greenacre & Blasius, 2006: 72). Therefore, if we had drawn frames and positions as principal variables, and actors as supplementary, the different categories would have had different scaling, making it hard to make sense of movements. Consequently, in the figures that describe the dynamic repositionings happening during fragmentation and settlement, we also draw *Frames* and *Positions*, and *Models* as supplementary variables. By doing so, the respective positions of categories are still comparable. These technicalities

do not affect the interpretation of the meaning space but permit us to compare the respective positions of different variables. The plotted positions are indeed comparable, as "in the graphical solution, the locations of all variable categories can be compared to each other: short distances imply high similarities and long distances high dissimilarities" (Blasius & Thiessen, 2001: 7).

11 No. L 86/76 Official Journal of the European Communities 31/03/1989.

12 Intriguingly, *Il Sole 24 Ore*, the most read Italian financial magazine, on 7th of May 2021, reported that the producers of steel cans located in the region of Campania, where Bagnoli plant was located, are running out the steel necessary to produce their products and are suffering increasing in the price of steel around 40%. This reveals the increasing dependence of Italian manufacturing on imported steel that followed the restructuring of Italian steel industry (*Il Sole 24 Ore*, 07/05/2021, No. 123).

13 17/02/1982.

14 31/05/1984.

15 Electric furnaces work by using metal scraps that are melted to produce steel. On the other hand, blast furnaces are used in the primary steelmaking that produces steel from ores by bringing to high-temperature coals and iron ore.

16 Gazzetta Ufficiale. Serie Generale n.273 (22-11-1989). DELIBERAZIONE 13/10/1989, Indirizzi di politica industriale per la reindustrializzazione delle aree di crisi siderurgica.

17 Quotes are translated from the original Italian. Also, we describe among square brackets the category of actors that pronounced each quote.

18 *Sole 24 Ore*, 10/07/1986.

19 In 1988–1994, Bruno Trentin was the secretary general of CGIL, the largest left-oriented union and one of the more powerful unions in the steel industry.

20 Parliament Proceedings, Senate of the Republic, Commission of Finance and Treasury. Intervention of IRI president Franco Nobili. Rome, 08/05/1991, p. 11. Quoted in Cavazzuti, F. (2013: 90).

21 Decision 89/218 of the 23/12/1989. OJEC, No. L 86/76, 31.3.1989, page 76–81.

22 The political weight of this act is well described as an overt attack to the legitimacy of the Italian government by the resented reply of the Minister of Labour, Mr. Rino Formica, who declared that "the letter was a worrying document that aims at delegitimising the Italian government in respect to the European Economic Community" (*Sole 24 Ore*, 29/05/1988).

References

Acemoglu, D., & Robinson, J. A. (2006). De facto political power and institutional persistence. *American Economic Review*, 96(2): 267–288.

Balconi, M. (1991). *La siderurgia italiana (1945-1990)*. Bologna: Il Mulino.

Barca, F., & Magnani, M. (1989). *L'industria tra capitale e lavoro*. Bologna: Il Mulino.

Berta, G. (2001). *L'Italia delle fabbriche. Ascesa e tramonto dell'industrialismo nel Novecento*. Bologna: Il Mulino.

Blasius, J., & Thiessen, V. (2001). Methodological artifacts in measures of political efficacy and trust: A multiple correspondence analysis. *Political Analysis*, 9(1): 1–20.

Bourdieu, P. (1991). *Language and symbolic power*. Cambridge, MA: Harvard University Press.

Castronovo, V. (2011). Un profilo d'insieme. In V. Castronovo (Ed.), *Storia dell'IRI. Dalle origini al dopoguerra: 1933-1948* (pp. 162–268). Bari, Italy: Editori Laterza.

Cavazzuti, F. (2013). Le privatizzazioni: L'IRI tra parlamento, governo e dintorni. In R. Artoni (Ed.), *Storia dell'IRI* Vo (4). Bari: Editori Laterza Crisi e privatizzazione.

Curli, B. (2013). Il "vincolo Europeo": Le privatizzazioni dell'IRI tra Commissione Europea e governo Italiano. In R. Artoni (Ed), *Storia dell'IRI*, Vol (4). Bari : Editori Laterza Crisi e privatizzazione.

D'Antone, L. (2011). Da Ente Transitorio ad Ente Permanente. In V. Castronovo (Ed.), *Storia dell'IRI. Dalle origini al dopoguerra: 1933-1948* (pp. 332–419). Bari: Editori Laterza.

Doria, M. (2011). I trasporti marittimi. La siderurgia. In V. Castronovo (Ed.), *Storia dell'IRI. Dalle origini al dopoguerra: 1933-1948* (pp. 332–419). Bari: Editori Laterza.

Gourevitch, P. A., & Shinn, J. (2010). *Political power and corporate control: The new global politics of corporate governance*. Princeton, NJ: Princeton University Press.

Gramsci, A. (1975). *Quaderni dal carcere* Torino: Giulio Einaudi Editore.

Greenacre, M., & Blasius, J. (Eds.). (2006). *Correspondence analysis in the social sciences: Recent developements and applications*. Academic Press.

Howell, T. R., Noellert, W. A., Kreier, J. G., & Wolff, A. W. (1988). *Steel and the state*. Boulder and London: Westview.

Ingram, P., & Clay, K. (2000). The choice-within-constraints new institutionalism and implications for sociology. *Annual Review of Sociology*, 26: 525–546.

Johnson, C. (1982). *MITI and the Japanese miracle*. Stanford, CA: Stanford University Press.

Laclau, E., & Mouffe, C. (2014). *Hegemony and socialist strategy: Towards a radical democratic politics*. Verso Trade.

Lanza, O., & Lavdas, K. (2000). The disentanglement of interest politics: Business associability, the parties and policy in Italy and Greece. *European Journal of Political Research*, 37(2): 203–235 LA-English. 10.1023/A:100701 7624486

Meyer, R. E., & Höllerer, M. A. (2010). Meaning structures in a contested issue field: A topographic map of shareholder value in Austria. *Academy of Management Journal*, 53(6): 1241–1262. 10.5465/amj.2010.57317829

Mollona, E., & Pareschi, L. (2020). A Gramscian perspective on field dynamics. The case of the privatization of Italian steel industry. *Scandinavian Journal of Management*, 36(4): 101128. 10.1016/j.scaman.2020.101128

Mucchetti, M. (2013). L'ultimo decennio, revisione di una liquidazione sommaria. In Artoni, R. (Eds.), *Storia dell'IRI, Vol (4): Crisi e privatizzazione*. Bari: Editori Laterza.

Petrini, R. (2013). L'IRI nei tre anni fatali: La crisi del paese e la svolta delle privatizzazioni (1990-1992). In R. Artoni (Ed.), *Storia dell'IRI* (pp. 147–180). Vo (4). Bari: Laterza.

Silva, F. (2013). Un profilo d'insieme. In F. Silva (Ed.) *Storia dell'IRI*. Italy: Editori Laterza, Bari.

Trentin, B. (1977). *Da sfruttati a produttori, lotte operaie e sviluppo*. Bari: De Donato.

Verhoeven, A. (1996). Privatisation and EC Law: Is the European Commission "Neutral" with respect to public versus private ownership of companies? *The International and Comparative Law Quarterly*, 45(4): 861–887.

Wilson, G., & Grant, W. (2010). Business and political parties. In D. Coen, W. Grant, and G. Wilson (Eds.), *The Oxford handbook of business and government*. New York, NY: Oxford University Press.

7 Settlement of the historical bloc

7.1 Heading towards the settlement of the field: how to re-align actors' economic interests

7.1.1 The material pressures agitating the steel field

In the first half of the 1990s, the competition in the steel industry increased due to the fall in the demand for steel and the increase in global competition. As reported in Figure 7.1, in 1992 and 1993, a decrease in steel demand and production in Europe was associated with the increase in the volumes sold by the producers located in Asia. The quantity sold by Italian state-owned producers decreased along with the selling prices. Such a downturn in the European steel industry occurred while Italy was experiencing a deep monetary crisis with a strong devaluation of the Italian Lira and a connected worsening of national financial indicators. To give a feeling of the mounting pressures in Italy, we already mentioned the financial law worth nearly 100,000 billion of Italian Liras issues in July 1992 by the Prime Minister, Mr. Amato, the largest in the period post WWII to cover the public deficit.

This situation came after the enthusiasm that had characterised the steel industry at the end of the previous decade in which the growing demand had stimulated optimistic investments by ILVA, the company that was now incorporating all the state-owned steel production capacity previously owned by Finsider.

In 1991, the investments of ILVA were equal to 1,341 billion liras, the cash flow amounted to 142 billion and only marginally contributed to cover such investments (11%). Invested capital grew 19% to reach 9,311 billion liras that included 7,236 billion in net fixed investments, 32% of which was covered by the equity while the remaining 68% was covered by 6,338 billion of debt. Consequently, financial costs increased by 22.7%, growing to reach 847 billion liras. The workforce increased to 50,244 employees, with an increase of 556 workers.

A difficult competitive position associated with the financial burden of such an investment campaign drove ILVA into a deep financial crisis.

DOI: 10.4324/9780429438516-7

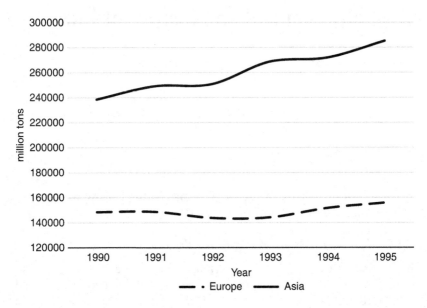

Figure 7.1 Crude steel production ('000 tonnes)

Source: elaborated on International Iron and Steel Institute, Steel Statistical Yearbook, 1995.

From the positive income of 115 billion liras in 1990, ILVA reported a loss of 499 billion liras the following year and, between 1991 and 1992, the loss grew fourfold, from 499 to 2,310 billion (Figure 7.2).

In 1993, the CEO of ILVA, Hayao Nakamura, in a letter[1] to IRI chairman, Romano Prodi, clearly stigmatised the dramatic situation of the company by remarking the burden of the accumulated debt. The analysis of the operations highlighted the increase in efficiency. Within the first semester of 1993, the unit sales had increased by 10% and the industrial margin had increased from 40 to 100 billion liras. However, the CEO continues, the company could not improve the income due to the burden that financial costs brought about in the economic report. At the beginning of 1993, the company had an accumulated debt equal to 7,600 billion Liras, and financial costs had increased to 100 billion per month (12% of sales). The CEO lamented that the 1993 budget foresaw the need for further financial funds amounting to 3,510 billion. As the owner of ILVA, IRI had already covered financial needs relative to the first semester that were equal to 1,080 billion. Remarking that such dramatic financial conditions made it impossible for ILVA to search for funding in the market, the letter advised that the only way to restore the company's credibility and solvability was the decision by IRI, as the owner, to rapidly implement a restructuring plan.

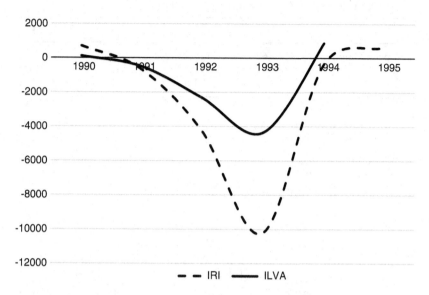

Figure 7.2 Income of IRI and ILVA (billion liras)
Source: elaborated on IRI Consolidated balance sheet.

7.1.1.1 The economic interests of field's actors: why private producers liked privatisations

The instability that characterised the steel industry in the first half of the 1990s launched ambiguous signals. To the fall in consumption of steel, which occurred in 1992–1993, a growth followed in 1994 (see pattern in the apparent consumption of crude steel in Table 7.1). Such volatility triggered inaccurate investment policies in many European countries, thereby creating oscillations in the utilisation of installed production capacity.[2]

Given this landscape, the existence in the European steel market of such a large company as ILVA stimulated political reactions from foreign and national competitors. On the one hand, foreign producers lamented the unfair state support to the inefficient state-owned Italian steel producer and pressed the European Union to impose the reduction of installed capacity as a rebate for the given out state aids. On the other hand, private producers had an interest in the advancement of the privatisation process since, despite the debts that burdened ILVA's balance sheet, and the connected financial costs that distressed the economic report, the company owned a number of firms that were endowed with excellent technology and know-how.

In this light, privatisation would contribute to accommodate the interests of private producers. For example, as reported by Affinito et al.

Table 7.1 Apparent crude steel consumption ('000)

	1991	1992	1993	1994
European Union[*]	123,624	119,757	103,880	120,192
Asia[**]	268,640	270,829	325,352	318,376
World	726,959	701,425	716,418	724,337

[*]   Belgium, Luxembourg, Denmark, France, F. R. Germany, Greece, Ireland, Italy, Netherlands, Portugal, Spain, United Kingdom.

[**] Bangladesh, China, India, Indonesia, Hong Kong, Japan, Malaysia, Myanmar, North Korea, Pakistan, Philippines, Singapore, South Korea, Sri Lanka, Taiwan, Thailand, Viet Nam.

Source: elaborated on International Iron and Steel Institution. Steel Statistical Yearbook 1991–1992–1993–1994–1995.

(2000: 33–34), the acquisition of AST, a state-owned producer located in Terni, a town in the centre of Italy, was strategic for any steel producer aiming at competing in the global market for flat stainless products. Before the privatisation, AST was endowed with valuable know-how, technology, and a rich repertoire of technical skills that ranged from the production of stainless and magnetic flat products to titanium products. In the area of steel forging, AST operated through Società delle Fucine; this latter was a company entirely owned by AST that was endowed with valuable technology and owned the largest Italian, and the most modern European, mould for steel and the 12,600-tonne world's most powerful printing press. In 1994, considering the market share for stainless and magnetic products, AST was the third producer in Europe and the fifth globally with more than 450,000 tonnes sold per year of which 410,000 was stainless steel.

Steel pipes producer Dalmine, as well, was an interesting firm. Built at the beginning of the 20th century close to the city of Bergamo, one of the area in the north of Italy that traditionally specialised in the production of iron and steel products, Dalmine had a long tradition in the production of steel seamless pipes. In the variegated system of state-owned companies, Dalmine represented a very tasty morsel for whoever was willing to build a competitive position in the European and global market of steel pipes. In 1994, the year before privatisation, Dalmine was in a relative financial health with earnings before taxes in 1994 and 1995, respectively, equal to 3.3 and 13.9 billion Liras (Dringoli, 2000: 123). Being the fourth seamless steel pipes producer in the world, with a 24% market share, and the second in Europe after the German Mannesman, Dalmine displayed an enviable competitive position as well.

7.1.2 *Discursive opportunity structure during settlement*

As for the discursive opportunity structure, the key constraining cultural elements do not change much moving from the fragmentation (1984–1992) to the settlement phase. In Figure 7.3, we report again our portrait of the discursive space that puts into relation actors, frames, and attitudes towards privatisation. In the picture, by employing arrows that describe actors' movements, in Figure 7.3 we highlight how actors changed their positions in the discursive space moving from the fragmentation to the settlement phase. From a graphical point of view, the positions of actors during fragmentation are indicated by the number "1" in the categories' label, and by the use of grey colour for the label. Actors' positions during settlement are indicated by the number "2" in the label. To highlight movements, a grey arrow connects the positions in the first period with the positions in the second period. We can notice that actors in the left camp of the map basically did not change their stance in the shift from fragmentation to settlement. Just for these cases, we removed the label referred to in the first period to improve the readability of the map. As for the actors in the right camp of the map, both *Public Managers* and *Centre Politicians* move towards the neoliberal pole of the map, embracing the *Continental Capitalism* frame and leaving behind the *Developmental State*. Also, *Unions* move to the left, but they basically remain around the frame *Labour versus Capital*. The only category of actors that moved against the tide is composed of *Leftwing Politicians*: we can interpret this movement as a quest for political space. Indeed, as privatisations were underway, leftwing politicians took a clear political position against privatisation in the hope that brushing against their traditional political repertoire might have granted some political consensus in the ranks of leftwing voters.

7.1.3 *Political opportunity structure during settlement*

In the period running from 1992 to the beginning of 1993, Italy experienced the peak of a strong economic and political turmoil. As seen, mounting public debt had raised international concerns on the robustness of the Italian economy and currency. This was especially dramatic in the face of the constraints to accomplish the financial and economic parameters set by the Maastricht Agreement to be included in the European Union. This complex tangle of political and economic pressures was exacerbated by the fact that a large part of the political ruling class was implicated in a vast anti-bribery investigation known as *mani pulite* (clean hands), from the name of the trial. At the same time, in the summer of 1992, the battle against the Mafia in South Italy experiences one of its most dramatic phases when two magistrates, who were considered leaders in the war against criminality, Giovanni Falcone and

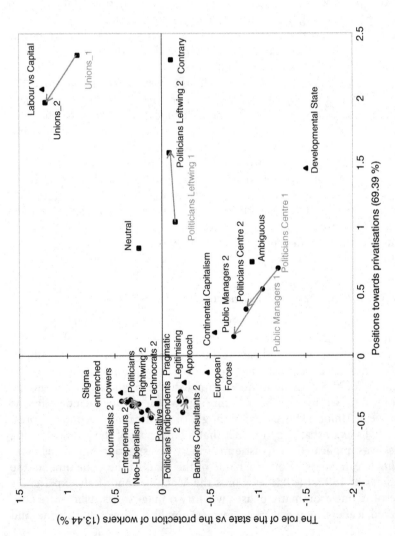

Figure 7.3 Frames, actors, and positions – detail of actors' positions during fragmentation and settlement

Paolo Borsellino, were killed in two attacks taking place in May and July 1992.

The emerging political landscape was one clearly portraying the final collapse of a political system and a connected historical bloc. Yet, the situation, we advocate, was as well reaching its climax and the seeds were planted for a new settlement of the field. In this light, the account of the political opportunity structure unveils a number of significant signals of change between 1992 and 1993.

Two governments that lasted 1 year each were formed in sequence to manage the described economic and political shocks. Despite the fact that the coalition of parties supporting the two governments was almost the same (only the PRI decided to leave the coalition), a difference was in the men asked to lead the coalitions: Giuliano Amato (from June 28, 1992 to April 22, 1993) and Azelio Ciampi (from April 28, 1993 to January 13, 1994). The former was a socialist who had worked in the preceding governments as an economic expert and who had been Treasury Minister; the latter had been governor of the Bank of Italy and was renowned as belonging to the elite of the Italian technocracy. Mr. Ciampi was considered an independent politician; that is, a member of technocracy asked to enter the political arena but independent of political parties.

The change from Amato to Ciampi, from a politician coming from the Socialist Party, this latter a central element of the largely delegitimised political class, to Ciampi, who was considered a knowledgeable technician with an outstanding career as governor of the Bank of Italy, signalled the will to find a truce to settle a dramatically conflicting social and political landscape. As well, agreeing to support a technician was for the members of the Parliament tantamount to admit the evident loss of legitimacy of the ruling political class. Aiming at a new settlement, in 1993, during the Ciampi government, a pact among the government, the unions, and Confindustria was signed. The pact came after 2 years of strong industrial conflicts around the *scala mobile* (salary scale), the mechanism that automatically adapted salaries to the rate of inflation, which Confindustria wanted to eliminate. The pact defined the rules for the dialogue among the parties and created a mechanism articulated along two layers. The first layer was an agreement on salaries set at the national level; the second layer involved agreements set at the local or organisational level. The national layer, to be renewed every 2 years, was aimed at preserving the purchasing power of salaries considering the trend in inflation within a wide set of considerations involving the state of the economy, the income policy, the state of the labour market, and the context of specific industries.

The government of Mr. Ciampi, however, lasted one year. In 1994, new political elections were organised to give to the country the possibility to select a new political coalition. Thus, in the last period of the settlement phase, from 1994 to 1995, a new coalition came to power, led by Mr. Silvio Berlusconi. The coalition was supported by newly created parties, such as Forza Italia (created by Mr. Berlusconi himself), Lega Nord (that supported a federal organisation of the state), and two small parties that inherited the tradition of the dissolved Christian Democrats. Mr. Berlusconi's government lasted for only 1 year and was substituted by a government led again by independent technocrats in which the prime minister was Lamberto Dini, who was asked to lead the government while he was the General Director of the Bank of Italy. Once again, the Bank of Italy proved to be a precious reservoir of technocratic skills to draw fully from in order to find support for a weak political class.

In order to settle the field, and to build a new historical bloc, our account suggests this old political class, which had among its most representative political parties the Christian Democrats and the Socialist Party, had to be delegitimised and dismissed.

7.1.3.1 The European Union, the discipline on state aid, and the pressure of privatisation

Another central element of the political opportunity structure that constrained actors' strategising in the Italian steel industry regards the relationship between the Italian government and the European Union. Specifically, the issue of state aids continued to represent the critical force that moulded the territory where the tensions between the Italian government and the European Commission occurred. In the fragmentation phase, a sort of agreement had been reached to bargain financial support to state-owned steel producers with reductions in the Italian installed capacity. Only in the first half of the 1990s, however, the matter found a definitive settlement.

In July 1993, after years of quarrels between the European Commission and a number of Italian governments that came in succession to lead the country, an agreement was signed between Karel Van Miert and Beniamino Andreatta, the former the European Commissioner to Competition, the latter the Minister for Foreign Affairs in the Italian government lead by Azelio Ciampi. The agreement, however, did not come without strong efforts by the Italian government to maintain its sovereignty on the national economic policy. The release of the new code for state aid in 1991 had further reinforced a neo-liberal approach to market competition and had advocated a harsher restriction of the role of the European governments in their economies. The release of the code animated a heated debate on what was to be considered state aid and what, on the other hand, was to be considered a physiological and legitimate state intervention. Thus, the first half of the 1990s saw the recrudescence of the debate on the correct interpretation of the state aid discipline. The Commission led by Delors was keen to cut back the territory of legitimate state intervention, whereas a number of countries, Italy was one of these, claimed that the discipline on state aid, as enacted by the Commission, implied a preference for privatisation. In this light, these countries reiterated the argument that neither the Treaty of Rome, instituting the European Economic Community, nor the Treaty for the functioning of the Common Market, which was issued in 1986, included any indication regarding state ownership.

On the verge of this theoretical debate, in February 1993, the Directorate General for Competition of the European Commission revealed the intention to launch infringement proceedings against the Italian government for the violation of the state aid discipline. Yet, a key turn point in the quarrel between the European Commission and the Italian government concerning the discipline on state aid occurred in conjunction with the bankruptcy and the liquidation of EFIM,[3] a large state-owned company operating as financial harm of the Italian government to support manufacturing companies. The European Commission opened another infringement proceeding against the Italian government for alleged violation of the discipline of state aid in liquidating the company.

Interestingly, the proceeding unveiled the deep gap that separated the logic underpinning the action of the Commission and the deep-seated institutions of the Italian government. Specifically, the contested issue revolved around article 2362 of the Italian civil law. The law protected the creditors of EFIM (and of any other state-owned company) with the financial guarantee of the Italian government. More specifically, article 2362 required that when a company went bankrupt, for the labilities created in the period in which a sole proprietor existed of the equity, this proprietor was held accountable. The Commission intervened, arguing that a private investor would have never invested with such an unlimited responsibility without requiring an adequate rate of return.

Along this line of interpretation, the Commission asked the* government to eliminate the effect of article 2362 for state-owned enterprises. The proposal initially put forward by Minister Andreatta included three elements. The first element was the commitment of the Italian government to keep the state ownership below 10% for future acquisitions, in order not to trigger the consequences of article 2362. The commitment to reduce the debt was the second element. In exchange, the Italian government asked, as a third central element of the proposed agreement, the maintenance of the state guarantee connected to article 2362 for the debt of the state-owned companies as certified at a specific date. Commissioner Van Miert, however, insisted on the elimination of the guarantee provided by article 2362 based on the supremacy of the communitarian law over the national one. In the perspective of the Italian government, the position of the

European Commission, in the person of Van Miert, was seriously at risk of being perceived as invasive in the Italian sovereignty over its economic policy. The perceived penchant of the Commissioner towards the privatisation of the Italian economy bothered many who emphasised how the European Commission could not impose a specific form of ownership of economic activities. Specifically, Van Miert replied to the proposal of the Italian government by requiring three commitments. First, the Commission's plan required the Italian government to sell portions of equity in state-owned firms in order not to maintain a share in companies greater than 70%. A second requirement was the elimination of the guarantee provided by article 2362. Finally, Van Miert's list of obligations included the commitment to freeze and to reduce the debt of all the companies completely owned by the state. A time period was assigned to the Italian government to implement the described privatisations and, during this period, the renegotiation, the renewal, and the extensions of the terms of the existing debt had to be communicated and agreed upon with the European Commission. In Italy, the top management of IRI fiercely rebutted the conditions set by the Commission. A very cogent argument of IRI's top management, among others, was that the elimination of the guarantee provided by article 2362 would have triggered a sudden request of reimbursement by creditors of about 27,000 billion liras (14 billion euros) (Curli, 2013: 226). After months of intense diplomatic interactions among the Italian government, the top management of IRI, and the European Commission, at the end of July 1993, an agreement was reached.

The Italian government committed to quantifying, by December 31, 1993, the debt of companies 100% owned by the state; for this stock of debt, the Commission allowed the guarantee by article 2362. The Italian government committed to reduce the mentioned debt to a physiological level, this latter defined as the debt that a private investor operating in a competitive market economy would be ready to bear. In addition, the Italian government committed to reducing below 100% its share of ownership so as to neutralise the guarantee of article 2362. Lastly, the Italian government accepted to devise, along with the Commission, a monitoring scheme of the agreement.[4] As Curli reports (2013: 252), the agreement left on the ground the issue of privatisations, while the Commission leveraged on the agreement to ask the privatisation or liquidation of IRI, the Italian government and, more resolutely, IRI top management interpreted the decrease in state ownership as described in the agreement as solely intended at deactivating the guarantee of article 2362.

7.2 Strategic manoeuvring in the field

7.2.1 Discoursive manoeuvring: sedating antagonising logics of equivalence

When analysing the discursive manoeuvring leading to settlement, interesting dynamics surface. While field's actors seem strongly embedded and constrained by the DOS, they display the ability to strategise in the discursive space by modifying their support for privatisation models. Thus, despite the stability of the connections between actors and the frames that they adopted to interpret the privatisation issue, actors are able to change their interpretation of how the privatisation process ought to be managed. It is in this specific dimension of the discursive space–the proposal of different privatisation models–that field's actors found room for discursive strategising.

More interestingly, we are able to capture a specific trend that characterised the settlement phase; actors converged towards a behaviour that was apparently aimed at smoothening extreme discursive positions in the attempt to find out a viable discursive alliance. In doing so, of course, the repertoire of logics of equivalence that have been put in place in the fragmentation phase needed to be simplified to converge towards a logic of equivalence able to include the possible largest number of actors.

From this perspective, moving from fragmentation to settlement, in Figure 7.4, all the actors moved leftwards, towards the "controlled" side of privatisation, in which the role of the government in orchestrating the process is preserved in some proportion, thus leaving behind the support for *Market Driven*. Along this line, *Centre Politicians* and *Leftwing Politicians* joined the *Government Controlled* area in the top left quadrant, while *Independent Politicians* moved to the extreme corner of the same quadrant. *Technocracy* moved slightly towards the left but remained around the horizontal axis.

On the right of the map, *Public Managers*, *Bankers and Consultants*, and *Journalists* moved as well to the left towards the side of the map in which actors concede to the government the role of the pivotal player in the privatisation process. What is relevant is that *Entrepreneurs*, as well, abandoned the right side of the map, that is the camp in which actors advocated that the market is the most efficient mechanism to guide the privatisation process. This is probably the most significant and revealing movement: they crossed the horizontal axis and moved towards the position occupied by *Unions,* thereby positioning on the side of the map where the intervention of the government in the privatisation process was welcome. The *Rightwing Politicians* followed the entrepreneurs, moving to the left. In the lower left quadrant of the map, *Unions* moved slightly towards the bottom. This movement, as well, crystallises a

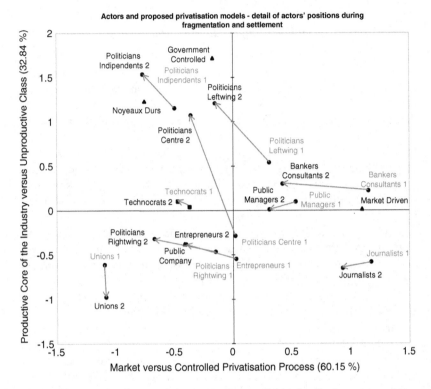

Figure 7.4 Actors and proposed privatisation models – detail of actors' positions during fragmentation and settlement

relevant piece of discursive manoeuvring. The movement downward implies that unions were increasing their distance from the logic of equivalence that, on the vertical dimension, associated the actors that do not belong to the productive core in the steel industry.

Overall, shifting from fragmentation to settlement, all the actors moved towards the left side of the map. Therefore, a simplification of the discursive space occurred: the horizontal dimension of the debate, which portrays the opposition between selling SOEs in the free market, or let the government control privatisations, lost traction.

We advocate that such mutation in the meaning space reveals the rhetorical and ambiguous nature that characterised the discourse on the "prodigious" benefits of the market when this latter was originally mobilised in the Italian debate on privatisations. Indeed, we argue that the global neo-liberal discourse that at the end of the 1980s allowed the local mobilisation of market principles against the intrusiveness of the Italian state in the economy was rhetorically mobilised by some actors in the fragmentation phase in support of the hegemonic practice that we labelled *Against the party state*. In describing the discourse occurring in the Italian Parliament and in the economic elite in the 1990s, Cavazzuti confirms that it was a common understanding that in Italy the Anglo-Saxon neo-liberalism had no real footing (2013: 62). As Trentin suggested, Italian entrepreneurs contemporaneously looked for "laissez faire" and state support.[5] Thus, as the privatisation process in the steel industry reached its completion, the actors who had interests in keeping the dialogue alive with the government and the political parties gradually abandoned the state-market antagonising discourse. In particular, *Entrepreneur* walked off the market-driven rhetoric to discursively re-vitalise the "Pact of Producers". It is worth noting that, in Figure 7.4, *Journalists* are the actors that changed their position less in the discursive space. A possible interpretation is that, not being involved in the economic consequences of privatisations, *Journalists* could preserve their original ideological inclination.

In this antagonism, the *Noyaux Durs* model, in the middle way between *Government Controlled* and *Public Company*, emerged as the frame that mediated between two logics of equivalence. More precisely, while a logic of equivalence was increasingly pooling together the actors that recognised the role of technocracies in bringing under control the perils that a privatisation left to the market could have brought about, another logic of equivalence emerged that kept together those who felt a sense of belonging to the productive core of the industry. In this light, in reporting the movement downwards of unions, we had already noticed that the vertical dimension of the debate, which captures the opposition between productive and unproductive classes, remained relevant in the discursive space. The analysis of this vertical dimension brings light on the discursive alliance between unions and entrepreneurs. The discursive strategy of this alliance was built around the suspect that the interests of those directly involved in production might have been ignored. From this angle, we explain the support that this alliance offered to the model of *Public Company*, which, in the words of its advocates, represented a transparent way to make available the equity of the privatised companies to citizens and to transform workers into shareholders.

7.2.2 Political manoeuvring: the emerging of a winning alliance

The second Delors Commission, beginning from 1989, and, specifically, the Commissioner to Competition, Leon Brittain, was animated by a fervour to apply the discipline of market economy and competition and to curb the practice of state aid. The white paper of the Commission on Growth, Competitiveness, Employment, in 1993, gave a further push to such an ideological stance. Overall, we may say that in the first half of the 1990s the European Union provided a political context in which the market discipline was dominant and in which countries were invited to privatise and to reduce the role of the state in their economies. In the case of Italy, this pressure was especially strong for three reasons. First, as anticipated, the Commission's census on state aid, in 1989, had revealed that Italy accounted for 55% of all the state aids distributed by European countries (Curli, 2013: 206). Second, the critical financial conditions and the alleged inefficiency of the Italian system of state-owned companies were considered a point of the fragility of the overall European economy and an isle of state activism and an obstacle to the creation of a European market economy. Finally, to what the steel industry is concerned, Italian state-owned companies still occupied large market shares and European competitors seized the opportunity to claim that such market position was maintained through anti-competitive state support.

In particular, the infringement proceeding for the violation of state aid discipline that was menaced in February 1993 by the Directorate General for Competition of the European Commission had a major impact on the steel industry. The reply of the Italian government was to advocate that the state aid discipline was not to be applied strictly but needed to take account of the enormous effort that the government was undertaking to transform the Italian economy. The strategy of the Italian government was to tackle separately the issue of restructuring, on the one hand, and the dispute on the closure of production capacity, on the other. The Commission, on the other hand, insisted that the reorganisation of the Italian steel industry had implied state aid and, therefore, required to be compensated with plant closures.

Indeed, the Italian government, beginning in the first half of the 1990s, was taking key steps to privatise the economy. The Amato government pushed forward the privatisation process by transforming in law no. 359 August 8 1992 the decree no. 333 of July 11 1992 that transformed large state holding owned directly by the Minister of Treasury–IRI, ENEL, and ENI[6] – into limited responsibility companies private companies whose equity could be held by the same Ministry. This technical step was meant to be preparatory to the re-organisation of state-owned holdings to be conducted through mergers and privatisation of firms owned by the state holdings. The Ciampi government laid down another further pillar to privatisation by issuing law no. 537 on December 24, 1993, that delegated the government to create an agency for the regulation of the strategic industries undergoing privatisations, such as public utilities. At the same time, in 1993, with decree 174/1993, the Ministry for state ownership, which was in charge to coordinate state ownership was abolished. Finally, the following government, lead by Silvio Berlusconi, further refined the institutional framework necessary for privatisation by issuing law no. 474 on the 30th of July 1994 to accelerate privatisations.

The general trend toward privatisations of the Italian government was partially moved by the necessity to abide by the constraints imposed by the European Union and partially advocated by a group of technocrats in the country. The latter could rely upon general support by a large portion of the public opinion that was influenced by a dominant hegemonic discourse that praised the holy benefits of the market economy.

Yet, in the management of privatisations, different interests, and ideological inclinations emerged not only in the political manoeuvring by the three mentioned governments (Amato, Ciampi, and Berlusconi) but among different members of the same governments. In this light, particularly telling is the quarrel between the Ministry of Industry and the Ministry of Finance in the Amato government in the writing of law no. 359. The privatisation plan of Giuseppe Guarino, the Ministry of Industry, clearly embodied a model of privatisations in which the government maintained a pivotal role in the economy. Privatisations were considered as a means in the repertoire of possible tools to implement an economic policy aimed at making the Italian economy efficient without necessarily moving towards a complete exclusion of the state. The plan of Minister Guarino advised gathering companies to be privatised in two state-owned holdings: one including the shares owned by the Ministry of Treasury in financial companies and the other including the Minister's shares in non-financial companies. The plan recommended 25% of the equity of the profitable-companies-holding to be assigned to a hard core of Italian entrepreneurs and another 25% to remain in the hands of the Ministry of Finance, so that the government, through the Ministry of Finance, was able to maintain a grip on profitable companies; the rest of the equity would have been put on the market (Cavazzuti, 2013: 103). In this version, the plan assigned to the Ministry of Finance the role of coordinating the financing of the two *super-holding* by orchestrating the placement of shares, warrants, and convertible bonds in the market through a partnership of banks.

On the other hand, the Minister of Finance Piero Barucci, along with the Ministry General Director Mario Draghi, wanted to centralise the power to manoeuvre privatisation policy without sharing responsibility with the Minister of Industry and, more importantly, refused the privatisation approach based on Minister Guarino's model of *super-holdings*. While the Minister of Industry interpreted privatisation policy as an element of a broader intervention of industrial policy, the Minister of Finance looked, on the one hand, at privatisations as the spearhead of a more drastic liberalisation of the Italian economy and, on the other, as the necessary tool to counter a threatening and pending fiscal deficit.

Of course, the quarrel as well crystallised a power struggle in which the Minister of Industry represented the will of a portion of politicians to maintain control over the economy while the Minister of Finance embodied the motives of another group more reactive to the financial constraints posed by the European Union and motivated by a penchant toward the merits of financial discipline. As Cavazzuti suggests, the Minister of Finance was, probably, as well influenced by the interests of large financial firms eager to yield rich remunerations as brokers, intermediaries, and consultants (Cavazzuti, 2013: 99).

It was evident that the choice of a privatisation model was enmeshed in the wider problem of what new power system would have ensued. Three different models were on the table: the constitution of public companies, the direct sale of shares, or the sale through auction. In addition, a key issue pending was whether the government was willing to orchestrate the sales in order to constitute stable cores of investors (*noyaux dur*). As Cavazzuti reports (2013: 117), connected to the issue of how to privatise was the selection of a new class of top managers, especially in those companies in which the state had some shares. The choice was between new administrators, probably belonging to the highly skilled technocracy or the experienced members of the old bureaucracy.

Given the broader institutional context that was going to be created to put in place steel privatisation, a key actor in the process, and a centre of power and interests, was the state-holding IRI, the holder of the equity in the state-owned steel producers.

In the period 1991–1995, three chairmen came in succession: Franco Nobili (1989–1993), Romano Prodi (1993–1994), and Michele Tedeschi (1994–1997). The latter was as well the CEO of the company during Prodi's chairmanship. Franco Nobili, as previously reported, was a strenuous defender of IRI autonomy in the management state holding's necessary restructuring. Romano Prodi was chairman for the second time after a first period during 1982–1989, in which he had strongly contributed to restoring the financial balance of the company. Both Romano Prodi, in his second mandate as chairman, and the following chairman, Michele Tedeschi, had to manage the state holding in between the perils of a worsened financial situation, the constraints to strategic manoeuvring introduced by the discipline on state aids, and the impending pressures to privatisation. In this context, in the period 1992–1993, Romano Prodi, contemporaneously tried to preserve the strategic and organisational autonomy of IRI and to improve the efficiency of operations. In particular, Prodi, in 1993, appointed Hayao Nakamura, previously consultant of the Italian government with experience as a manager in Nippon Steel, as CEO of ILVA in substitution of Giovanni Gambardella.

In this framework, the CEO of IRI, Michele Tedeschi presented a project to restructure ILVA. The plan, approved by the IRI Board of Directors on the 28th of April 1993, was articulated along three main axes.[7] The first axis was the focusing on core business, flat products, with the sale of the activities connected to long and special steel products, and pipes, as well as real estate, energy, engineering, and R&D.

These non-core activities were mainly owned by two companies, AST and Dalmine. The sale of non-core activities was necessary and urgent in order to cover the increase of debt and the connected reduction of equity of ILVA. Yet, the IRI management had to cope with limited manoeuvring. On the one hand, selling assets to private investors would have required the time that IRI had not under the pressure to stop up the company's, and the country, financial haemorrhage. On the other hand, IRI could not directly cover the debt of the participated company ILVA without incurring in the infringement of the discipline on state aids. The solution was for ILVA to sell assets directly to IRI with the value of these assets assessed by independent experts. A second axis of the plan mentioned the creation of a new company, Nuova Siderurgica, that would have incorporated the activities in the core business. Yet, still in June 1993, the interpretation of the IRI plan regarding the privatisation of Nuova Siderurgica was unclear. The plan devised the involvement of private investors, even in the role of majority holders of the equity of the resulting company and a progressive dismissal of state ownership was prefigured. Finally, the plan foresaw the liquidation of residual assets.

The plan envisaged the agreement of unions in the restructuring of ILVA. Specifically, the plan envisioned 6,300 further layoffs, and IRI management, together with unions, appealed to the government for the implementation of early retirement plans, standby plans, and direct investments in a specific area characterised by high unemployment risk.

However, the reaction of the European Commission to the described plan forced IRI to clearly state the intention to privatise Nuova Siderurgica. Specifically, the argument of the Commission was that the debt of ILVA, and the connected guarantee offered by the holding IRI, was to be considered an instance of state aid requiring the cut of installed production capacity by an overall volume of 3 million tonnes of flat steel. This would have implied the dramatic reduction of installed capacity of Nuova Siderurgica in the plant of Taranto, in the South of Italy. Yet, the cut of such capacity, continued the Commission, would have impaired the opportunity of Nuova Siderurgica to find investors willing to buy the company in a scenario of privatisation. In other words, the Commission interpreted the plan, rather than aimed at restructuring state-owned steel production, as the design for the complete privatisation of the industry. In this light, the Commission asked IRI the official commitment of the Italian government to privatise Nuova Siderurgica. The privatisation would have implied the redrafting downwards of the assessment of Italian state aids with a connected reduction in the necessary cuts of installed capacity. Therefore, without the cut in capacity, Nuova Siderurgica would have been an appetising object for interested investors.[8] To respond to the requests of the Commission, in a second version of the restructuring plan, IRI officially planned to create another company that would include special steel products. The rationale behind the creation of two companies – Nuova Siderurgica for flat products and another company for special steel products – was to prepare them for the market by starting immediately a restructuring programme in order to prevent the intensification of organisational and managerial problems. The idea was to be able to realise the most from the sale of the firms by the means of competitive auctions.[9]

In this light, when assigned to the state-owned bank IMI (Istituto Mobiliare Italiano), the counselling to accomplish the evaluation of the two company branches, IRI expressly mentioned a mandate to privatise.[10]

Under the pressure of dramatic financial conditions, the General Assembly of ILVA, on the 31st of October 1993, decided the liquidation of the company and the allocation of assets to two newly created companies; ILP (ILVA Laminati Piani), operating in the business of flat steel products (with the assets previously owned by Nuova Siderurgica), and AST (Acciai Speciali Terni), the latter operating in the business of special steel products.[11] The newly created ILP included, along with the plants in the North West of Italy, these latter the sites that harboured the rise of steel production at the beginning of the century, the large integrated plant of Taranto, with the largest furnace in Europe.

Beginning operations on 1 January 1994, Acciai Speciali Terni (AST) was privatised in December of the same year when the company was sold for 600 billion liras through a direct sale to the newly constituted company Kai Italia. Created to apply for the privatisation of AST, Kai Italia was a company owned by German and Italian steel producers. Along with the German Krupp Thyssen, which owned 50% of the equity, another group, Far Acciai Srl, composed of the Italian Agarini, Falck, and Riva, participated in the equity with the remaining 50%. In December 1995, Riva and Falck sold their share of, respectively, 44% and 16% of the equity of Far Acciai Srl to Krupp that, as the consequence of this sale, came to hold 75% of the equity of Kai.

In April 1995, ILP, the larger state-owned company that included a large part of the remaining state-owned capacity for flat products, was sold to a private producer, Riva. The company was sold for 2,500 billion liras (approximately 1.3 billion euros) including the profit relative to 1994; this abates the selling price to 1,689 billion Liras (approximately 0.9 billion euros) (Dringoli, 2000: 78). More specifically, in July 1995, ILP is incorporated in RILP, whose main shareholder is the Riva group that holds 57.14% of the equity. The sale to Riva, however, was supported by a pool of state-owned banks that converted 200 billion of their credits towards Riva into shares of the new company undersigning part of the increase in equity by 700 billion realised in May 1995. As a result, for example, three banks–San Paolo of Turin, Banca Nazionale del Lavoro, and Cariplo–came to hold, respectively, 6%, 3%, and 2.14% of the equity. In addition, three minority shareholders of RILP were industrial partners; two were Italian steel producers, Acciaierie Valbruna and Metalfer; the third one was the Indian group Essar. Gradually, Riva acquired the shares held by the banks and other shareholders to reach 85.36% of the equity at the end of 1997.

Finally, in 1996, Dalmine, a pipe producer, was privatised by direct sale of 84% of the equity to the Techint Investment Netherlands (owned by the Rocca family). The sale was the product of an articulated political manoeuvring among elite groups. In late 1995, Techint stipulated a syndicate agreement with the bank of Rome, which was owned by the Ministry of Treasury through IRI. With a planned time horizon of 5 years, the agreement expressed the intention of the partners to maintain the ownership of the majority of the equity of Dalmine. Along with the Bank of Rome, a number of small Italian entrepreneurs joined in the ownership of Dalmine as well. In June 1997, 3 years before the planned time horizon, the syndicate agreement was taken to an end, allowing Techint to buy from the Bank of Rome the share owned by the bank in order to reach the majority of the equity.

7.3 Weaving together political and discursive manoeuvring to re-align the interests of field's actors: A hegemonic practice emerges to solidify a new historical bloc

While we described three hegemonic practices at work during fragmentation, in the phase of settlement, the simplification of both discursive and political structures paved the way for the selection of a new hegemonic practice able to solidify field's actors in a new historical bloc.

Observing the evolution of the hegemonic practices enacted by field's actors, the most important process that we noticed is the simplification of the repertoire of alliances. To create a historical bloc, actors needed to select among the possible interest alignments available.

As anticipated, in the discursive opportunity structure, the association between actors and frames did not really change, moving from fragmentation to settlement, but this result does not have to mask a profound change that happened at the level of hegemonic practices, where almost all of the actors abandoned the support for market-oriented privatisation models. Consequently, during settlement, the hegemonic practice *Against the party state* faded away, while the other two practices, *Party State* and *Pact of Producers,* apparently converged toward a new practice, which we called *National Interest First* (Figure 7.5), based on the voicing of a theory of "national interest" that recurs in our data in this period.

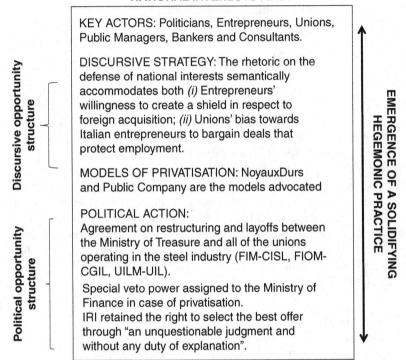

NATIONAL INTERESTS FIRST

Discursive opportunity structure

Political opportunity structure

KEY ACTORS: Politicians, Entrepreneurs, Unions, Public Managers, Bankers and Consultants.

DISCURSIVE STRATEGY: The rhetoric on the defense of national interests semantically accommodates both *(i)* Entrepreneurs' willingness to create a shield in respect to foreign acquisition; *(ii)* Unions' bias towards Italian entrepreneurs to bargain deals that protect employment.

MODELS OF PRIVATISATION: NoyauxDurs and Public Company are the models advocated

POLITICAL ACTION: Agreement on restructuring and layoffs between the Ministry of Treasure and all of the unions operating in the steel industry (FIM-CISL, FIOM-CGIL, UILM-UIL).
Special veto power assigned to the Ministry of Finance in case of privatisation.
IRI retained the right to select the best offer through "an unquestionable judgment and without any duty of explanation".

EMERGENCE OF A SOLIDIFYING HEGEMONIC PRACTICE

Figure 7.5 Hegemonic practices in settlement phase: *National Interests First*

Discursively, this new hegemonic practice was aimed at building a logic of equivalence that sutured the differences among the elites involved in the battle to assign the meaning to the privatisation issue in the steel field. By stressing the need to exclude foreign investors and enterprises from the privatisation of Italian SOEs, this logic attempted to weave together a political identity that promised to accommodate the interests of the key elite actors involved, such as politicians, unions, and entrepreneurs.

In particular, the *Noyaux Durs* model emerged as a mediation between *Government Controlled* and *Public Company*, as it was able to reduce the antagonism between the *Party State* and the *Pact of Producers* by refuelling an old corporatist pact. This model was a good candidate to work as a compromise between supporters of both models since it did not contradict any of the two: *Noyeaux Durs* promised to preserve political control over the privatisation process, while at the same time was likely to make it available to carefully selected private producers the equity of SOEs. The advantages of selecting a stable core of investors were justified by the principle that "in conducting efficient privatisations, the conditions leading to the defence of national interests[12]" need to be considered to create a "new system of command of the Italian capitalistic system". We found several occurrences of the expression "national interest" in the statements analysed. More specifically, among the statements that we used for reconstructing proposed privatisation models, we found 1 occurrence of "national interest" during fragmentation, and 16 occurrences during settlement, when this concept is explicitly invoked in reference to the *Noyeaux Durs* model as the following statement of a technocrat suggests: "when the political authority thinks that selling an enterprise to foreign entrepreneurs is not politically saviour, then a *noyeaux dur* of Italian entrepreneurs must be created, so that the State can confer them the responsibility for a strategic enterprise".

We find four occurrences of "national interest" also in the statements that were coded to the *Pragmatic Legitimising Approach*, where they are used to balance the need to privatise, and the fact that some sort of governmental control must remain in place, as in this quote from a journalist implies: "ENEL and ENI are SOEs operating as monopolists. Even if they are transformed into a stock company, they will continue to represent a "national interest". Therefore, the State will not be able to simply withdraw from the strategic and financial control".

The rhetoric of national interests was revived but was already subtly infiltrated in the political debate. As Cavazzuti reports (2013: 119), in 1992, in the parliamentary debate on privatisations, a Committee on industrial policy focusing on the guidelines and objectives of privatisation, in the Senate, disclosed a report in which two key pillars were put forward. First, the protection of national interests was a key constraint of the privatisation process. Second, privatisations ought to contribute to creating national industrial and technological hubs, integrating public and private ownership, able to compete globally. The report as well reminds the need for the creation of large popular ownership, possibly including workers of the companies to be privatised.[13] The report is a revealing example of the complex yarn of interests, motivations, and feelings that both reflected the awareness of the need to modernise the Italian economy and preserved a historical bloc that was clearly defined within national borders. The very figure of the speaker of the mentioned report, Senator Luigi Granelli, is interesting in understanding the forces that were at work to preserve the glue that kept together the country during the laborious process of post Second World War growth. Senator Granelli, who had been a blue-collar metalworker who started his political activity in the Christian Democratic Party, was the example of those politicians in the ruling coalition who always maintained an intense dialogue with workers' representatives and the left.

For the hegemonic practice to be effective, the discourse needed to be associated with the intervention on the regulatory framework. The deliberation of the *Inter-Ministry Committee for Economic Planning* (CIPE) on the 30th of December 1992 explicitly recommended organising public auctions to select stable cores of investors that guarantee stability and a coherent strategic intent to the ownership of privatised firms. Yet, public auctions clearly do not guarantee full control over the selection of acquirers. The concept of the auction, therefore, was gradually changed into the concept of direct selection, this latter more suitable to have complete control over the selection of investors. The idea of directly selecting among candidate acquirers was conveyed recurring to the narrative on Noyaux Durs that, discursively, could be easily adopted for two different purposes: on the one hand, it could be used to brush up a corporatist agreement in which large private investors are assigned the control on privatised firms within a pact that considers the interests of a large audience of stakeholders. Secondly, as the then Ministry of Finance explained,[14] the creation of stable groups of investors was functional to the retention of the ownership of firms in Italian hands since the government held the power to select acquirers with "an unquestionable judgment and without any duty of explanation".[15]

Following this tendency towards the selection of Noyaux Durs, decree 332 mentioned direct sales to a "stable nucleus of investors (article 1)" as a possible privatisation model, and when the decree was transformed into law 474/1994, a few months later, a clear reference to the "objectives of national industrial policy" was added.[16]

The evolution of the mentioned law no. 474/1994 captures the consolidation of a historical bloc around the rhetoric on national interests. The law was the transformation of the decree no. 332/1994. The decree delegated the government to select the companies owned, directly or indirectly, by the state in which special power (in Italian *poteri speciali*) had to be attributed to the Ministry of Finance in the case of privatisation. More specifically, in these companies, before privatisation, the general assembly of shareholders had to vote for the creation of a clause that assigned to the Ministry such power as veto power to transfer portions of the equity to specific subjects, to the conclusions of specific pacts or agreement, and to operations that could be considered as threatening national interests. The Ministry as well had the power to appoint a member of the board of directors.

The procedure defined for the privatisation of ILVA, for example, envisaged the selection among a number of potential investors. The selection was based on a preliminary offer that had to include, among others, the industrial and investment plan, and the description of the financial framework adopted to acquire privatised companies. In addition, IRI required candidates to be endowed with a minimum equity of 50 and 100 billion liras for the acquisition of, respectively, AST and ILP. The selection among preliminary offers of those meeting the requirements was to be made on the basis of its "unquestionable judgment".[17] Among the selected offers, after due diligence, IRI retained the right to select the best offer.

This hegemonic practice was able to accommodate the interests of a number of elite actors thereby paving the way for the coalescence of a new historical bloc. Politicians in the government maintained control in the selection of buyers and could mobilise the result of steel privatisations amounting to 4,000 billion liras for IRI (Ravazzi, 2013: 281) for preserving at least some portion of bargaining power in the face of the European Commission. Leftwing politicians could rebuild a political identity around the protection of the industry and of labour from the power of large global groups while rightwing politicians presented privatisation as a fundamental step toward the liberalisation of the economy and relaxation of political control over SOEs. On the other hand, unions were able to take part in the reorganisation of privatised firms working to preserve employment levels. Finally, bankers and consultants enjoyed their share in the settlement of the field as brokers and consultants. More specifically, the government selected a number of private financial institutions as advisors to evaluate companies to be privatised.[18] Before the mentioned intervention of IMI bank, the privatisations of AST and Dalmine were assigned to Barclay's, and a list of potential consultants was produced for the privatisation of ILVA.[19]

Yet, Italian entrepreneurs were probably the elite group that took a central position, and the largest share of benefit, in the historical bloc. Italian privatisations of the State steel were performed through direct sales to select private investors or through a mix of direct sales and auctions. The intent was clearly to follow the model of *Noyaux Durs*, leading to the creation of stable groups of investors. Between 1994 and 1995 the state steel was completely privatised, and Italian entrepreneurs, protected from foreign enterprises, took the lion's share. Italian entrepreneurs were definitively the winner of the process, from an economic point of view. Taking advantage of privatisations, both Riva and Rocca consolidated their competitive positions. In 1995, Acciaierie e Ferriere di Piombino was sold to Gruppo Lucchini and ILP was sold to Riva. As seen before, Dalmine was privatised by direct sale to the Techint Investment Netherlands, owned by the Rocca family.

The articulation of the agreement leading to the privatisation of Dalmine, in particular, reveals the intention to preserve the tangle of interests of the elites that were components of a consolidating, or re-consolidating, historical bloc. Under the shield of the *national interest* rhetoric, Techint along with the Bank of Rome, a bank firmly embedded in the state-owned economic system, led a consortium supported by a number of smaller Italian entrepreneurs. Officially a company based in Argentina, Techint was a company owned by an Italian family who emigrated to Argentina after the Second World War: the Rocca family had a profound acquaintance with the national steel industry. The founder of the group, Agostino Rocca, had been CEO of Dalmine before his departure to Argentina (Dringoli, 2000: 125).

Starting as a producer of steel rebar, before acquiring ILP, Riva was a medium-sized company with sales of around 3,000 billion liras (around 1.5 billion €). By acquiring ILVA, Riva added blast furnaces to electric furnaces to become a large producer of flat steel products. The privatisation plan had reduced the production capacity installed in the industry and increased the concentration so that, in 1995, with its 14.4 million tonnes of raw steel, Riva produced 52% of the national steel supply and was the first Italian producer. In addition, after the acquisition of ILP, Riva became the seventh global producer of raw steel and pig iron (2 years before, it was 27th). Sales grew from 3,000 to 11,496 billion liras in 1995, net income increased from 105 to 966 billion liras, investments escalated from 362 to 2,758 billion liras, and workers reached a level of 26,542 from 5,754. Overall, the acquisition of ILP allowed Riva to build up a powerful position in integrated steel production in both Europe and globally.

On the other hand, acquiring Dalmine, Techint was able to build a leadership in the business of seamless steel pipes growing in production volumes above direct competitors such as the German Mannesman, the French Vallourec, and the Japanese Sumimoto (Dringoli, 2000: 125).

The case of AST seems an exception, as in 1994 the company, producing stainless steel, was sold to Kai Italia, owned by Thyssen Krupp and by a few Italian entrepreneurs. Nonetheless, Italian entrepreneurs earned a large financial return also in this case, as 1 year later they sold their shares to Thyssen Krupp (Affinito et al., 2000: 30). With the acquisition of AST, Krupp could reach 35% of the aggregated European installed production capacity for stainless steel and 12.5 % of the global capacity reaching the production of 1,410,000 tonnes that allowed the German company to maintain the European and global leadership in the stainless business. In the privatisation of AST, those who had to drink from the bitter cup were the employees. In the first year of privatisation, employment fell from 4,451 in 1994 to 3,521 in 1995. The layoffs were distributed equally between blue-collar workers (−19%) and white-collar workers (−25%).

Yet, unions could enjoy some benefit from supporting the *National Interest First* hegemonic practice as well; for example, the privatisation of ILVA was preceded by an agreement on restructuring and layoffs between the Ministry of Treasury and all of the unions operating in the steel industry (FIM-CISL, FIOM-CGIL, UILM-UIL). In addition, the procedure adopted by IRI included that among the requisites for the acquirer was to accept the duty connected to the information and consultation procedures agreed with unions.[20]

In the privatisation of ILP, specifically, as for employment, most of the effort in downsizing the workforce had been conducted during the state ownership through the collaboration between IRI and unions. After privatisation, law no. 451 issued on the 19th of July 1994 allowed 1,352 workers to benefit from early retirement programmes in 1995 and 1,487 in 1996. Yet, during 1997, Riva increased the workforce in ILP by 3,406 workers to reach 13,546. This increase is the result of the incorporation of workers previously employed in state-owned companies now merged in the Riva group. In 1998, the workforce experienced further growth to reach the level of 14,100 with an increase of 554 workers. In 1999, the Ministry of Industry, Riva, and the unions reached an agreement that required Riva to hire 1,400 employees before 2001 and, in particular, to hire young employees with training contracts (Affinito et al., 2000: 106–107).

In the case of the privatisation of Dalmine, the agreement included an official commitment by Techint to preserve employment. Leveraging a consolidated dialogue between IRI and unions, and taking advantage of the retirement schemes funded by the government, state ownership had already taken the responsibility for the most painful cut in employment. The most dramatic reduction in the workforce of Dalmine occurred in 1989 and 1993 when ILVA owned Dalmine. During this period, employees fell from 3,004 to 2,492, and in 1995, after the liquidation of the company and before privatisation, the workforce dropped again to 2,366 (Dringoli, 2000: 158). On the contrary, during the first 2 years of Techint management, in 1996 and 1997, the workforce increased to reach 2,763 employees.

Only in the privatisation of AST, in which a foreign acquirer was involved, a clear reduction in workforce occurred. Overall, given the described discursive and the political opportunity structures–the dominating neo-liberal rhetoric, the constraints of the European Commission, and the financial pressures imposed by the bleeding balance sheets of SOEs–we can say that unions did not have much space for manoeuvring. Joining the emerging hegemonic practice, which we labelled *National Interest First*, was probably the best strategy to maintain the right of voice and to at least partially preserve employment. Between 1985 and 1995, the Italian steel industry reported a 36.7% reduction in jobs, while in France and Spain the reduction was 51% and 53.7%, respectively.

Notes

1 Notes for IRI Board of Director, meeting 3/12/1993. *Nota per il Consiglio di Amministrazione. IRI Spa Consiglio di Amministrazione (08/07/1993) – Problematiche ILVA – CEE.* RP-05, Historical Archive of the European Union (HAEU).

2 Apparent consumption is calculated by subtracting exports and the increase of inventories to the sum production + imports + decrease of inventories.

3 Ente Partecipazioni e Finanziamento Industrie Manifatturiere.

4 Notes for IRI Board of Director, meeting 3/12/1993. *Nota per il Consiglio di Amministrazione*. *IRI Spa Consiglio di Amministrazione (03/12/1993)– Accordo tra il governo italiano e la commissione CEE sull'applicazione dell'art. 2362*. RP-05, Historical Archive of the European Union (HAEU).

5 Rinascita, vol. 47: p. 4, 1985.

6 ENEL (Ente Nazionale per l'energia ELettrica) was the state-owned utility that provided electricity and ENI (Ente Nazionale Idrocarburi) was the state-owned utility operating in a number of businesses such as chemicals, gas and petrol extraction and infrastructure building.

7 Nota per il Consiglio di Amministrazione. IRI Spa Consiglio di Amministrazione (17/06/1993). *Stato di attuazione del Piano di risanamento – problematiche connesse*: pages 1–2 RP-05, Historical Archive of the European Union (HAEU).

8 Nota per il Consiglio di Amministrazione. IRI Spa Consiglio di Amministrazione (22/07/1993). *Negoziato CEE – Piano ILVA,* RP-05, Historical Archive of the European Union (HAEU).

9 Nota per il Consiglio di Amministrazione. IRI Spa Consiglio di Amministrazione (22/07/1993). *Processo di ristrutturazione dell'ILVA,* RP-05, Historical Archive of the European Union (HAEU).

10 Nota per il Consiglio di Amministrazione. IRI Spa Consiglio di Amministrazione (22/07/1993). *Processo di ristrutturazione dell'ILVA*. RP-05, Historical Archive of the European Union (HAEU).

11 Nota per il Consiglio di Amministrazione. IRI Spa Consiglio di Amministrazione (31/08/1993). *ILVA. Revisione del piano di risanamento e privatizzazione*, RP-05, Historical Archive of the European Union (HAEU).

12 Industry and Tourism Commission of Italian Senate, Document XVI, no.2, 13/11/1992. Reported in Cavazzuti (2013: 119).

13 Industry and Tourism Commission of Italian Senate, Document XVI, no.2, 13/11/1992.

14 Sole-24ORE, 17/11/1992.

15 Nota per il Consiglio di Amministrazione. IRI Spa Consiglio di Amministrazione (15/12/1993). *Procedure relative alla cessione delle società ILVA Laminati Piani e Acciai Speciali Terni,* RP-05, Historical Archive of the European Union (HAEU).

16 Law 474/1994 (article 2).

17 In Italian, in the notes for the meeting of the Board of Directors of IRI of the 15/12/1993. *"insindacabile giudizio"*. Nota per il Consiglio di Amministrazione. IRI Spa Consiglio di Amministrazione (15/12/1993). *Procedure relative alla cessione delle società ILVA Laminati Piani e Acciai Speciali Terni,* RP-05, Historical Archive of the European Union (HAEU).

18 CIPE 30/12/1992 (point 7).

19 A list of companies was created that included the Italian branch of Morgan Grenfell, Samuel Montagu, Kleinwort Benson, and the Italian companies Sopaf, Sofipa, and Cofilp e Akros. Nota per il Consiglio di Amministrazione. IRI Spa Consiglio di Amministrazione (15/12/1993). *Procedure relative alla cessione delle società ILVA Laminati Piani e Acciai Speciali Terni,* RP-05, Historical Archive of the European Union (HAEU): page 7.

20 Nota per il Consiglio di Amministrazione. IRI Spa Consiglio di Amministrazione (15/12/1993). *Procedure relative alla cessione delle società ILVA Laminati Piani e Acciai Speciali Terni,* RP-05, Historical Archive of the European Union (HAEU): page 7.

References

Affinito, A., De Cecco, M., & Dringoli, A. (2000). *Le privatizzazioni*. Roma: Donzelli Editore.

Cavazzuti, F. (2013). Le privatizzazioni: L'IRI tra parlamento, governo e dintorni. In R. Artoni (Ed.), *Storia dell'IRI*, Vol 4, (pp. 59–146). Bari: Editori Laterza.

Curli, F. (2013). Il "Vincolo Europeo": Le privatizzazioni dell'IRI tra Commissione Europea e governo Italiano. In R. Artoni (Ed.), *Storia dell'IRI*, Vol 4, (pp. 182–256). Bari: Editori Laterza.

Dringoli, A. (2000). Le privatizzazioni nel settore siderurgico. In Affinito, M., De Cecco, M., & Dringoli, A. (Ed), *Le privatizzazioni nell'industria manifatturiera italiana*. Donzelli Editore.

Ravazzi, P. (2013). Le privatizzazioni del gruppo e la liquidazione dell'IRI. Valutazioni, orientamenti, alternative. In R. Artoni (Ed.), *Storia dell'IRI*, Vol 4, (pp. 257–335). Bari: Editori Laterza.

Trentin, B. (1977). Relazione introduttiva al XV congresso nazionale della Fiom-Cgil. *Da sfruttati a produttori, lotte operaie e sviluppo*.

8   Stabilisation

As an appendix to the work described in the previous chapters, we also used Topic Modeling (Hannigan et al., 2019) to analyse about 70,000 newspaper articles about privatisations in Italy, as Topic Modeling is suited to deal with such big corpora of texts (DiMaggio et al., 2013). The scope of this endeavour was twofold: first, we were able to discuss a long stabilisation period in the steel industry after the privatisation season; second, we were able to enlarge our zoom and to take into account the whole public sphere, not only the segments focused on state steel. As for the state steel, our analysis sheds light on a long period of stabilisation (1996–2014), and also for fragmentation and settlement we were able to see the field through a different vantage point, as we now focus on a wider amount of data. More in general, this approach permitted us to describe the evolution of the overarching public debate regarding privatisations in Italy.

8.1 Topic modeling

Before processing data, we had to clean our textual sources to improve the quality of our results (Hannigan et al., 2019); as data were already in .txt format, we only removed special characters from texts. Then, we developed a stopword list, which is the list of all the words that are not meaningful, and must not be analysed, as they would add noise to the results. Typically, this list includes articles, pronouns, adverbs, and the like (Hannigan et al., 2019). Also, we decided to avoid the lemmatisation of words, as this technical step outdistances the topics from the original corpus, which can be counterproductive for the inductive interpretation of topics (Ferri et al., 2020). After removing stopwords, our corpus of 67,086 articles consisted of 22,411,532 words, with the longest articles being composed of 21,079 words. For analysing our data with Topic Modeling, we used Mallet (McCallum, 2002), a state-of-the-art software (Hannigan et al., 2019).

A sensitive decision regards the number of topics to be elicited by the software. Some scholars define the value based on metrics, such as

DOI: 10.4324/9780429438516-8

coherence (Schmiedel et al., 2019), or perplexity score (Fligstein et al., 2017). Nonetheless, not only are these measures usually not concordant, but research also describes how topic models, which are better from the point of view of these measures, are not always the best models according to the judgment of human experts (Chang & Blei, 2009). The reason is that Topic Models act like a lens that reduces complexity for analytical reasons (DiMaggio et al., 2013), and a computational best is not necessarily the best for interpretability, since "all models are wrong, but some are useful" (Box & Wilkinson, 1979: 202). Actually, DiMaggio et al. (2013: 582) say that "when topic modeling is used to identify themes and assist in interpretation [...], there is no statistical test for the optimal number of topics", so they suggest selecting the number of topics based on interpretative purposes. Therefore, we prioritised interpretability and saliency over the development of a formal – but not necessarily useful – measure (Grimmer & Stewart, 2013) and, following a standard qualitative procedure, we developed models with 15, 20, 25, 30, 35, and 40 topics. We then assessed three main outputs to examine the quality of each model (Ferri et al., 2020):

1. A list of the most important words for each topic, which is defined based on the prevalence of each word in a topic over the prevalence of that word in the entire corpus.
2. A matrix where rows are the original textual sources and columns are the topics. This matrix details the percentual contribution of each topic to each article.
3. A detailed list of the coding of each word in the corpus.

For each model, we independently analysed the aforementioned items, and each author read at least the ten most representative articles per topic. A discussion followed, to identify the model with the greater interpretive power. It was soon apparent that topic models with more than 25 topics presented topics that were very similar to each other, while models with less than 20 topics resulted in bags of words that were too aggregated, thus mixing different meanings. Therefore, we also developed the models with 21, 22, 23, and 24 topics, and went through another iterative and inductive cycle of analysis and testing, similar to the one described above. After an autonomous interpretation, followed by discussions among the authors, we ended up selecting the 23 topics.

In the following step, we engaged again with the most important outputs of the 23 topics model: we report in Table 8.1 the ten most representative words for each topic, together with a descriptive label, which we induced based mainly on Topic Modeling's output.[1] We also run descriptive analyses to better understand data: we identified, in particular, the average prevalence of each topic in our corpus, which describes the presence of each topic across the sample. Large topics represent recurrent themes, while smaller topics represent niche themes (Ferri et al., 2020).

8.1.1 Clusters of topic

Topics in Table 8.1 are presented according to the ID produced by the software, but this order has no substantive meaning. Therefore, we make sense of the topic models by describing a second-order clustering, which we performed as a result of our inductive phase.

A general and expected result is that topics are ontologically different (DiMaggio et al., 2013): while some topics can elicit discourses, others just point at specific themes. Therefore, aware of this feature of topics, we clustered the topics in higher-order thematic clusters. In Table 8.2, the first column details the cluster of topics, the second column lists the inductively developed labels, and the third details the prevalence of each topic. The cluster *Industries* collects topics dealing with the privatisation of specific industries; the cluster *Economics* groups topics dealing with the economic effects of privatisations; the category *Governance* has to do with topics that tackle the governance of the privatisation process. *Geography* collects topics used to refer to privatisations in other countries, while *Technical issues* deals with topics about the technicalities of privatisations. *Resistance* collects topics dealing with the protests against privatisations. Finally, the category *Other* collects topics that cannot be clustered in any of the previous groups. As we elicited 23 topics, if all of them were used in the same way, all the topics would account for about 4.3% of all the words in our corpus (1,000/23=4.3%). Nonetheless, by analysing the average prevalence, we notice that some topics are used more than others: these topics constitute wide discourses, which tend to fill a great number of articles. Conversely, niche topics are seldom used and tend to be used only in articles specifically dealing with the issues represented by those topics (Ferri et al., 2018). In our case, topics in the cluster *Economics* are used above average, thus constituting diffused discourse, while it is the opposite for topics within the cluster *Geography*, which indeed are used only for articles dealing with these foreign countries. Topics in the cluster *Technical issues* are smaller, while in the cluster *Resistance* there are two small topics and two big ones. After Table 8.2, we describe in more detail the topics pertaining to the cluster *Industries* and *Resistance*.

8.1.1.1 Industries

TOPIC 10 – TRANSPORTATIONS

Topic 10 is used in articles reporting the debate and the proposals regarding the privatisation of public transportation. Among the most

Table 8.1 Ten most important words per topic²

Topic 0 – Italian economy and privatisations as a tool of industrial policy	Italian	governo, debito, economia, crescita, anno, italia, pil, spesa, miliardi, inflazione
	English	government, debt, economy, growth, year, Italy, pil, expense, billions, inflation
Topic 1 – Privatisation and economic reforms in Russia	Italian	russia, dollari, economia, governo, paese, mosca, milioni, presidente, eltsin, ministro
	English	Russia, dollars, economy, government, country, Moscow, millions, president, Yeltsin, minister
Topic 2 – Local services and municipal utilities	Italian	comune, sindaco, regione, privatizzazione, milano, acqua, locali, milioni, servizi, gestione
	English	municipality, mayor, region, privatisation, Milan, water, locals, millions, services, management
Topic 3 – Investment funds	Italian	obb, bond, italia, azionario, europa, monetario, america obbligazionario, oasi, sanpaolo
	English	bond, bond, Italy, equity, Europe, monetary, America, bond, oasis, sanpaolo
Topic 4 – Stigma privatisations	Italian	anni, grande, tempo, mondo, storia, paese, potere, crisi, ormai, politica
	English	years, great, time, world, history, country, power, crisis, now, policy
Topic 5 – Labour and unions	Italian	lavoro, sindacati, lavoratori, dipendenti, cgil, riforma, governo, pubblico, personale, sindacato
	English	work, labour unions, workers, employees, cgil, reform, government, public, personal, trade union
Topic 6 – Stock market chronicles	Italian	borsa, mercato, titoli, azioni, investitori, prezzo, mercati, affari, piazza, lire
	English	stock, market, titles, actions, investors, price, markets, business, square, lire
Topic 7 – Public management of SOEs	Italian	presidente, consiglio, direttore, generale, amministratore, delegato, amministrazione, nuovo, assemblea, roma
	English	president, council, director, general, administrator, delegate,

(Continued)

Table 8.1 (Continued)

		administration, new, assembly, Rome
Topic 8 – Protests, students, and the civil society	Italian	contro, scuola, città, piazza, studenti, privatizzazione, centro, cultura, beni, persone
	English	against, school, city, square, students, privatisation, centre, culture, goods, people
Topic 9 – Economics of privatised firms	Italian	miliardi, milioni, anno, lire, netto, utile, bilancio, euro, pari, capitale
	English	billions, millions, year, lire, net, profit, balance, euro, even, capital
Topic 10 – Transportation	Italian	alitalia, compagnia, privatizzazione, societ, autostrade, milioni, piano, aeroporti, air, trasporti
	English	alitalia, company, privatisation, company, highways, millions, plan, airports, air, transport
Topic 11 – Manufacturing firms	Italian	gruppo, iri, miliardi, societa, eni, azienda, finmeccanica, sme, settore, privatizzazione
	English	group, iri, billions, society, eni, company, finmeccanica, sme, sector, privatisation
Topic 12 – Italian politics and italian parties	Italian	governo, politica, partito, maggioranza, sinistra, berlusconi, elezioni, presidente, elettorale, partiti
	English	government, policy, party, majority, left, berlusconi, elections, president, electoral, parties
Topic 13 – Privatisations and international competition	Italian	imprese, italia, sviluppo, mercato, investimenti, settore, paesi, europa, anni, paese
	English	businesses, italy, development, market, investments, sector, countries, Europe, years, country
Topic 14 – Microhistories of privatisations	Italian	società, già, così, può, cento, però, attività, cioé, dovrà, possibilità
	English	society, already, so, can, one hundred, however, activities, that is, will have to, possibility
Topic 15 – Legal technical vocabulary	Italian	articolo, legge, decreto, comma, enti, dicembre, ministero, entro, anno, presente
	English	article, law, decree, paragraph, entities, December, ministry, within, year, current
Topic 16 – Telecommunications and utilities	Italian	telecom, enel, mercato, energia, societ, italia, rete,

(*Continued*)

Table 8.1 (Continued)

	English	telecomunicazioni, privatizzazione, stet
	English	telecom, enel, market, power, company, Italy, network, telecommunications, privatisation, stet
Topic 17 – The credit system	Italian	banca, banche, mediobanca, istituto, credito, capitale, banco, gruppo, azionisti, comit
	English	bank, banks, mediobanca, institute, credit, capital, banco, group, shareholders, comit
Topic 18 – Laws, decrees, and the Parliament	Italian	legge, commissione, camera, senato, esame, corte, decreto, riforma, governo, approvato
	English	law, commission, chamber, senate, exam, court, decree, reform, government, approved
Topic 19 – Privatisations in Europe	Italian	francese, gruppo, parigi, franchi, francia, miliardi, governo, privatizzazione, francesi, germania
	English	French, group, Paris, francs, France, billions, government, privatisation, Germany
Topic 20 – Privatisations in the rest of the World	Italian	dollari, milioni, usa, londra, miliardi, anno, governo, anni, sterline, british
	English	dollars, millions, USA, London, billions, year, government, years, pounds, British
Topic 21 – Values of developmental state	Italian	mercato, sistema, pubblico, imprese, pubblica, politica, controllo, gestione, servizi, caso
	English	market, system, public, enterproses, public, policy, control, management, services, case
Topic 22 – Governance of the privatisation process	Italian	governo, ministro, tesoro, iri, privatizzazione, privatizzazioni, consiglio, presidente, roma, piano
	English	government, minister, treasure, iri, privatisation, privatisations, council, president, Rome, plan

relevant words, we find the names of the companies to be privatised, such as *Alitalia*, *FS* (national railway), *Tirrenia* (ferry). We also find the words *highways*, *airports*, *port*, *transport*, and *railways*, together with the names of firms involved in the privatisation process.

Table 8.2 Clusters of topics, topics, and their average prevalence (1984–2014)

Cluster	Topic	Average Prevalence
Industries	Topic 10 – Transportations	4.0%
	Topic 11 – Manufacturing firms	3.8%
	Topic 16 – Telecommunications and utilities	3.9%
	Topic 17 – The credit system	4.6%
	Topic 2 – Local services and municipal utilities	4.3%
Economics	Topic 9 – Economics of privatised firms	4.7%
	Topic 0 – Italian economy and privatisations as a tool of industrial policy	5.7%
	Topic 13 – Privatisations and international competition	5.8%
Governance	Topic 22 – Governance of the privatisation process	7.6%
	Topic 12 – Italian politics and Italian parties	4.3%
	Topic 7 – Public management of SOEs	3.4%
Geography	Topic 1 – Privatisation and economic reforms in Russia	3.4%
	Topic 19 – Privatisations in Europe	3.4%
	Topic 20 – Privatisations in the rest of the world	3.2%
Technical issues	Topic 3 – Investment funds	0.7%
	Topic 15 – Legal technical vocabulary	2.6%
	Topic 18 – Laws, decrees, and the Parliament	2.7%
	Topic 6 – Stock market chronicles	5.4%
Resistance	Topic 5 – Labour and unions	3.8%
	Topic 8 – Protests, students, and the civil society	3.1%
	Topic 21 – Values of developmental state	8.1%
	Topic 4 – Stigma privatisations	6.3%
Other	Topic 14 – Microhistories of privatisations	4.7%

TOPIC 11 – MANUFACTURING FIRMS

This topic is used for discussing the privatisation of state-owned industrial manufacturing firms, and of the enterprises controlled by these gigantic industrial holdings: for example, one of the most relevant articles starts with the sentence "During the last year, ENI sold 27 firms, earning 833 billion. The selling of other 54 smaller controlled firms is underway".[3] Among the most relevant words for this topic are the names of the firms, such as *IRI, ENI, Finmeccanica, Sme,* and *ILVA,* together with words referring to economic issues, such as *billions, revenue,* and *financial.*

TOPIC 16 – TELECOMMUNICATIONS AND UTILITIES

Topic 16 is used for discussing privatisations of telecommunication infrastructure and services, and to deal with the privatisation of state-owned utilities. In the list of the most relevant words are names of the firms, such as *ENEL, Stet, Rai, Poste, Eni,* and *Telecom,* and words related to the utilities being discussed, such as *energy, natural gas, electricity,* and *tlc,* together with words referring to economic issues.

TOPIC 17 – THE CREDIT SYSTEM

This topic deals with privatisations and/of the credit system, as both are used to emphasise the role of the banks in the privatisation process and to describe their privatisations. Indeed, the names of banks are among the most relevant words: *mediobanca, istituto, credito, banco, san paolo, generali*, and *cariplo*. In this list we also find *comit*, known also as Banca Commerciale Italiana (or BCI), which was a bank owned by IRI since 1934. This institution was particularly relevant as a lender to the iron and steel industry and was finally privatised in 1999.

TOPIC 2 – LOCAL SERVICES AND MUNICIPAL UTILITIES

This topic is used to deal with the privatisation of local services and local public utilities, run by municipalities, such as water, local public transportation, and the management of waste. One of the most representative articles for this topic deals with an offer, by two private firms, to manage eight municipal graveyards in Florence for 25 years, while up to that moment it was the municipality in charge for the cemeteries. Among the most relevant words for this topic we find references to the political apical roles at the local level: *mayor, municipality, regional local government, province, president, local*, and *council*.

8.1.1.2 Resistance

TOPIC 5 – LABOUR AND UNIONS

Topic 5 is used mainly in articles discussing the union's position on privatisations. Protests, strikes, and resistance to privatisations are described through this topic, also in relation to retirement and the privatisations of specific Social Security schemes. Among the most representative words are *work, unions, employees, strike, pension*, and the name of the most important labour unions (*CGIL, UIL,* and *CISL*).

TOPIC 8 – PROTESTS, STUDENTS, AND THE CIVIL SOCIETY

This topic is mostly used to report demonstrations against privatisations: while the emphasis of topic 5 is on unions, topic 8 focuses on students and on the civil society in general. Several papers report rallies against the "privatization of knowledge", as protesters wanted the university system to remain completely public. Among the most important words are *against, school, students, privatisation, centre, culture, university, citizens, movements*, and *manifestations*.

TOPIC 21 – VALUES OF DEVELOPMENTAL STATE

This topic is mostly used in opinion articles that promote the character-istics of Developmental State, where industrial activity and economy are partly regulated by the State. Therefore, this topic emphasises the good values of state control over economics. A quote by one of the most re-levant articles says, indeed, that "public administration exists because it permits safeguarding the interests of the whole society, and not the ones of individual persons only. Objectives to be met are social ones, and often only state-owned organisations can pursue these objectives". Also, from another article, "the aim of the state-owned enterprise – whether it is in the condition of oligopoly or monopoly – is not profit only, as it is the case for private firms. The aim is much more general, and economists call it social well-being: as public and private firms have different aims, they necessary have different behaviours". Among the most important words are *system, public, enterprises, society, interest, state, community, control, system, intervention,* and *politics*.

TOPIC 4 – STIGMA PRIVATISATIONS

This topic is often used in opinion articles that do not necessarily deal with economic issues only, but more generally, discuss societal condi-tions through a historicised perspective. Also, we find articles written by literary authors or interviews with movie directors and intellectuals in general. Privatisations appear, in these articles, just to be stigmatised. We find words with a humanistic flavour, such as *history, world, country, scope, capitalism, family, home, power,* and *policy*.

8.2 Validation: privatisation of specific industries

In order to validate our model, and check the soundness of our inter-pretation, we focus on predictive validation (Grimmer & Stewart, 2013): the idea is to see whether particular topics respond in predictable ways to news events that should affect their prevalence, if our interpretations are correct (DiMaggio et al, 2013). In particular, as trend plays a crucial role in the interpretive process (Ferri et al., 2020), we analyse the evolution over time of the topics referring to the privatisation of specific industries. Figure 8.1 reports the prevalence trend over time for these topics. It's good to see that the evolution of the presence of each topic in the debate reflects the actual privatisation process that took place in Italy; for example, topic 10, Transportation, has a clear peak in 2008, when the privatisation of Alitalia, the Italian airline company, was discussed in the Italian discursive space. The ruling government decided to privatise Alitalia at the beginning of 2007, but the tender offer failed due to lack of possible buyers. In 2007, the administrators approved a survival plan

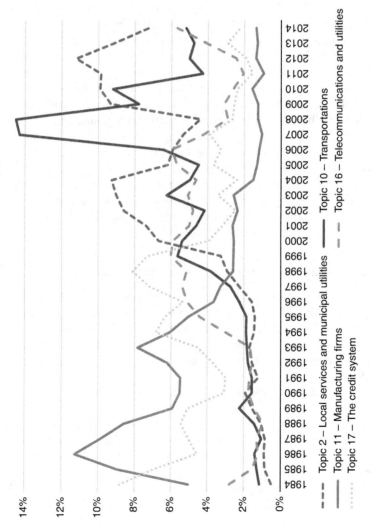

Figure 8.1 Trends for the topics referring to privatisations of specific industries

for Alitalia. Nonetheless, at the end of 2007, a second attempt to proceed to privatisation occurred, and Air France-KLM, Lufthansa, and other enterprises were involved. In 2008, the offer by Air France-KLM was accepted. This offer was conditioned to some terms, among which was a deal that had to be approved by unions. Alitalia's privatisation was a key issue during the 2008 political campaign, with all the parties involved in the debate. The agreement, however, failed and on the 21st of April 2008, the offer by Air France was withdrawn by its CEO.

Similarly, also the other trends reflect what happened in the Italian public sphere and political debate: the first and most debated industry corresponds to topic 11, manufacturing firms, which has a peak in 1996, and a smaller one in 1993. Topic 17, which refers to banks, has a peak in 1984, which reflects the role played by banks in other privatisation processes. Then, in 1998, another peak occurs, which refers to the privatisation of the banking system itself. Topic 16, which refers to telecommunications and utilities, has had a plateau since 1996 for about 10 years. In 2004, there is the first peak for local services' privatisation (topic 2 – local services and municipal utilities). This topic will have a greater peak in 2012. This progressive development of privatisations in the public discourse unveils a path that starts by privatising firms that hardly can be protected from privatisation by politicians, as they are burdened by debts and bad managing: this is the case for the manufacturing firms. Also, the first industries to be privatised are the ones where privatisations' effects are less tangible for citizens: only when privatisations get to be legitimised as a means of the industrial economy, also industries where privatisation directly impact citizens will be privatised: this is the case with transportation (topic 10), but also with local services and municipal utilities (topic 2).

8.3 Resistance to privatisations in public discourse

Even if privatisations were eventually performed in the time range under analysis, Topic Modeling permits us to trace the evolution of the forms of discursive resistance to privatisations in the Italian discursive sphere (Hardy & Maguire, 2012). We grouped in the cluster *resistance* four topics where the confrontation against the privatisation process takes different shapes.

Topic 5, Labour and unions and topic 8, Protests, students, and the civil society are two small topics that deal with protests by organised groups of workers and by citizens and students. Topic 21, Values of developmental State and topic 4, Stigma privatisations are bigger topics that have to do less with the stories of specific events and strikes and more with values and ideas.

Figure 8.2 presents the trends over for the former two topics. As for topic 5, there is no clear trend in the 30 years under analysis, as the eight

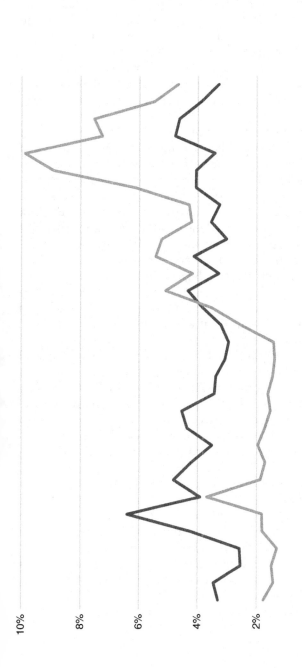

Figure 8.2 Trends over time for topic 2, local services and municipal utilities and topic 8, protests, students, and the civil society

peaks follow one another, although the highest one is in 1989, and is followed by other two peaks in 1991 and 1995. Indeed, the number of strikes increased dramatically starting in 1985 until the end of the decade (Balconi, 1991: 464) and this increase is reflected in the topics debated in the public sphere. As for the protests by citizens, the prevalence of topic 8 exceeds topic 5 in 2001, and after that year topic 8 becomes more and more prevalent, until reaching its maximum exposure between 2009 and 2012. There are several events that explain this trend: the most important one is a series of four referendums, held in 2011; two of the four questions concerned the repeal of laws regarding the privatisation of water services and the criteria to determine the price for the water. The debate around these questions was very heated in the months before the consultation.

Also, at the end of the first decade of the new millennium, different reforms started questioning and changing the traditional funding and organisation of public education. The most important of these reforms is probably the Gelmini Law (2010), which profoundly changed the organisational structure of the university, the career paths for researchers, and the curricula offered to students. Two years before, on the 6th of August 2008, law number 133 opened the way for the transformation of the public universities in private foundations, with the transfer to these foundations of all the previously state-owned infrastructures. Also, in the same period, several reforms targeted high school. An increasing trend for topic 8 in these years reports the increasing number of articles dealing with protests by students against the "privatization of knowledge", and also by citizens supporting the idea that water is a "common good", and its supply cannot be delegated to market laws.

Topic 4, stigma privatisations, and topic 21, values of developmental State are used to voice resistance to privatisations in a way that is less connected to reports of specific events. These two topics differ according to the period in which they arise, the words they are composed of, the meanings they bear upon, and the shared consciousness they refer to. By focusing on these two topics, we now focus on how different vocabularies can be used to resist privatisations in different phases of institutional change.

Figure 13 shows the respective prevalence of both topics in our corpus over time: values of developmental state is more prevalent from 1984 to 2003, while since that moment stigma privatisations becomes more present in the debate. The discourse built around topic 21, values of developmental state opposes privatisations from a theoretical and value-based point of view: it is used in opinion articles and editorials that support state intervention in the economy and that tackle neo-liberalism. These articles explicitly refer to the organisation of the state, and the words that constitute the vocabulary used by this topic and that compose the discourse against privatisations speak to the socioeconomic theory: *public, control, management, society, rules, government,* and *state.* An example of the use of this discourse in context is provided by the following quote, which is extracted from one of the most representative articles for this topic. Here, the author of the editorial, a journalist working for *Il Sole 24 Ore,* warns against possible backlashes due to the retirement of the State from the involvement in industrial production: "Privatization policy wants to free firms and markets from the presumption of the state of being able to create social benefits [leveraging industrial production]. Nonetheless, we must decide whether this is the only objective to be pursued, or if we want to pursue the aim, stated by the Italian Constitution, of a balance between freedom for the firms and attention to positive outcomes for the whole society". This topic is used by those that want to preserve the role of the state in the economy, even if privatisations will be performed, as another quote by a journalist confirms: "Create strong regulatory agencies is very important if privatizations must be performed: the state must shift from property of public utilities to a strong role of control". On the same line of thought is the intervention of a politician, that highlights the importance of performing an effective control of firms operating in industries where the public interest is strong: "in other countries, organizational forms exist, for private firms, where managers can be identified as responsible of specific activities of the firms. This is very important for firms operating in industries where the public interest is involved".

Topic 21 embodies the resistance toward privatisations during the first years of the period under analysis. Nonetheless, resistance to privatisations is not successful, and while privatisations are performed, also the discourse that opposes them through the values of the developmental state loses traction. Starting at the beginning of the new millennium, and more effectively since 2003, another discourse becomes the most important for opposing neo-liberal values and privatisations. Within articles built especially through topic 4, the words *privatisations* and *privatisation* do not appear in technical or economic articles anymore. Conversely, the term *privatisation* is now part of a wider societal vocabulary, which is used in a panoply of contexts, which are not often related to the economic and political fields. Through the use of Topic 4, stigma privatisations, resistance materialises in articles that deal with literature, movies, theatre, or other cultural fields, and where any sort of influential intellectual can define privatisations as something that ruined societal cohesion and society in general. Through this topic influential speakers, such as film directors or literary authors, blame privatisations. An example is an interview with Mauro Corona, a successful Italian author of books, who speaks about Vajont, a region where in 1963 a massive landslide, due to failures in a dam, caused a man-made tsunami that destroyed several villages and towns and killed 1,917 people. The

Italian electrical company and the Italian government dismissed evidence: "they did not learn from Vajont [the government]. After losing the biggest lake in the region, they sacked the Sacred River of the Homeland; they bled it dry through pipes and dams. And, worst, they privatized here water, the single most important resources for the country". In the same vein, we find interviews with foreign authors, blaming privatisations, such as the Chilean Luis Sepulveda: "troubles, for Argentina, started with dictatorship, that imported neoliberalism and wild industrialization. Privatizations impoverished regions that used to be rich. [...] I remember Rosario: that city had a quality of life similar to the one of Paris. Now it is as poor as some Mexican cities...". Another explicative quote is from the literary author Paolo Rumiz, who discusses the backlashes of privatisations, while describing a report in Romania: "this is the consequence of the Big Fraud: industrialization forced by Stalinism, fraud-privatizations during post communism, market forces that deprives towns faster than the planned economy: now Romania has no more industries, nor fields". Finally, another example is a quote from director Ken Loach, in a long retrospective interview: "then Thachter arrived. And with her, her politics arrived, composed of liberalism without rules, wild privatizations, uncontrolled favors to firms, unions' ruin. If I look back at myself in those years, I see a poor man, in his tie, desperately searching for money for my screenplays. My movies were a taboo".

Trends of topics over the years tell us that Developmental State became delegitimised in the public debate, as it was not possible to support it in public utterances by journalists and politicians. But resistance to privatisations did not disappear: it just changed shape, vocabulary, and vocal actors. Intellectuals and artists, endowed with symbolic capital, were more free to oppose privatisations. Starting from 2003, topic 4 is the most used in discourses against privatisations (Figure 8.3).

8.4   A long stabilisation

The beginning of the new millennium, and especially the year 2003, is a key temporal milestone regarding the discourse around privatisations in the public sphere in Italy. Beginning from 2003, the discursive resistance to privatisations ceases to be conveyed through the values of the developmental state, as the discourse that resists privatisations is framed within a wider and more general topic. Before 2003, it was still possible, for the political elite and in general within the mainstream media, to despise privatisations. The political elite framed the mounting privatisation wave as an undiscriminating attack on the developmental state, being the bulk of the political and economic power of the Italian economy since the Second World War. In particular, from this point of view, the specific historical economic development of Italy legitimised

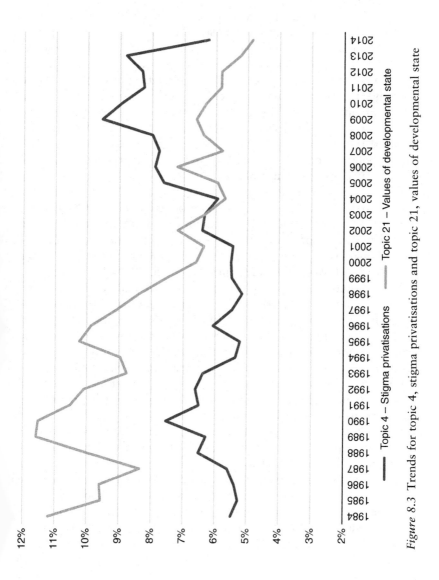

Figure 8.3 Trends for topic 4, stigma privatisations and topic 21, values of developmental state

the role of the state as an entrepreneur. Nonetheless, the discourse on developmental state lost its strength, also because of the vast anti-bribery investigation known as *mani pulite* (clean hands) or *Tangentopoli* (City of bribes), which are the names that journalists gave to this system based on bribery that involved large parts of the political leading class in the previous decade. In addition, the unfolding of the privatisations, the larger part of which was completed with the end of the 1990s, took out economic capital from political elites. The resistance to privatisations that hinged on the rhetoric on the developmental state weakened and was marginalised with the loss of economic, social, and symbolic capital by the political elite.

On the other hand, a new discourse animated the resistance to privatisation. This discourse mobilised the frame based on topic 4, stigma privatisations. Intellectuals, who were disconnected by the social and economic capital that the privatisation wave was dismantling, supporting the discourse grounded on the Privatisations' Stigma. More precisely, intellectuals from all over the world reprised the discourse against privatisation, mobilising their symbolic capital grounded on the cultural capital. In Gramscian terms, a hegemony was in place that determined a state of relative stability in which not only the dominant class aligned political control, through State apparatus, and economic control of material resources, but molded the discourse in the civil society as well, claiming mutuality of interests. Oppressed social actors cannot attempt to directly overturn relations of productions without having first recognised their own interests as separate from those of the hegemonic class. This process of consciousness needs to be preceded by intellectual critique (Gramsci, 1975) into the cultural superstructure to erode the stabilised intellectual and moral unity (Gramsci, 1975: 458).

Privatisations are a series of policy interventions that revolutionised economies all over the world. As a consequence, often entrenched political elites were, at least partially, dismantled. Their legitimisation, their political connections, and the economic power that they derived from the control of large portions of economies were damaged, if not destroyed. Moreover, the privatisation movement deprived public discourse of a rich repertoire of frames previously employed. Nowadays, especially in Western countries, hardly anyone can be found who overtly supports the argument for nationalising sectors of the economy. In the sense of Bourdieu (1991), a pedagogic discourse is hegemonic that associates private ownership with efficiency and that weakens discourses that resist such a hegemonic narrative. We highlighted two specific topics that convey discourses against privatisations. In particular, we observe that the discourse on the virtues of the developmental state, which was grounded on economic and social capital, lost its strength. On the other hand, we discovered that the issue fields protected by cultural capital were able to accommodate and preserve the discourse against privatisation. Although relegated in not-technical fields, and often referred to as the daydreams of idealistic intellectuals, discourse against privatisation resisted. The prestige of intellectuals as Ken Loach or Luis Sepulveda preserved words and vocabularies that could be used to animate the discourse against privatisations.

Notes

1 For sake of space, in this chapter we will not describe all the topics, as we will focus only on those that validate our analysis (topics referring to the privatisation of other industries), and on those that are essential to our description (topics where resistance to privatisations materialises). For the same reason, we present only ten words per topic. More data are available on request to the authors.

2 Original words are in Italian, so we added an English translation for each word. Topic order has no meaning in this table.

3 All the quotes were originally in Italian, so we translated them for the sake of understandability.

References

Balconi, M. (1991). La siderurgia italiana (1945–1990). Bologna: Il Mulino.

Bourdieu, P. (1991). *Language and symbolic power*. Harvard University Press.

Box, G. E. P., Launer, R. L., & Wilkinson, G. N. (1979). Robustness in the strategy of scientific model building. In Launer, RL and Wilkinson, GN (Eds.) *Robustness in Statistics* (pp. 201–236). New York: Academic Press.

Chang, J., & Blei, D. M. (2009). Relational topic models for document networks. *Journal of Machine Learning Research*, 5: 81–88.

DiMaggio, P., Nag, M., & Blei, D. (2013). Exploiting affinities between topic modeling and the sociological perspective on culture: Application to newspaper coverage of U.S. government arts funding. *Poetics*, 41(6): 570–606. 10.1016/j.poetic.2013.08.004

Ferri, P., Lusiani, M., & Pareschi, L. (2018). Accounting for Accounting History: A topic modeling approach (1996–2015). *Accounting History*, 23(1–2). 10.1177/1032373217740707

Ferri, P., Lusiani, M., & Pareschi, L. (2020). Shades of theory: A topic modelling of ways of theorizing in accounting history research. *Accounting History*, 26(3): 484–519. 10.1177/1032373220964271

Fligstein, N., & McAdam, D. (2011). Toward a general theory of strategic action fields. *Sociological Theory*, 29(1): 1–26.

Fligstein, N., Stuart Brundage, J., & Schultz, M. (2017). Seeing like the Fed: Culture, cognition, and framing in the failure to anticipate the financial crisis of 2008. *American Sociological Review*, 82(5): 879–909. https://doi.org/10.11 77/0003122417728240

Gramsci, A. (1975). *Quaderni dal carcere* (G. E. Editore (Ed.)). International Publishers.

Grimmer, J., & Stewart, B. M. (2013). Text as Data: The promise and pitfalls of automatic content analysis methods for political texts. *Political Analysis*, 21(3): 267–297. DOI: 10.1093/pan/mps028

Hannigan, T. R., Haan, R. F. J., Vakili, K., Tchalian, H., Glaser, V. L., Wang, M. S., Kaplan, S., & Jennings, P. D. (2019). Topic modeling in management research: Rendering new theory from textual data. *Academy of Management Annals*, 13(2): 586–632.

Hardy, C., & Maguire, S. (2012). Institutional entrepreneurship. In *The Sage handbook of organizational institutionalism* (pp. 198–217). SAGE Publications Ltd. 10.4135/9781849200387.n8

McCallum, A. K. (2002). *MALLET: A machine learning for language toolkit.* http://mallet.cs.umass.edu

Schmiedel, T., Müller, O., & vom Brocke, J. (2019). Topic modeling as a strategy of inquiry in organizational research: A tutorial with an application example on organizational culture. *Organizational Research Methods*, 22(4): 941–968. 10.1177/1094428118773858

9 Conclusion

9.1 The pedagogy and rhetoric of privatisations

In the 1980s and in the 1990s, the period in which the facts that we report occurred, the global diffusion of neo-liberal economic policies, as crystallised in the 1990 so-called Washington Consensus, initiated a heated political and cultural battle. The Washington Consensus, as christened by the economist John Williamson at the Institute for International Economics (1993), constituted the typical package of economic policies that the International Monetary Fund (IMF), the World Bank, and the U.S. Department of the Treasury considered to be propaedeutic to recover economies in crisis. The set of policies included, among others, trade liberalisation, liberalisation of inward foreign direct investment, privatisation of state enterprises, and deregulation.

Despite being primarily directed at restructuring economies in third-world countries, the Washington Consensus came to crystallise the very substance of neo-liberal policies, and the label – Washington Consensus – became the signifier of the hegemonic neo-liberal ideology.

Initially embraced by the Reagan and Thatcher governments, respectively in the USA and United Kingdom, the neo-liberal ideology, which was behind the Washington Consensus, diffused globally to build up what Wilks called the "fairy-tale" of the TINA (There Is No Alternative) (2013: 255), and the hegemonic discourse on the thaumaturgical properties of markets and on the market economy as the highest level of civilisation available for humankind (Fukuyama, 1992). This hegemonic discourse weakened the shared consciousness that considered state ownership as a naturalised institution. Mobilising these principles, Mazzuccato (2013) suggests, "the State has been attacked and increasingly dismantled, through its bureaucratic, inertial, heavy-handed character". This cultural shock was particularly strong in those countries, like Italy, in which the role of the state as the backbone of the economy of the country was particularly well-entrenched.

As Feigenbaum, Henig, and Hamnett argue (1998; Feigenbaum & Henig, 1994), the privatisation issue may be framed in different ways.

DOI: 10.4324/9780429438516-9

First, privatisations may be thought of as a taken-for-granted pragmatic solution to immediate problems (: 44). Second, they might be interpreted as "tactical", when they occur in situations that are directly, if not necessarily overtly, political and are intended for the short-term political interests of those backing the policy (: 46). Finally, privatisations may be presented as "systemic", when they are ideological in their origins and the most widespread in their intended impact and, rather than being a solution to a discrete number of specific problems, systemic privatisation aims at permanently changing power structures, institutions, values, and culture (: 50–51).

Following this scheme, in Europe, we argue, the framing of privatisations integrated a systemic and a pragmatic framing. Systemic framing, as for example in the United Kingdom during Thatcher's government, depicted privatisations as policy interventions aimed at a deep transformation and, supposedly, modernisation of the economy. Pragmatic framing reconstructed privatisation policy as the natural avenue to follow to restructuring financial budgets in bad conditions.

The concentration of symbolic capital, that is the legitimisation and the right to speak (Bourdieu, 1991), in the hands of the champions of neo-liberal principles, contributed to the deployment of a form of "symbolic violence", that is, a gentle, invisible form of violence (Bourdieu, 1977). This monopoly of symbolic capital in economic literature allowed advocates of neo-liberal policies to transform policy-making into a pedagogic practice (Bourdieu & Passeron, 1977; Oakes et al., 1998) in a way "that diminishes the possibility of resisting because the process appears neutral and normal, 'technical'" (Oakes et al., 1998: 272).

Because of the pedagogical normalisation of the battlefield, it was possible to make a vested inculcation of privatisations as the "right" solution to the deleterious involvement of politicians in state-owned enterprises. Yet, once constituted, this ideological order tended to reproduce itself globally through a process of naturalisation that depicted the transition from state to private ownership as an irreversible and unquestionable process, a purely technical exercise to be globally applied independently of idiosyncratic institutional arrangements.

In this book, we analysed how this globally spreading narrative, and connected political order, interplayed with locally entrenched economic relations and political and cultural structures. By investigating these structures at the local level, the book made an effort to emphasise the rhetorical and political components of economics. What is often described as a context-neutral and globally indisputable technical solution is the outcome of intense, context-dependent, discursive, and political battles that dramatically rearrange local economic relations.

9.2 Using Gramscian theory of hegemony for explaining local variations in globally spreading policies

In his 1971 paper, Davis (1971) described the logical underpinning of interesting theories in social sciences. Among the others, one of the features that differentiate interesting theorising is the capability to elicit the local or general nature of phenomena. Namely, through the process of *lòcalisation*, an interesting theory may explain how "[w]hat seems to be a general phenomenon is in reality a local phenomenon" (1971: 317). In our research, we take issue with the rhetoric that looks at privatisation as a desirable technique to be applied generally. More importantly, we aim at emphasising the dramatic political implications of privatisations. These implications, we argue, need to be carefully investigated in order to design privatisation programmes.

For the sake of completeness, it is fair to say that within the entourage of those who embraced this "privatization mantra", some made an effort to explain how local outcomes may depend on the features of political and administrative structures and processes. In addition, global consulting firms showed their skills to select from a panoply of privatisation techniques, each supposedly more adapted to the specific local context.

Yet, in this book, our specific aim is to demonstrate that to fully capture and anticipate the outcomes and the unfolding of privatisation processes, social scientists need to approach privatisations as a local phenomenon that activates locally entrenched symbolic, material, and political structures. Put in Davis' words, the outcome of privatisations is a local phenomenon. Despite globally spreading cultural and political pressures influenced, and still influence, how policies are locally applied, and often produce the main trigger for such policies, the consequences of such policies can be understood only by looking at the local tangle of power relations.

Taking this perspective, in this book, we suggest that the Gramscian theory of hegemony, and in particular the concept of the *historical bloc*, provide a useful conceptual framework for investigating the idiosyncratic configuration of local variation of globally spreading policies.

More specifically, within our theoretical construction, we used the concept of the historical bloc to explain why and how do countries privatise their industries. We suggest that it is important to make available a theory that diverges from, and provides an alternative explanation to, mainstream analysis of privatisation processes. The topic has been widely explored in the economic literature. Recurring arguments for privatising state-owned firms refer to the increased efficiency of the incentives brought about by private ownership in competitive markets (Bos, 1991: 7; Vickers & Yarrow, 1997: 9), to the control on management operated through capital markets (Vickers & Yarrow, 1997: 11), and to the relief that revenues from privatisation provide for states with high deficits and limited capability of bond sales (Vickers & Yarrow, 1991: 119).

In economic theory, a typical narrative suggests that privatisations intervene to improve the efficiency of industries plagued by the inefficiency of state ownership. Based on our analysis of Italian steel privatisations, we suggest that this line of enquiry may reveal three weaknesses.

First, privatisations often unfold, rather than as the result of planning, as the emergent compromise among the interests of elite actors, and their relative power determines the features of privatisations processes. Yet, actors and their policies are constrained by the resources they can rely upon, including their political manoeuvring, and on what is ideologically acceptable. Therefore, this is the second critical point in the analysis of privatisations, power relations are dynamic and depend on the endowment of economic resources as well as on the discursive legitimacy that hegemonic ideologies confer to specific social actors. Third, inferred from our first and second remarks, privatisation is an emergent process whose outcome is only partially desired and expected.

In sum, the outcome of privatisation processes is the result of a truce built upon a socially constructed narrative on the desirability of the process itself. Without the analysis of these mechanisms, it may be difficult to explain the often idiosyncratic, local, context-dependent results of privatisation processes.

9.3 Privatisations as the emerging configuration of a historical bloc

By modifying the entrenched socio-political and cultural-symbolic institutions, and by transforming the economic relationships by reallocating property rights, privatisations bring about a dramatic change in power relations in the contexts in which they occur. Once threatened, the historical bloc that dominates a specific field reacts by reorganising and by finding new economic and political compromises and new discursive configurations. Alternatively, a new historical bloc may emerge, eventually saving some elements of the previous power structure. The emergent reconfiguration of a field's historical bloc, we suggest, explains the idiosyncratic outcome and features of a privatisation policy.

The model that we sketched in Figure 9.1 captures the dynamics of such an evolution. Privatisation policies imply the reallocations of property rights that typically produce the reorganisation of an industry with connected modifications of the industrial relations, layoffs, and reallocation of resources. These movements fire up competition among the previously settled economic interests of the field's actors. This pressure creates fractures in the historical bloc that trigger misalignments in

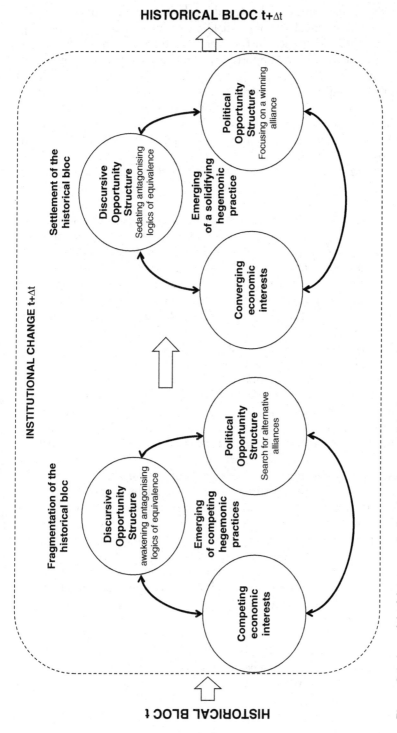

Figure 9.1 A model of fragmentation and settlement of the historical bloc

both the socio-political and cultural-symbolic structures of the field. As for the socio-political dynamics, field's actors mobilise the political opportunity structure to search for alternative alliances. In parallel, actors work in the discursive opportunity structure to evaluate alternative discursive alliances. To do so, they need to brush up on the political identities using available narratives. To this aim, field's actors awake dormant antagonising logics of equivalence and dormant enemies.

The formation of these cracks in the alignment of the elements of a historical bloc leads to the most unstable phase in the evolution of the field to which privatisations are applied. In this phase, which we call *fragmentation*, we suggest the field is agitated by competing hegemonic practices aimed at producing a variety of alternative, not necessarily coherent, alliances.

More specifically, in this phase, the processes occurring in the field interact dynamically to amplify the fissures in the historical bloc. Competing economic interests encourage both the awakening of the dormant logics of equivalence and stimulate the search for alternative political alliances. Competing discursive alliances, on the other hand, and the fragmentation of political alliances reinforce each other. Finally, both discursive and political alliances emphasise the clash among different economic interests.

How do these fractures are sutured to stabilise the field?

For the field to regain a state of equilibrium, a re-alignment needs to be achieved among the economic, socio-political, and cultural-symbolic elements of the historical bloc. In other words, a new structure of power needs to emerge that represents a truce in which a winning alliance is able to realign economic incentives of field's actors, to create new socio-political arrangements, and to take together the alliance with an appropriate discourse that produces a political identity and a shared consciousness. The first step in this phase of *settlement* is the envisioning by field's actors of the possibility to create an alliance among actors who may reach an acceptable compromise among their economic interests. For a field to reach a state of settlement, however, a solidifying hegemonic practice needs to emerge. Grounding on our field study, we suggest that such a hegemonic practice unfolds through two key interweaved processes. First, a cultural-symbolic process occurs in the discursive opportunity structure and operates to produce the suturing of the fractures created by the antagonising logics of equivalence. To produce a viable truce, the winning alliance protects the realignment of economic interests by producing a discourse that emphasises the benefits from a new economic order. This implies sedating the antagonising logics of equivalence that had been embraced in the fragmentation phase as a weapon for the battle for hegemony. A second process is socio-political in nature and occurs when actors consolidate a winning alliance by building up appropriate formal institutions and political alliances.

Differently from what happens during the phase of fragmentation, in the phase of settlement, the field-level processes work to increasingly suturing the fractures and to realigning the elements of the historical bloc. The converging of economic interests suggests sedating antagonising logics of equivalence and focusing on a winning political alliance. Given the focus by field's actors toward a unique alliance, sedating the antagonising logics of equivalence and focusing on a single political alliance reinforce each other. Finally, both discursive and political alliances emphasise the compatibility among different economic interests.

9.4 A contribution to the theory of institutional change

The outcome of a privatisation process is an instance of the broader concept of institutional change; that is, a transformation of a specific institutional arrangement. Thus, the analysis of the dynamic alignment or misalignment of a historical bloc supports the explanation of institutional change as fields' fragmentation and settlement. Traditionally, accepted definitions of fields' settlement refer to the emergence of epiphenomena, such as a "generalised sense of order and certainty" (Fligstein & McAdam, 2012: 10), or agreement about field rules (Rao & Kenney, 2008), or also aligned views (Litrico & Davis, 2017: 989). Yet, how and when such epiphenomena emerge remains unclear. In this work, conversely, we propose a structural notion of fields' settlement that depends on the concept of alignment among the components of a historical bloc. According to our model, the process of misalignment is an endogenous explanation of why processes of institutional change start, while alignment, or, better, re-alignments, explain why and how fields settle after an institutional change.

More generally, the concept of alignment, which is central in the Gramscian framework, makes available a perspective to connect fields' dynamics with in-depth analysis of the interaction between the cultural and political mechanisms underpinning institutional change.

In neo-institutional literature, as said in the foregoing, a growing thread of research addresses fields as arenas of power dependencies and strategic interactions where actors' politics shape institutional settings (Schneiberg & Bartley, 2001; Ingram & Clay, 2000; Fiss & Zajac, 2004; Henisz & Zelner, 2005).

When addressing institutional change, this perspective highlights the role of exogenous jolts in awakening dormant fields' fragmentation (Greenwood et al., 2002; Clemens & Cook, 1999; Hoffman, 1999) and in generating diverging incentives in social actors who are committed differently to the status quo (Greenwood & Hinings, 1996: 1035). Field's fragmentation generates opportunities for political manoeuvring and field's actors may pursue these opportunities by widening fractures in logics (Thornton et al., 2012: 2; Friedland & Alford, 1991) and divergence in interests

(Hoffman, 1999; Morrill et al., 2003). Fields settle when actors reach truces that, at least partially, suture the fragmentation (Rao & Kenney, 2008). These truces are fragile (Meyer & Höllerer, 2010: 1254) and seldom consensual (Morrill et al., 2003), and represent the domination of specific interests and power structures (Lawrence, 2008).

To explain fields' upheaval, a discursive perspective emphasises how fragmentation and settlement result from the struggles that fields' actors pursue over the framing of the reality (Benford & Snow, 2000) and the meaning to be assigned to contested issues (Seo & Creed, 2002; Meyer & Höllerer, 2010).

From this point of view, fragmentation is considered a "framing contest" (Ryan, 1991) in which the previously accepted frames are not perceived as appropriate anymore (Fligstein, 2001; Maguire et al., 2004). In these cases, fragmentation can be sutured through "compromise frames" (Fligstein & McAdam, 2012), bridging frames (Snow & Benford, 1988), and integrating frames (Rao & Kenney, 2008). The effectiveness of such a suture depends on the endowment of skills of field's actors who "take what the system gives" (Fligstein, 2001: 106), recombine "available discursive elements" (Hensmans, 2003: 362), and mobilise the knowledge of the societal beliefs and practices (Friedland & Alford, 1991) within a field. Also, the ability of a discourse to integrate antagonising frames depends on the characteristics field's "latent meaning structure" (Meyer & Höllerer, 2010), including the "multiplicity" of logics (Hoffman, 1999: 2001) and their "relative incoherence" (Ansari et al., 2013; Granqvist & Laurila, 2011) or ideological incompatibility (Rao & Kenney, 2008). These factors affect whether and how discursive alliances might coalesce (Meyer & Höllerer, 2010; Hensmans, 2003). As a consequence, Cornelissen and Werner propose to focus on "the opportunity provided by salient discourses that are alive and have momentum at a particular point in time" (2014: 210), which is the *discursive opportunity structure* (Koopmans & Statham, 1999: 231; McCammon et al., 2007: 745).

Yet, neo-institutional research acknowledges that such discursive struggles are "embedded in more comprehensive political struggles" (Meyer & Höllerer, 2010: 1254) and power relations (Rao & Kenney, 2008). The diffusion of texts itself depends on resources, formal authority, and centrality of the institutional entrepreneurs who voice that text (Phillips et al., 2004: 648). Moreover, since and social actors produce "judgements about the types of power within a field that might facilitate or impede adoption" (Gray et al., 2015: 131), the imbalance of power is of paramount importance to anticipate the destiny of frame adoption processes. As a matter of fact, "change can be blocked through a concentrated power structure (elite domination)" (Greenwood & Hinings, 1996: 1046) or facilitated by fragmented political elites (Zelner et al., 2009). The consequence is that the composition of elites

(McAdam, 1996: 27) and the size of political coalitions (Rao & Kenney, 2008) are crucial for the success of discursive practices. Therefore, to account for the differences in "political interests between actors and groups" (Cornelissen & Werner, 2014: 211), and to explore the mechanisms to integrate these interests in large alliances, is key for explaining the success of framing struggles and emerging settlements.

In this perspective, neo-institutional scholars (Meyer & Höllerer, 2010: 1254; Gray et al., 2015: 118) recognise the role of *political opportunity structures* (Tarrow, 1994; McAdam, 1996; Tarrow, 1996; Diani, 1996; Hargrave & Van de Ven, 2006; Meyer & Höllerer, 2010; Gray et al., 2015) as the "signals to social or political actors which either encourage or discourage them" in conducting political activity (Tarrow, 1996: 54).

Despite notable attempts to explore how field dynamics emerge from the interaction of cultural and political pressures (Gray et al., 2015; Rao & Kenney, 2008), how field's settlement finds its way by weaving together opportunities that are both discursive and political is still under-researched. Consequently, the nature of the "coalitions of entrepreneurs" (Rao & Kenney, 2008) that emerge to stabilise fields remains vague. It is not clear whether these groups are "discursive alliances" (Hensmans, 2003; Meyer & Höllerer, 2010), which coalesce, more or less intentionally, around a shared discourse, or political alliances that bargain over shared objectives and control influential resources (Rao & Kenney, 2008).

By emphasising the analysis of the alignment, misalignment, or re-alignment among the cultural and political elements of the historical bloc, our model highlights the interaction of DOS and POS as the endogenous source of a selection of alternative trajectories of settlement.

For example, the "pact of producers", which was a cultural element that offered a discursive opportunity, became the anchor of a hegemonic practice aiming at an alliance between entrepreneurs and unions. The logic of equivalence that emerged between unions and entrepreneurs made available a rhetoric that was employed to make sense of their converging interests. These latter coalesced in political action aimed at protecting the field from foreign investors. Furthermore, this alliance set the basis for the National Interest First hegemonic practice in the settlement stage of the field.

9.5 The revision of the concept of agency

Our work, we suggest, offers a new perspective to address the nature of agency in institutional change. Despite the rich portrayal that neo-institutional literature offers of the cultural and political complexity of fields when it comes to describing political dynamics, the prevalent research focuses on the opposition between agency and resistance. Often, members of the field that are not the champions of the proposed change tend to be ignored, and if they are not ignored, they are just objects of persuasion, and re-aggregation of interests and preferences (Hardy & Maguire, 2008). As a consequence, the typical narrative, within the neo-institutional theory, is about how institutional entrepreneurs can overcome opponents (Greenwood et al., 2002; Greenwood & Suddaby, 2006), despite lacking "resources, power, and legitimacy" (Hargrave & Van de Ven, 2006: 865) as if they were "hypermuscular" agents, able to subvert the entrenched power relations to force an institutional change. Other authors focus on the centrality of the field position of institutional entrepreneurs to explain the change (Hardy & Maguire, 2008). Few works, however, present a more nuanced picture, such as the one of Fligstein and McAdam (2012), who describe challengers temporarily accepting institutional arrangements not aligned with their interests.

In general, however, in the neo-institutional narrative, there is a clear distinction between challengers and incumbents, between those who want the preservation of extant institutions, and those who aim at overturning the latter. The consequence is that change occurs within a simplified ontology that is populated by "protagonists, antagonists, and an audience of uncommitted but potentially mobilised supporters of a course of action" (Creed et al., 2002: 481). In this description, agents can only choose "one institutional model over another" (Kim et al., 2007: 288), with the institutional change that is often considered an improvement in respect to the original arrangement (Hardy & Maguire, 2008) with almost no regard for the unintended consequences of institutional change (McGaughey, 2013). In particular, "studies rarely focus on how changes to the field can serve the interests of dominant actors who may adopt new practices, but typically retain their dominance" (Hardy & Maguire, 2008: 213).

Conversely, agency has a more articulated description within Gramscian theory. For a historical bloc to settle, it is necessary to build alliances (Burgio, 2014) and recompose "fragmented elements" (Filippini, 2017: 67) within structures that are not only discursive but consist of material and political forces as well. The picture that Gramsci conveys is one in which agency is not just about fighting incumbents and convincing a neutral audience; rather, political action must evaluate the "homogeneity, self-awareness, and organization" of social actors (Filippini, 2017: 102). In the light of Gramscian theory, adopting a logic of diffused agency, we propose, implies recasting the antagonism between challengers and incumbents into a space of relative distances among groups. Adopting these conceptual lenses, we assume that steel privatisation was a dramatic institutional change and agency materialised into the repertoire of efforts to drive the process into one among the many desired models. Yet, the joint efforts, the relative bargaining power, and the variegated interests of different social actors (Unions, Entrepreneurs, and Politicians), rather than the action of one actor, an institutional entrepreneur, explain the outcome of the change. Social actors may be opposed given conflicting interests, yet, they continuously assess their relative distances in discursive, political, and material terms in order to join possible alliances. A corollary of our theory of institutional change, is that agency, rather than fully guided by a social actor with a stable goal, is distributed and, at least partially, emerging and unintended. On the other hand, our theorising gives back a picture of hegemonic practices that is, as well, a process that is evolving and distributed. As material interests of social actors and their respective positions within discursive and political spaces change, different social actors may decide to converge to support similar models or combinations of models at different points in time. Hegemonic practices evolve, adapting to the change in material interests and the transformation of discursive and political opportunities.

In proposing our hybridisation of neo-institutional theory with Gramscian theoretical elements, we are not neglecting the relevance of an individual institutional agency. Rather, we are giving more emphasis to field-level structural and inertial forces. In our analysis, the association of large entrepreneurs (Confindustria), for example, in reframing (Gray et al., 2015) the privatisation issue, maintained an ambiguous position between joining the neo-liberal wave of criticism directed toward the entrepreneurial state (opponents of the party state) and joining the pact of producers as connoisseurs of the inner dynamics of the field. For sure, as powerful actors in the steel industry and legitimated forerunner of the interests of private capital against state intrusiveness in the economy, entrepreneurs enjoyed a favourable structural position. Yet, it is actors' capability to interpret the advantages of such a position and to organise their discursive and political action that make the position valuable.

Another direction in which, we propose, our theorisation contributes to investigate agency concerns the conceptualisation of alliances. In neo-institutional theory, groups acting as entrepreneurs (Wry et al., 2011) or coalitions of entrepreneurs (Rao & Kenney, 2008: 353) form alliances that play a central role for institutional change. Nonetheless, such alliances are predominantly discursive (Hensmans, 2003; Meyer & Höllerer, 2010). What we suggest, conversely, is that we need to acknowledge the underpinning political composition and the stability of elites (McAdam, 1996: 27) to fully understand the role of alliances in explaining fields' stabilisation. While received literature concedes that "the extent to which ruling political elites are tightly organized in a stable alignment has been emphasised as a key dimension of the political opportunity structure that may severely constrain change" (Kim et al., 2007: 299), we argue that an alliance needs to become a historical bloc to stabilise a field. A successful alliance needs to acquire political influence, which is a prerequisite for achieving governmental power (Gramsci, 1975: 2010). Successful coalitions, then, are those in which "ideological compatibility" (Rao & Kenney, 2008) comes with an alignment among political structures and economic interests (Gramsci, 1975: 41). Along these lines, in our work, we take issue with the predominantly cultural approach of Laclau and Mouffe (2014) to hegemonic theory. Whereas they emphasise the "autonomization of the political" from the economic base (2014: 25), in our model, economic relations are focal for interpreting social dynamics. Yet, we propose, economic relations and forces are interpreted differently and leveraged depending on the political and cultural structure of a field and the respective positions of actors. As "economic and discursive dimensions are mutually reinforcing" (Levy & Scully, 2007: 977), we develop our model and propose that the political organisation of a historical bloc crystallises the compromise between economic and cultural pressures that appear "inextricably linked" (Fligstein & McAdam, 2012: 43).

References

Ansari, S. S., Wijen, F., & Gray, B. (2013). Constructing a climate change logic: An institutional perspective on the "tragedy of the commons." *Organization Science*, 24(4): 1014–1040. 10.1287/orsc.1120.0799

Benford, R., & Snow, D. (2000). Framing processes and social movements: An overview and assessment. *Annual Review of Sociology*, 26 (1): 611–639.

Bos, D. (1991). *Privatization. A theoretical treatment*. New York, NY: Oxford University Press.

Bourdieu, P. (1977). *Outline of a theory of practice*. Trans. Richard Nice. Cambridge: Cambridge University Press.

Bourdieu, P. (1991). *Language and symbolic power*. Cambridge, MA: Harvard University Press.

Bourdieu, P., & Passeron, J. C. (1977). *Reproduction in education, society and culture*. Beverly Hills, CA: SAGE Publications.

Burgio, A. (2014). *Gramsci. Il sistema in movimento*. Roma: DeriveApprodi.

Clemens, E., & Cook, J. (1999). Politics and institutionalism: Explaining durability and change. *Annual Review of Sociology*, 25: 441–466.

Cornelissen, J. P., & Werner, M. D. (2014). Putting framing in perspective: A review of framing and frame analysis across the management and organizational literature. *The Academy of Management Annals*, 8: 181–235.

Creed, W. E. D., Scully, M. A., & Austin, J. R. (2002). Accounts and the social construction of identity clothes make the person? The tailoring of legitimating accounts and the social construction of identity. *Organization Science*, 13(5): 475–496.

Davis, M. S. (1971) That's interesting: Towards a phenomenology of sociology and a sociology of phenomenology. *Philosophy of the Social Sciences*, 1(2): 309–344.

Diani, M. (1996). Linking mobilization frames and political opportunities: Insights from regional populism in Italy. *American Sociological Review*, 61(6): 1053–1069.

Feigenbaum, H., Henig, J., & Hamnett, C. (1998). *Shrinking the state: The political underpinnings of privatization.* Cambridge University Press.

Feigenbaum, H. B., & Henig, J. R. (1994). The political underpinnings of privatization: A typology. *World Politics*, 46(2): 185–208. http://www.jstor.org/stable/10.2307/2950672

Filippini, M. (2017). *Using Gramsci.* PlutoPress: London.

Fiss, P. C., & Zajac, E. J. (2004). The diffusion of ideas over contested terrain: The (non)adoption of a shareholder value orientation among German firms. *Administrative Science Quarterly*, 49(4): 501–534.

Fligstein, N. (2001). Social skill and the theory of fields. *Sociological Theory*, 19: 105–125.

Fligstein, N., & McAdam, D. (2012). *A theory of fields.* Oxford: Oxford University Press.

Friedland, R., & Alford, R. (1991). Bringing society back in: Symbols, practices, and institutional contradictions. In W. W. Walter, & P. J. DiMaggio (Eds.), *The new institutionalism in organizational analysis* (pp. 232–263). Chicago: University of Chicago Press.

Fukuyama, F. (1992). *The end of history and the last man.* New York, NY: Free Press.

Gramsci, A. (1975). *Quaderni dal Carcere.* Torino: Giulio Einaudi Editore.

Granqvist, N., & Laurila, J. (2011). Rage against self-replicating machines: Framing science and fiction in the U.S. nanotechnology field. *Organization Studies*, 32(2): 253–280.

Gray, B., Purdy, J. M., & S. Ansari (2015). From interactions to institutions: Microprocesses of framing and mechanisms for the structuring of institutional fields. *Academy of Management Review*, 40(1): 115–143.

Greenwood, R., & Hinings, C. R. (1996). Understanding radical organizational change: Bringing together the old and the new institutionalism. *Academy of Management Review*, 21(4): 1022–1054.

Greenwood, R., & Suddaby, R. (2006). Institutional entrepreneurship in mature fields: The big five accounting firms. *Academy of Management Journal*, 49(1): 27–48.

Greenwood, R., Suddaby, R., & Hinings, C. R. (2002). Theorizing change: The role of professional associations in the transformation of institutionalized fields. *Academy of Management Journal*, 45(1): 58–80.

Hardy, C., & Maguire, S. (2008). Institutional entrepreneurship. In R. Greenwood, C. Oliver, K. Sahlin, & R. Suddaby (Eds.), *The SAGE handbook of organizational institutionalism* (pp. 651–672). London: Sage.

Hargrave, T. J., & Van De Ven, A. H. (2006). A collective action model of institutional innovation. *The Academy of Management Review*, 31(4): 864–888.

Henisz, W. J., & Zelner, B. A. (2005). Legitimacy, interest group pressures, and change in emergent institutions: The case of foreign investors and host country governments. *The Academy of Management Review*, 30: 361–382

Hensmans, M. (2003). Social movement organizations: A metaphor for strategic actors in institutional fields. *Organization Studies*, 24: 355–381.

Hoffman, A. J. (1999). Institutional evolution and change: Environmentalism and the U.S. chemical industry. *Academy of Management Journal*, 42(4): 351–371.

Ingram, P., & Clay, K. (2000). The choice-within-constraints new institutionalism and implications for sociology. *Annual Review of Sociology*, 26: 525–546.

Kim, T.Y., Shin, D, Oh, H., & Jeong, Y. (2007). Inside the iron cage: Organizational political dynamics and institutional changes in presidential selection systems in Korean universities, 1985-2002. *Administrative Science Quarterly*, 52: 286–323.

Koopmans, R., & Statham, P. (1999). Ethnic and civic conceptions of nationhood and the differential success of the extreme right in Germany and Italy. In M. Giugni, D. McAdam, & C. Tilly (Eds.), *How social movements matter* (pp. 225–251). University of Minnesota Press.

Laclau, E., & Mouffe, C. (2014). *Hegemony and socialist strategy: Towards a radical democratic politics*. Verso Trade.

Lawrence, T. B. (2008). Power, institutions and organizations. In R. Greenwood, C. Oliver, K. Sahlin, & R. Suddaby (Eds.), *The SAGE handbook of Organizational Institutionalism*. London: Sage.

Levy, D., & Scully, M. (2007). The institutional entrepreneur as modern prince: The strategic face of power in contested fields. *Organization Studies*, 28: 971–991.

Litrico, J., & Davis, R. J. (2017). The evolution of issue interpretation within organizational fields: Actor positions, framing trajectories, and field settlement. *Academy of Management Journal*, 60(3): 986–1015.

Maguire, S., Hardy, C., & Lawrence, T. (2004). Institutional entrepreneurship in emerging fields: HIV/AIDS treatment advocacy in Canada. *Academy of Management Journal*, 47(5): 657–679.

Mazzuccato, M. (2013). *The entepreneurial state. Debunking the public vs. private myths*. UK: Anthem Press.

McAdam, D. (1996). Conceptual origins, current problems, future directions. In D. McAdam, J. D. McCarthy, & M. N. Zald (Eds.), *Comparative perspectives on social movements: Political opportunities, mobilizing structures and cultural framings* (pp. 23–40). New York, NY: Cambridge University Press.

McCammon, H. J., Muse, C. S., Newman, H. D., & Terrell, T. M. (2007). Movement framing and discursive opportunity structures: The political successes of the U.S. women's jury movements. *American Sociological Review*, 72(5): 725–749.

McGaughey, S. L. (2013). Institutional entrepreneurship in North American lightning protection standards: Rhetorical history and unintended consequences of failure. *Business History*, 55(1): 73–97.

Meyer, R. E., & Höllerer, M. A. (2010). Meaning structures in a contested issue field: A topographic map of shareholder value in Austria. *Academy of Management Journal*, 53(6): 1241–1262. 10.5465/amj.2010.57317829

Morrill, C., Zald, M. N., & Rao, H. (2003). Covert political conflict in organizations: Challenges from below. *Annual Review of Sociology*, 29: 391–415.

Oakes, L., Townley, B., & Cooper, D. (1998). Business planning as pedagogy: Language and control in a changing institutional field. *Administrative Science Quarterly*, 43(2): 257–292.

Phillips, N., Lawrence, T. B., & Hardy, C. (2004). Discourse and institutions. *The Academy of Management Review*, 29(4): 635–652.

Rao, H., & Kenney, M. (2008). New forms as settlements. In R. Greenwood, C. Oliver, K. Sahlin, & R. Suddaby (Eds.), *The SAGE handbook of organizational institutionalism* (pp. 651–672). London: Sage.

Ryan, C. (1991). *Prime time activism: Media strategies for grassroots organizing.* Boston, MA: South End Press.

Schneiberg, M., & Bartley, T. (2001). Regulating American industries: Markets, politics, and the institutional determinants of fire insurance regulation. *American Journal of Sociology*, 107(1): 101–146.

Seo, M. G., & Creed, W.E.D. (2002). Institutional contradictions, Praxis, and institutional change: A dialectical perspective. *The Academy of Management Review*, 27: 222–247.

Snow, D., & Benford, R. (1988). Ideology, frame resonance, and participant mobilization. In B. Klandermans, H. Kriesi, & S. Tarrow (Eds.), *From structure to action: Comparing social movement research across cultures*, vol. 1. JAI press.

Tarrow, S. (1994). *Power in movement: Social movements, collective action and politics.* Cambridge University Press.

Tarrow, S. (1996). States and opportunities: The political structuring of social movements. In D. McAdam, J. D. McCarthy, & M. N. Zald (Eds.), *Comparative perspectives on social movements: Political opportunities, mobilizing structures and cultural framings* (pp. 1–20). New York: Cambridge University Press.

Thornton, P. H., Ocasio, W., & Lounsbury, M. (2012). The Institutional Logics Perspective. *A new approach to culture, structure, and process.* Oxford: Oxford University Press.

Vickers J., & Yarrow, G. (1991). Economic perspectives on privatization. *Journal of Economic Perspectives*, 5(2): 111–132.

Vickers J., & Yarrow, G. (1997). *Privatization. An economic analysis.* Cambridge, MA: The MIT Press.

Wilks, S. (2013). *The political power of the business corporation.* Cheltenham, UK: Edward Elgar.

Williamson, J. (1993). Democracy and the "Washington consensus". *World Development*, 21(8): 1329–1336.

Wry, T., Lounsbury, M., & Glynn, M. A. (2011). Legitimating nascent collective identities: Coordinating cultural entrepreneurship. *Organization Science*, 22(2): 449–463.

Zelner, B. A., Henisz, W. J., & Holburn, G. L. F. (2009). Contentious implementation and retrenchment in neoliberal policy reform: The global electric power industry, 1989–2001. *Administrative Science Quarterly*, 54(3): 379–412.

Index

Printed in the United States
by Baker & Taylor Publisher Services